TUNING AND MODIFYING THE
ROVER V8 ENGINE

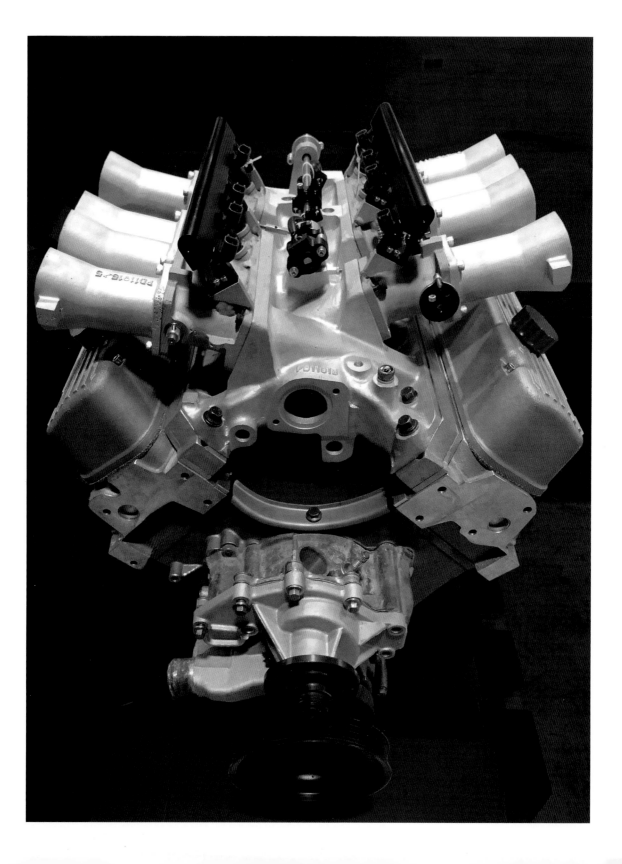

TUNING AND MODIFYING THE
ROVER V8 ENGINE

Daniel R. Lloyd & Nathan J. Lloyd

THE CROWOOD PRESS

First published in 2019 by
The Crowood Press Ltd
Ramsbury, Marlborough
Wiltshire SN8 2HR

enquiries@crowood.com

www.crowood.com

This impression 2023

British Library Cataloguing-in-Publication Data
A catalogue record for this book is available from the British Library.

ISBN 978 1 78500 603 6

Frontispiece: Rover V8 engine with Wildcat cylinder heads and modified Pierburg injection
manifold. ANTHONY DOWIE

Typeset and designed by D & N Publishing, Baydon, Wiltshire

Printed and bound in India by Thomson Press India Ltd.

CONTENTS

DEDICATION

This book is dedicated to Russell Robert Lloyd, who shared his
passion and knowledge of the Rover V8 engine with us.
We will always love you Dad.

ACKNOWLEDGEMENTS

We would like to acknowledge and thank the following individuals for helping us produce this book:

Alex Cochrane (Killerbytedesign), for the cover design and assisting with photographs.

Roland Marlow (Automotive Component Remanu-facturing Ltd), for providing technical advice and supplying photographs.

Sally Lloyd, Wendy Chard, Sandra Lloyd, Jason Starkings, Paul Brooks and Martin Howlett, for assisting with proof-reading.

Steve Cliff and Rob Steele, for assisting us with our Rover V8 development work.

Mark Everett, James Perkins (oldsmobilejetfire. com), SC Power, Eann Whalley (Torque V8), Rotrex AS, Patrick Stuart and Derek Beck, for supplying photographs or illustrations.

INTRODUCTION

The Rover V8 has been around for many decades now, and a few books have already been written about this very versatile and well-loved engine. The aim of this book is to provide the reader with a complete and comprehensive guide to tuning the Rover V8 engine. Although designed in the late 1950s and last produced for production vehicles in 2002, the Rover V8 engine lives on into the twenty-first century in the hands of many owners of classic and competition vehicles. Enthusiasts and specialists alike have developed the engine even further now, with modern engine management, supercharging, turbocharging and LPG conversions becoming much more commonplace in recent years.

In its original form as a Buick or Oldsmobile 215 V8, this engine powered hundreds of thousands of American cars. Various circumstances then led to the engine design and original tooling being sold to Rover in 1965, and the engine we know and love as the 'Rover V8' was born. First featured in the Rover P5B, the Rover V8 has gone on to power a huge range of vehicles, including the Rover P6, Rover SD1, Triumph TR8, Land Rovers, Range Rovers, LDV Sherpa, as well as various TVRs, Morgans, Marcos, Westfields and many more besides. This means that there are still a large number of vehicles around today that are powered by the legendary Rover V8 engine.

Nowadays the Rover V8 is naturally compared to more modern engines when considered as a transplant option for an engine conversion or kit car. Some people will therefore disregard this V8 engine as being relatively low on power compared to its cubic capacity, but when you also consider the relatively low weight and compact size of the Rover V8, it is easy to see why it is still a popular choice with car enthusiasts today. If you then factor in the glorious sound and the versatility of its broad spread of torque, it is clear that there is still life in the old engine yet!

MG RV8 engine bay.

Morgan Plus 8.

TVR Chimaera 400 on track. MARK EVERETT

Workshop manuals.

1954 Ferguson tractor with 3.5-litre Rover V8.

Ultra 4 buggy with 4.6-litre Rover V8.

This book is not designed to replace the original workshop manuals for this engine. There are already excellent factory workshop manuals readily available from Land Rover for the sole purpose of stripping and reassembling the Rover V8 in its standard specification. Although there will be some overlap in information, the main purpose of this book is to provide the reader with all the information required to tune and modify the Rover V8 for their particular application. Although this book is written in a manner that allows you to read it from cover to cover, each chapter or subsection can also be used as a standalone reference. If used in this manner

it is important to bear in mind that the different engine components need to work together properly in order to produce an engine that best meets your requirements.

The versatility of this marvellous engine makes it suitable for a very wide range of vehicles, from lightweight sports and race cars, to 4×4s used for towing or specialist off-road competition. This book should enable the reader to build or modify their Rover V8 engine to best suit their vehicle and its intended use. Although the engine is fairly versatile in most forms, tailoring it correctly for the application will yield significant benefits to the end user.

Ford Capri with 3.9-litre Rover V8.

Mercedes 190e with 4.6-litre Rover V8.

CHAPTER 1

ENGINE REQUIREMENTS AND SPECIFICATION

Before deciding on the specification of your engine build, or spending money on your existing engine, it is important to decide exactly what you require the engine for, and which characteristics are particularly important to you. By establishing your requirements at the beginning you will spend less of your hard-earned cash reaching your goal than if you change the requirements over the course of building or modifying your engine.

Be honest with yourself about your requirements. What are your priorities and where are you willing to compromise? Is maximum performance your main priority? Do you require good performance but also reasonable fuel economy and reliability? Does your engine have to meet certain emissions criteria? Is your vehicle likely to suffer from traction or transmission limitations? All engine specifications involve compromise in one or more areas. The aim is to balance these various compromises to suit your needs.

Planning your engine build carefully is also essential to ensure that you do not mismatch the various components: for example, spending money on big-valve cylinder heads but fitting an intake manifold that will not allow the heads to flow to their full capability; or fitting heads, intake and valvetrain that are capable of producing power up to 7,000rpm, but being limited by a crankshaft that will break at 6,200rpm. This may seem obvious, but many of us (authors included!) have been guilty of building or modifying engines in this way, costing more time and money in the long run to achieve the same desired result once the various limitations have been resolved.

PERFORMANCE

You have to be truthful with yourself about the type of 'performance' you require. Is there a particular peak horsepower figure that you are looking to achieve on the rolling road? A quarter-mile time you are looking to obtain? Or are you after the most significant 'seat of the pants' improvement within a given budget or specification?

Measuring the performance of an engine is a controversial topic and far from straightforward. This performance is usually measured whilst the engine is still in the vehicle, using a chassis dynamometer, drag strip, stopwatch or accelerometer. Measuring engine performance in the vehicle will obviously introduce a lot of potential for error, through transmission losses, rolling resistance, traction issues, driver reaction time, gear ratios, vehicle weight and aerodynamics. These errors must be correctly calculated to ensure an accurate measure of engine performance. A properly calibrated engine dynamometer is therefore a more accurate way of measuring the performance of the engine, with the torque being measured directly at the flywheel or crankshaft.

More often than not people focus on the *peak* horsepower or *peak* torque, but 99 per cent of the time the engine is not operating at this point, even when at full throttle. Unless we are purposely building a circuit-spec race engine with a narrow power-band, what we should focus on is the torque at the point you fully open up the throttle, until the point you let it off. Most drivers will be able to drive faster with an engine that has a broad spread of torque (a

Dyno screen showing 'before' and 'after' tuning.

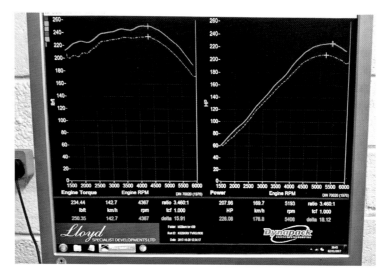

Rover V8 on engine dyno.
ROLAND MARLOW, AUTOMOTIVE
COMPONENT REMANUFACTURING
LTD

'rally-spec' engine) than they would with the circuit-spec engine, even if the circuit-spec engine has more peak horsepower. The engine with the broad spread of torque will always feel more powerful, even to a racing driver.

Deciding the engine speed range in which you want most of the torque (and by extension horsepower) to occur is a key part of the engine specification. The Rover V8 has a relatively 'flat' torque curve, but can be tuned for higher rpm torque if the engine builder is willing to sacrifice some lower rpm torque, drivability, and engine longevity. Likewise, if

the application requires additional low rpm torque (for example off-road, towing) the Rover V8 can be tuned to suit if you are willing to sacrifice some higher rpm power and drivetrain longevity.

The weight and available traction of the vehicle being used also plays a key part here. With a lightweight sports car or kit car (for example TVR, Marcos, Westfield) not only is it acceptable to sacrifice some lower rpm torque for higher rpm power, it is often advantageous, as the Rover V8 usually endows these vehicles with an excess of torque at lower engine speeds. This leads to traction issues, making it difficult for the driver to consistently extract the maximum performance out of the vehicle at lower engine and vehicle speeds.

Another consideration is the speed at which the engine itself is able to accelerate. Factors such as low reciprocating assembly weight, low frictional losses, lean-best torque fuel mixture, optimum ignition timing, optimum valve timing and high port velocities all help the engine's reciprocating assembly to accelerate quickly through the rpm range. Interestingly the Germans have a single word that best describes this: *Beschleunigungsleistung*, which means 'acceleration power'. An engine might have a high horsepower or torque figure – at, say, 5,000rpm – but if it takes twice as long for the engine to accelerate to that engine speed it will not perform so well in real-world terms.

Chassis Dynamometers

Most of us will use a chassis dynamometer (*aka* rolling road) to measure the performance of our Rover V8-engined vehicle. Many of us are aware that horsepower and torque figures not only vary between different cars, but also between different dynamometers, so we will briefly discuss some of the different methods of measuring horsepower and torque via a dynamometer to try and get a better understanding of what it all means.

The definition of horsepower is well publicized, but it is still worth printing the formula here to remind us that horsepower is a function of torque and engine speed:

$$\text{Horsepower (bhp)} = \frac{\text{Torque (lbft)} \times \text{Engine Speed (RPM)}}{5252 \text{ (Unit Constant)}}$$

Torque is the direct force that the engine applies to the drivetrain, or the direct force that the wheels apply to the ground – we will look at the differences later. Horsepower is usually more relevant to us, as this is a measurement of the work done by the engine or wheels in a given amount of time – this governs the rate of acceleration.

Car manufacturers usually always quote horsepower and torque figures at the engine's crank or flywheel; this is measured directly with the engine on an engine dynamometer. During testing some car manufacturers will use an engine that has been built to a better standard (blue-printed) and will not fit various ancillaries (including alternator, power-steering pump, and so on) to give higher publicized performance figures – TVRs of the 1990s are a prime example of this. Unfortunately there is not just one dynamometer measurement standard, either: common standards currently used include DIN 70020, SAE J1349, ISO 1585, and more besides. Different standards will give slightly different horsepower and torque figures, so it can be seen that there is already considerable variation between different horsepower and torque figures, even when measured directly at the flywheel or crankshaft.

V8-powered Westfield.

Westfield with 4.3-litre Rover V8.

Chassis dynamometers (or rolling roads) measure torque at the wheels or hubs, instead of at the engine's crank or flywheel, though the engine speed is still used to calculate 'wheel horsepower'. With a two-wheel drive vehicle using a manual gearbox, the difference between the wheel speed and engine speed can be very easily calculated using the differential (final drive) ratio:

$$\text{Engine Speed (RPM)} = \frac{\text{Wheel Speed (RPM)} \times \text{Differential Ratio}}{\text{Gear Ratio}}$$

If run in a 1:1 gear (for example, fourth gear), as is correct and normal practice where possible, this simplifies the calculation even further:

$$\text{Engine Speed (RPM)} = \text{Wheel Speed (RPM)} \times \text{Differential Ratio}$$

However, dynamometer operators often use the dyno software to calibrate the wheel speed to the engine speed, making it much simpler with automatic and four-wheel drive transmissions.

The horsepower or torque figures measured at the wheels or hubs are always lower than the figures measured at the flywheel – this is due to transmission losses. Transmission losses vary between different vehicles, and depend on a number of different factors, including number and type of differentials, type of gearbox, and viscosities of oil used in the drivetrain components:

$$\text{Flywheel Horsepower} = \text{Wheel Horsepower} + \text{Transmission Losses}$$

There are a few commonly used methods for estimating transmission losses, but as described, they are just estimates, adding even more variability between different rolling-road figures.

Many rolling-road operators will apply a transmission correction factor, in the form of a simple percentage multiplier, to the wheel horsepower and torque figures in order to provide the customer with flywheel horsepower and torque figures.

Some rolling roads do attempt to calculate transmission losses by measuring the horsepower used during a 'coast-down' phase, but this is still

TVR Chimaera 400 on Sun rolling road.

TVR Chimaera 400 on Dynapack hub dynamometer.

not accurate, as the losses are being measured with the gears within the differential and gearbox loaded on the opposite side to when the transmission is under maximum load in the forward direction. Interestingly, when we were using a local eddy-current type of rolling road we consistently recorded coast-down losses of about 45bhp at peak horsepower on a wide range of two-wheel-drive TVRs with a range of different manual transmissions, regardless of actual engine output. In other words, a TVR with 200bhp had virtually the same transmission losses as a TVR with 400bhp. This completely contradicts the idea that transmission losses are a simple percentage multiplier – if this is the case, then the TVR with 400bhp will have double the transmission losses of the TVR with 200bhp.

Perhaps it is more likely that a large proportion of the transmission losses are essentially a fixed amount with a small percentage variation to account for increased frictional losses with increased horsepower and engine speed.

ABOVE: *TVR Griffith 500 on Dastek rolling road.*

Supercharged TVR Chimaera 400 on Dastek rolling road.

The only way to know truly which method is correct would be through extensive testing. Despite numerous pages on the internet about dynos and transmission losses, such test information remarkably appears to be non-existent. In an ideal world we would test the engine on an engine dynamometer with all the ancillaries fitted (including complete intake and exhaust systems), and then test the car on a hub dynamometer (rather than a conventional rolling road) to measure the wheel horsepower without any variances due to tyre pressure, traction or ratchet-strap tension. If done using the same measurement standard, this would give us the most accurate measurement of transmission losses across the entire speed range.

Another consideration when comparing any dyno results is the effect of various atmospheric variables – this includes intake air temperature, ambient air temperature, barometric pressure and relative humidity. The performance of the engine will vary according to these atmospheric variables, so the dynamometer software will use various sensors to monitor these variables and calculate corrected horsepower and torque figures. The way in which the software calculates and corrects the effect of these atmospheric variables is dictated by the test measurement standard used (for example DIN 70020, SAE J1349, and so on). Unfortunately, even when using the same measurement standard, the results can

TVR Griffith 500 on Dynapack hub dynamometer.

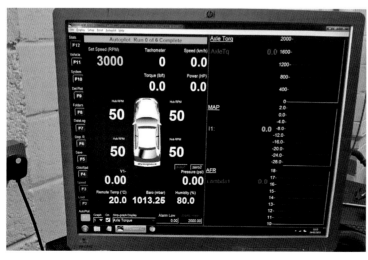

Dynapack software on screen.

vary (or can even be fiddled) by the location of the sensors – the location of the intake air temperature sensor in particular can cause a significant increase or decrease in calculated horsepower and torque.

So to summarize, chassis dynamometers are primarily useful for engine calibration (mapping), tuning and diagnostic purposes, not for comparing horsepower or torque figures between different dynos and cars. There are so many variables that we would be best to disregard flywheel horsepower altogether, and look solely at wheel horsepower – this way we remove the largest variable of all.

Although not commonly used by anyone outside professional engineering or race teams, there are a number of other ways of measuring or comparing engine performance. Some of these are slightly theoretical but can be useful when designing a new engine specification, comparing different engine specifications, or establishing whether the claimed performance of a particular engine specification is realistic.

Volumetric Efficiency

Volumetric efficiency is basically a measurement of how effectively the engine's cylinders are filled during a complete engine cycle (two rotations of the crankshaft). An engine that is operating at 100 per cent

volumetric efficiency (VE) at a particular engine speed is effectively filling its cylinders completely during each engine cycle. By plotting a graph of volumetric efficiency against engine speed we can see at which engine speeds the engine design is most efficient. Assuming that the fuel mixture and ignition timing have been fully optimized, the volumetric efficiency curve will be a similar shape to the engine's torque curve, with peak torque occurring at the engine speed at which peak volumetric efficiency starts to occur.

If the fuel mixture at maximum engine load is the same throughout the entire engine speed range, then the programmed pulse width of the fuel injectors will also plot a curve of similar shape.

Another parameter that corresponds directly to engine torque and volumetric efficiency is mass airflow. If the engine is fitted with a mass airflow meter, then measuring the mass airflow at maximum engine load throughout the engine speed range will also give a similar shaped curve and is therefore an excellent indicator of engine torque.

For the Rover V8, peak volumetric efficiency values are typically between 80 and 90 per cent. With aftermarket cylinder heads and careful selection of the other engine components it is theoretically possible to achieve a peak volumetric efficiency of more than 100 per cent, although this is very difficult to achieve in practice.

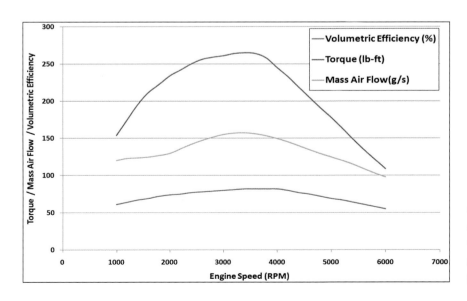

Graph showing the relationship between volumetric efficiency, mass airflow and torque.

Brake Mean Effective Pressure

Brake mean effective pressure (BMEP) is the mean average pressure to which a piston is subjected during one complete down-stroke (that is, from TDC to BDC). This measurement can be calculated from the torque output and the engine's displacement. Therefore it is useful when comparing Rover V8 engines with different capacities to ensure that the alleged power outputs are realistic with the components fitted.

$$\text{BMEP @ Peak Horsepower (psi)} = \frac{150.8 \times \text{Torque @ Peak Horsepower}}{\text{Engine Displacement (ci)}}$$

For the Rover V8 engine, BMEP values at the engine speed at which peak horsepower occurs are typically between 130 and 170psi, depending on the state of tune of the engine. As an example of a high-output Rover V8 engine, a 5-litre Rover V8 putting out a genuine 320bhp at 4,750rpm will have a BMEP value of 175psi.

With aftermarket cylinder heads and careful selection of the other engine components it is theoretically possible to achieve BMEP values of 200psi, although very difficult to achieve in practice.

DRIVABILITY

Drivability is difficult to quantify, but anyone who has driven a badly tuned Rover V8 with an aggressive camshaft will know all about poor drivability! Although this is particularly important for road-going vehicles, it should still be a consideration for competition vehicles as well. In many cases this is due to incorrect ignition timing, incorrect fuelling, or faulty components, but poor component choice can also be the cause of a Rover V8 engine that has flat spots in its power delivery.

As the Rover V8 engine is so cylinder head restricted as standard, it is fairly common practice to fit a camshaft of much more aggressive profile to try to achieve a particular horsepower target, by effectively opening the valves for longer in an attempt to overcome the head restrictions. In many cases this is a compromise too far, and the fact that the valves are open for longer makes the engine lose a great deal of cylinder pressure at low engine speed conditions. This low cylinder pressure means that the engine has distinctly less torque at lower engine speeds, and might even struggle to idle properly at a normal idle speed. An engine fitted with such a camshaft will have a noticeable flat spot at the lower engine speeds, and when the engine does 'come on song' there will be a noticeable switch in behaviour and engine output. This type of engine does not have a smooth transition in power output with increasing rpm, and will be difficult to drive at low vehicle speeds.

In many cases the Rover V8 owner will select a camshaft that has too much overlap and too much lift for the application – in some instances we have even obtained more power and torque by 'downgrading' the camshaft!

RELIABILITY/ LONGEVITY

It is easy enough to build an engine that produces a lot of power and torque for a short amount of time, but much more challenging to build such an engine that will last 100,000 miles (160,000km) or more. Again, component selection plays a big part here, and there is usually a compromise to be made between performance and longevity in particular. Going back to the camshaft as an example, a high lift camshaft will provide more horsepower, but there will be a substantially increased load on the valvetrain, significantly reducing the life of the camshaft, followers, rocker gear and so on. The high lift camshaft may even ultimately lead to the failure of the short engine.

Naturally, good quality components should always last longer than cheap components, and it is always worthwhile doing your research before purchasing engine components. Certain markets (for example, the Land Rover aftermarket) are very price driven, and as a consequence a number of components within that market are of a sub-standard quality.

Regular service intervals are very important if you want your engine to last a decent amount of time, with regular oil and filter changes being a minimum requirement. The air filter is a service item that is often neglected, and this should be replaced or cleaned/oiled as part of an annual service regime.

Engine oil and oil filter.

A well built and regularly serviced Rover V8 engine is likely to last an appreciable length of time. These engines can easily cover more than 100,000 miles (160,000km).

FUEL ECONOMY

Economy is not a word usually associated with the Rover V8, but a number of ways can be employed to improve significantly the fuel economy of these engines. These include camshaft selection, cylinder head modifications, optimizing ignition and air-fuel mixture, increasing compression ratio, and the use of alternative fuels. The various methods will be discussed in the following chapters, but again, if you want the best fuel economy, it is important to choose carefully the components and/or modifications to best suit your fuel economy target.

Measuring fuel economy is much more straightforward than measuring performance: it is simply the ratio of distance covered for a given amount of fuel, or vice versa – for example, miles per gallon

(mpg) or litres per 100 kilometres (ltr/100km). To enable us to measure fuel economy we simply need an accurate odometer, usually a part of the vehicle's speedometer, and an accurate measure of fuel used. Modern cars often already have a built-in fuel economy display, so you don't even have to do the basic maths to work out the fuel economy.

It is worth noting that certain aspects of both performance and economy tuning work hand in hand – for example, optimizing the compression ratio, fuel mixture and ignition timing will improve both engine performance and fuel economy, whilst other aspects are mutually exclusive. Camshaft selection is a good example of an area where a compromise is made to suit the end user's requirements – one particular camshaft will provide relatively good fuel economy but have very poor top-end performance, whereas another camshaft will give much better top-end performance but with poor fuel economy and idle quality.

SUMMARY

It is easy to assume that the original engine or vehicle manufacturer did not select the best components, but in many cases they actually selected the best combination of engine components for the application, with a well thought out compromise between reliability, drivability, fuel economy, emissions, performance and cost. Changing one of these components for an 'upgraded' item can adversely affect this optimized combination, so that you may have gained a little performance, for example, but to the significant detriment of the other factors – namely reliability, drivability, fuel economy and emissions. If you had fully understood that this was going to be the case beforehand, you may well have decided that the little extra performance was not worth the sacrifice!

The aim of this book is to provide you with the information to understand fully the Rover V8 engine, so that you can carefully build or modify the engine that will suit your application best.

CHAPTER 2

SHORT ENGINE

The Rover V8 engine block is a compact aluminium design, with steel liners and a single camshaft located between the two cylinder banks. Apart from being largely aluminium, it is similar in design to many classic American V8 engines – including the Chevy small block. This is not surprising when you consider that the Rover V8 originated from the Buick and Oldsmobile 215 V8 engines.

This chapter will look at the various Rover V8 short engines that are available, and how to select the ideal one for your application. This will cover the engine block, crankshaft, pistons, piston rings, conrods and bearings.

ENGINE BLOCK

A range of different capacity Rover V8 engines is available; the standard Rover/Land Rover ones are as shown in Table 1.

There is also a wide range of alternative capacity Rover V8 engines that have been made throughout the years; Table 2 lists a selection of them.

A number of slight variations of these engine capacities are also available, depending on the specific over-bore chosen. For example, a standard 4.6 (4553cc) with a 0.5mm over-bore (94.5mm bore) will give a capacity of 4601cc.

If you are trying to decide on a specific engine capacity for your particular application there are a number of factors to consider:

Torque requirements/limitations: How much torque do you require for your particular application? The larger capacity Rover V8s produce fairly significant amounts of low-down torque. This is usually beneficial, particularly for 4×4 applications, but can be a disadvantage if the vehicle is particularly light and lack of traction becomes an issue. Is the existing drivetrain capable of handling the torque level of your chosen engine capacity? Can you afford to replace and upgrade the drivetrain components to handle the torque of your chosen engine capacity?

RPM requirements/limitations: Choosing an engine with a longer stroke will limit the engine's maximum reliable rpm limit. For example, 6,000rpm should be considered as the maximum safe rpm limit for a TVR-spec 5-litre with its 90mm stroke. Increasing the stroke for any given engine speed will

Table 1: Standard engine capacities

Capacity	Bore	Stroke	Notes
3.5 litres (3528cc/ 215ci)	88.9mm/ 3.5in	71.12mm/ 2.795in	Most early OEM applications
3.9 litres (3947cc/ 241ci)	94.04mm/ 3.702in	71.12mm/ 2.795in	Early 1990s OEM – 30A block
4.0 litres (3947cc/ 241ci)	94.04mm/ 3.702in	71.12mm/ 2.795in	1994–2002 OEM – 38A block
4.2 litres (4275cc/ 261ci)	94.04mm/ 3.702in	77mm/ 3.032in	Early 1990s OEM – 30A block
4.6 litres (4553cc/ 278ci)	94.04mm/ 3.702in	82mm/ 3.228in	1994–2002 OEM – 38A block

Table 2: Alternative engine capacities

Capacity	Bore	Stroke	Notes
2.0 litres (1999cc/ 122ci)	88.9mm	40.25mm	Built by TVR for the Italian market, fitted with Eaton supercharger in the TVR S-series
3.5 litres (3498cc/ 213ci)	94mm	63mm	Short-stroke, big-bore version of the 3.5-litre
3.5 litres (3499.9cc/ 214ci)	88.5mm	71.12mm	Built for rallying, where regulations dictated 3500cc limit
4.4 litres (4415cc/ 269ci)	88.9mm/ 3.5in	88.9mm/ 3.5in	Leyland P76 engine, Australian
4.45 litres (4445cc/ 271ci)	94.04mm/ 3.702in	80mm/ 3.15in	Built by TVR for Tuscan challenge race series and 450se road car
4.8 litres (4748cc/ 290ci)	96mm	82mm/ 3.22in	Common aftermarket option. 4.6-litre 38A block with 96mm bore
5.0 litres (4997cc/ 305ci)	94.04mm/3.702in	90mm/3.54in	Built by TVR for the Griffith and Chimaera 500
5.0 litres (4995cc/ 305ci)	96mm	86.26mm	Short-stroke 5-litre
5.2 litres (5217cc/ 318ci)	95mm	92mm	

consequently increase the piston speed. Increasing the piston speed will reduce the reliability and increase the likelihood of major engine failure. Therefore engines with a shorter stroke will naturally be more suitable for high-revving applications.

Parts availability: Choosing a more obscure engine capacity may lead to issues with parts availability.

Parts reliability: Some of the engine capacities shown use stronger components as standard. For example, the 4.0-litre 38A engine has larger crank journals and main bearings. This makes it inherently stronger than the equivalent 3.9-litre 30A engine.

Engine Block Identification
Engine blocks have the engine number stamped on the outside edge of the block deck, and this can be seen with the cylinder heads still in place, adjacent to the dipstick tube (*see* opposite page, top).

The various factory engine numbers are shown in a table in the appendix at the back of this book. This table shows the main factory engine numbers, but aftermarket engines may have different numbers stamped into the block. As an example, many of the earlier Rover V8 engines fitted to TVRs have engine numbers starting with NCK, standing for 'North Coventry Kawasaki' (*see* opposite page, middle).

Other aftermarket engine numbers include JE or V8D, standing for 'John Eales' or 'V8 Developments' respectively.

There are also a number of key visual differences between the various Rover V8 engine blocks that have been produced. Here we will put them into two main categories, differentiated according to their bore diameter: 3.5in, or 88.9mm, small-bore engine blocks, and 3.702in, or 94mm, big-bore engine blocks.

3.5in or 88.9mm Small-Bore Engine Blocks
The first engine blocks, as fitted to Rovers and early Range Rovers from 1967 to 1980, utilize 3.5in-diameter cylinder bores and fourteen-bolt cylinder heads. The two-bolt main caps that retain the crankshaft are located via block registers on either side; these registers are 0.200in tall, and the ends of the main cap are 0.250in tall. On these early engine blocks the main cap to register contact area is only 0.090in tall. This is due to the design of the main caps on these early engine blocks.

Another key visual difference with these early Rover V8 blocks are the three valley ribs, which are thin compared to the ribs on later engine blocks.

In 1980 the later 'stiff block' was introduced, the key visual difference being the thicker valley ribs (approximately 14–15mm) common to all Rover V8 engine blocks from this point forwards. This later block with

OEM 4.6 P38A engine number.

TVR 420 SEAC engine number – North Coventry Kawasaki.

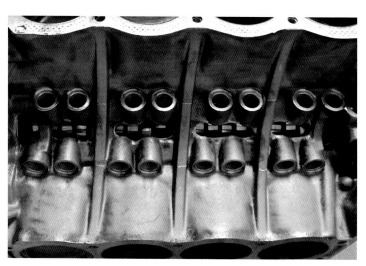

Later Rover V8 block, showing thicker valley ribs.

the 3.5in bore also uses different two-bolt main caps that have taller ends (0.650in), with a slightly increased main cap to register contact area (0.105in tall).

In 1995 a version of the 3.5in small-bore engine block was produced for the military; these particular engine blocks are often referred to as 'service' engine blocks. These blocks were based on the big-bore 38A engine-block castings, but used cylinder liners and the crankshaft from the 3.5in small-bore engine. These engine blocks are only compatible with the later ten-bolt cylinder heads, and use the later 38A main caps but without the cross-bolts, effectively using only two bolts with the four-bolt main caps. These 'service' blocks can be easily modified by drilling out the castings to produce a cross-bolted 3.5-litre engine.

Although rarely seen in the UK, it is worth briefly mentioning the other 3.5in small-bore engine block that was produced, for the 4.4-litre Leyland P76 engine. Produced in Australia from 1973 to 1980, this engine block has larger main bearings (2.55in in diameter) and a taller block (0.540in taller than the standard 3.5 Rover V8). These engine blocks only use ten-bolt fixings for the cylinder heads.

3.702in or 94mm Big-Bore Engine Blocks

The first of the 'big-bore' engines was produced in 1989 and utilized 3.702in diameter cylinder bores and fourteen-bolt cylinder heads. These engines still retained the two-bolt main cap design from the 'stiff block' 3.5in bore engines, primarily used for the 3.9-litre engines fitted into the Range Rover Classic, but also used with a different crankshaft and pistons to make the 4.2-litre engine fitted into the Range Rover Classic LSE.

In early 1994, the 'interim' engine was introduced, using the same block casting as the later 38A engine. The earliest of these 'interim' engine blocks used the same two-bolt main caps as the first of the 'big-bore' engines, as well as being drilled and tapped for fourteen-bolt heads (although still fitted with ten-bolt heads). However, most of these 'interim' engine blocks used the later 38A main caps, but without the cross-bolts, just like the 'service' 3.5-litre engines. This means that these engine blocks can be easily modi-

fied to produce a cross-bolted 3.9- or 4.2-litre engine. They are also usually drilled and tapped for the later ten-bolt cylinder heads from mid-1994 onwards.

The 'interim' engines use a 'short-nose' (70mm long) crankshaft, as per all early Rover V8s, but have

Interim crankshaft nose, with longer keyway.

Threaded Cam Location Plate Holes

Threaded camshaft location plate holes on interim engine block.

a longer key-way machined into the crank nose to accommodate a 60mm long Woodruff key. This is to drive the crank-driven oil pump, a key feature of all big-bore Rover V8 engines from this point forwards. Another key feature of this 'interim' engine is the use of a camshaft thrust plate, which can be bolted to the block via two tapped holes and prevents any axial movement of the camshaft.

In late 1994 the 38A block was introduced and used for the 4.0- and 4.6-litre engines fitted into the Range Rover P38A. These engines use a 'long-nose' (90mm long) crankshaft to drive a crank-driven oil pump and four-bolt (cross-bolted) main caps as standard. The 38A crankshafts also have larger main bearings (2.5in diameter) and larger big ends (2.185in diameter). These 38A engine blocks are all drilled/tapped for the later ten-bolt cylinder heads, and use stretch-bolts with composite head gaskets as standard. This type of engine is also fitted with a camshaft thrust-plate as standard, and has the provision for two knock sensors on the outside of the block.

The 38A engine block technically represents the best Rover V8 production short engine ever made.

Potential Problems and Solutions

One well-known issue with the 38A engine block in particular is liner slippage. Aluminium and steel have different rates of thermal expansion, so any over-heating issues can potentially lead to a slipped liner. The Range Rover P38A and Discovery 2 had

38A engine block and crankshaft.

Location of knock sensor bosses on P38A engine.

revised cooling systems that ran at higher operating temperatures for emissions purposes, but unfortunately this led to a significantly increased number of engine failures due to slipped liners or block cracking.

There are two ways of preventing the slipped liner problem occurring on any Rover V8 engine: the first is to ensure that your cooling system is in perfect working order, with no coolant leaks, and the second is to fit top-hat flange liners.

Top-hat flange liner.

A number of different companies offer this service, including ACR and Turner Engineering. These top-hat flange liners are a good 'insurance policy' in case your Rover V8 engine over-heats, but they are not a substitute for ensuring that the cooling system is in good condition. Although they will ensure that the cylinder liners are not able to slip, overheating can still cause other major issues such as warped cylinder heads, warped block, cracked block.

With a P38a cooling system, another approach is to reduce the operating temperature by retrofitting a lower temperature thermostat.

Block cracking behind the liner is another well known issue with the 38A engine block, although some of the earlier 3.9- and 4.2-litre engines also had this problem. The early 3.5-litre engines did not have this issue, as the smaller 88.9mm bore has more material around the outside of the cylinder liner. Although there is always a certain amount of core shift with cast aluminium engine blocks, there is always plenty of material left around the cylinder

liner on a 3.5-litre engine. The nominal diameter of 93.25mm (without the liner) leaves a minimum of 5.5mm wall thickness in the surrounding aluminium.

With larger 94mm-bore engines, the nominal diameter of 98.6mm (without the liner) leaves about 3mm wall thickness in the aluminium around the cylinder liner and the waterways that pass between the different cylinder bores. With some core shift during the casting process, this wall thickness can be reduced to the point where the aluminium surrounding the cylinder liners is quite thin. If the engine then gets a little too hot, or goes through a number of extreme heat cycles, the aluminium behind the liner can crack, allowing the liner to move. Coolant can then leak from around the liner into the cylinder, and the cylinder pressure can pressurize the cooling system. This is often noticed as a slight coolant loss that gets progressively worse.

From 1993 onwards Land Rover ultrasonically tested this wall thickness on all their engine blocks, and wrote the minimum wall thickness in the valley of the engine block. So, for example, if you see '2.5' written in the valley of your 3.9-litre engine block, it means that the minimum wall thickness on that engine is 2.5mm. Further to this, from 1997 Land Rover marked the 38A engine blocks (again, in the valley) with a colour instead – blue, yellow or red.

Any engine blocks that had less than the 2.2mm minimum requirement were scrapped at the factory.

Table 3: 38A engine-block colour codes

Colour	Wall thickness range (mm)	Notes
Blue	2.2–2.5	Used for 4.0-litre engines
Yellow	2.5–2.8	Used for both 4.0- and 4.6-litre engines
Red	2.8–3.0	Used for 4.6-litre engines

Alternative/ Aftermarket Engine Blocks

Apart from Land Rover or Rover, there have been a number of aftermarket suppliers of alternative Rover V8 engine blocks. Top-hat linered engine blocks have become very commonplace over the last ten years, due to the liner slippage issues with the 38A engine. TVR produced the 5-litre Rover V8, using a longer stroke crankshaft, fitted to the TVR Griffith 500 and later to the TVR Chimaera 500: these engine blocks have been modified specifically to accommodate the increased crankshaft stroke. Throughout the 1990s, Wildcat Engineering also produced a wide range of different engine capacities – even a 6-litre version using a modified Ford V8 crankshaft with a 101.6mm bore and 92mm stroke! This engine block had no waterways between the cylinders to allow for the larger bore diameter, and used six head studs per cylinder.

Camshaft Bearings

When rebuilding a short engine we always recommend replacing the camshaft bearings. These are located in the centre of the block, and are replaced using a specific tool. If required, this tool can be easily made by your local machine shop.

Camshaft bearings.

Worn camshaft bearings lead to low oil pressure and eventually loss of oil pressure, so these should be replaced during every engine rebuild.

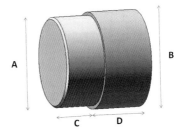

	'A' Dim. (mm)	'B' Dim. (mm)	'C' Dim. (mm)	'D' Dim. (mm)
Bearing 1	45	48.3	20	25
Bearing 2	44.3	47.5	20	25
Bearing 3	43.5	46.8	20	25
Bearing 4	42.8	46	20	25
Bearing 5	42	45.3	20	25

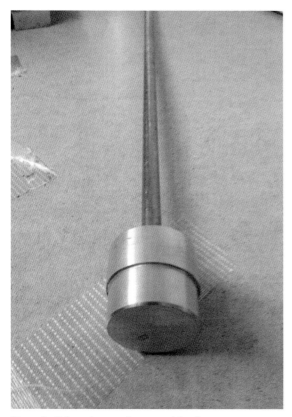

Camshaft bearing replacement tool.

Dimensions of camshaft replacement tool.

Core Plugs and Oil Gallery Plugs

If you are stripping and rebuilding your short engine, it is well worth removing the coolant core plugs and oil-gallery plugs prior to cleaning the engine block. This allows the coolant and oil passageways to be thoroughly flushed and cleaned prior to reassembly. The coolant core plugs are readily available and should be replaced. The threaded oil-gallery plugs can be reused.

Core plugs and oil gallery plugs.

PISTONS AND PISTON RINGS

The Rover V8 is fitted with cast aluminium pistons as standard, most of which were made for Rover by Hepolite. The later specification hypereutectic cast aluminium pistons (as found in the 38A-specification engine) are more durable than the earlier cast aluminium pistons, due to the higher silicon content.

In terms of piston and cylinder-bore wear with most road-going applications, the Rover V8 is usually very durable and long lasting. As with any engine, regular oil and filter changes will help prolong the life of the engine. If you need to retain very good piston-to-bore sealing with your road-going Rover V8, we would recommend a rebore with new pistons and rings every 50,000 to 75,000 miles (80,500 to 120,700km). It is worth noting, however, that the Rover V8 is capable of covering significantly higher mileage without any noticeable problems with the short engine. Significant factors that have an impact on engine longevity include:

- service regularity: a regularly serviced engine will always last longer
- engine loads: heavy loads, including towing and off-road, reduce the life of the engine
- engine speeds: lots of high rpm use reduces the life of the engine
- engine temperature: a cold engine will wear more quickly, so an engine that spends a higher proportion of its time at full operating temperature will last longer. Conversely, an excessively hot operating temperature, or over-heating, will reduce the life of an engine

If your engine has excessive piston-to-bore clearance you may be able to hear 'piston slap', the dull slapping sound of the piston skirt making contact with the cylinder bore.

Early cast pistons should be considered to have a maximum safe engine speed limit of approximately 6,000rpm, with the later hypereutectic cast pistons okay for use up to 6,500rpm. Note that these engine speed limits do depend on how long the engine spends at those particular speeds. For example, an earlier piston will last longer if only taken to 6,000rpm in short bursts, compared to a later hypereutectic piston held above 6,000rpm for sustained and repeated periods of time. If cast pistons are to be used for racing applications, they will have a significantly shorter life than road-going applications.

Forged pistons are a great upgrade for race-specification engines that consistently see engine speeds above 6,000rpm, as well as for supercharged or turbocharged engines. These are available from a number of different suppliers, with larger diameter 96mm pistons readily available for the 4.6-litre 38A-specification engine, giving an increased capacity of 4.8 litres. Custom-forged pistons are

96mm forged pistons.

also available from a number of different suppliers, including Ross Racing, Diamond, and so on.

A standard piston on a freshly rebuilt engine will have a piston-to-bore clearance between 0.001in and 0.002in, but forged pistons usually require more clearance to allow for their higher rate of thermal expansion. Forced induction applications also usually require increased piston-to-bore clearances due to the higher combustion temperatures present at the piston.

If your engine is going to have a lot of valve lift, you also need to try and establish whether or not you will require valve reliefs or cutouts in the top of your pistons, to allow sufficient piston-to-valve clearance on both the intake and exhaust valves.

The location of the gudgeon pin in the piston is another consideration, particularly with custom engine builds. There are two main dimensions to take into account – the pin height and pin offset.

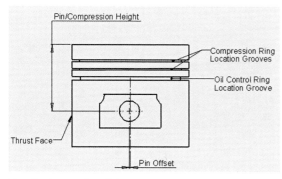

Key features of a piston.

The 4.0-litre and 4.6-litre 38A engine uses a 0.6mm gudgeon pin offset to reduce the side loads on the piston and therefore reduce the stress/wear on the entire rotating assembly. Earlier Rover V8 engines have zero pin offset.

The pin height is also known as the compression height, and it varies between the different engine capacities.

The piston-dish volumes shown in Table 4 are for the standard quoted compression ratio of 9.35:1, unless otherwise stated.

Table 4: Standard piston dimensions

Engine capacity	Compression height	Piston-dish volume examples
3.5-litre	46.8mm	8.5cc for 9.6:1CR, 11.2cc for 9.35:1, 15.3cc for 8.13:1
3.9-litre	49.5mm	22.5cc
4.0-litre 38A	35.9mm	13.2cc
4.2-litre	45mm	22.5cc for 8.94:1
4.6-litre 38A	35.9mm	22.3cc

The piston-dish volume also varies between the different engine capacities. Interestingly, this can sometimes be used to our advantage. For example, a 4.6-litre engine fitted with 4-litre pistons will have a fairly significant compression ratio increase. So when using non-standard components, or when mixing and matching components, it is important to check that the piston dimensions are correct for your combination of block height, rod length, stroke, and desired compression ratio.

Each piston has two compression rings and an oil-control ring. Naturally the different piston rings not only vary in diameter but also in thickness. A range of different compression and oil-control ring thicknesses were used in standard engines, as well as in aftermarket engine builds.

CONNECTING RODS

The length and type of connecting rod fitted to your engine depends on the original or current engine capacity.

Table 5: Standard con-rod dimensions

Engine capacity	Con-rod length	Big-end bearing diameter	Small-end diameter
3.5-litre	143.8mm (5.66in)	50.8mm	22.2mm (.875in)
3.9-litre	143.8mm (5.66in)	50.8mm	22.2mm (.875in)
4.0-litre 38A	155.2mm	55.5mm	24mm
4.2-litre	143.8mm (5.66in)	50.8mm	22.2mm (.875in)
4.6-litre 38A	149.7mm	55.5mm	24mm

Standard con-rods are rarely a limitation on the Rover V8, and are quite durable enough for most applications, even at higher engine speeds. Naturally, the con-rods fitted to the longer stroke engines – for example the TVR-spec 5-litre – will undergo more dynamic load than the con-rods fitted to shorter stroke engines. Even so, the con-rods are usually not an issue with engine speeds below 6,800rpm on naturally aspirated applications.

If you are building a very high specification engine with forced induction, high engine speeds or an alternative stroke, you may require aftermarket con-rods. Due to parts commonality with some American V8 engines, forged I-beam and H-beam con-rods are readily available for the Rover V8 engine from a wide range of suppliers.

Rod ratio is the length of the connecting rod divided by the stroke. This relationship affects the behaviour of the engine: the higher rod ratio will have fewer side loadings on the piston, and will therefore be subjected to less friction between the piston skirts and cylinder walls. The higher rod ratio will also slightly increase the amount of time the piston spends at TDC (the piston dwell time), which also increases power at mid to high engine speeds.

The disadvantage with the higher rod ratios is that the intake vacuum is reduced slightly at lower engine speeds, which affects torque and engine response. Other potential disadvantages of higher rod ratio is that the gudgeon pin will need to be located higher in the piston, closer to the piston crown, and might entail the use of a shorter piston, which can lead to piston stability issues if you go too far (only really relevant with custom pistons).

The maximum rod ratio is limited by the height of the block deck.

When working out the fundamental engine speed capability of a particular short engine, the mean average piston speed is another useful factor to consider. In isolation, the mean piston speed is fairly meaningless, but is more relevant when comparing different engine specifications and their engine speed capability. For example, the rpm limit of a particular 5-litre Rover V8 short engine is 6,000rpm, at which point the piston has a mean average speed of 18 metres per second. In theory this means that if a 4-litre short engine is built with the same component materials, it will be capable of reaching a heady 7,593rpm before it reaches the same 18 m/s piston speed!

So the 38A 4-litre engine has the highest rod ratio with standard components, as well as the joint lowest piston speed. Therefore it is safe to assume that this particular short engine derivative has the highest engine speed capability out of all the standard Rover V8 short engines.

Table 6: Rod ratios and mean piston speeds

	Rod ratio	Mean piston speed @ 6,000rpm (m/s)
3.5-litre	2.02	14.2
3.9-litre	2.02	14.2
4.0-litre 38A	2.18	14.2
4.2-litre	1.87	15.4
4.6-litre 38A	1.83	16.4
5.0-litre TVR-spec	1.55	18

CYLINDER HEAD BOLTS

There are two standard types of head bolt fitted to the Rover V8, as well as some aftermarket options. Up to 1993, Rover V8 engines were fitted with head bolts that are technically reusable, although if doing so, it is always worth checking them for overall length, inspecting the threads for damage, and checking that the thread pitch is still correct. From 1994 onwards, engines were fitted with stretch-type bolts instead; these are not reusable and should be replaced every time they are removed after use.

ARP cylinder head stud versus standard head bolt.

ARP head stud kits are also available for the Rover V8, and these are superior both in terms of clamping force and due to the fact that you can thread the studs into the block before fitting the heads. They are also reusable, but they are not without potential issues. If there are any issues with the threads in the engine block, then you will encounter them sooner with the ARP studs. There are also some ARP stud kits that are sold as being suitable for the Rover V8, but are not entirely correct. The thread lengths are not correct, so it is important to check that the thread lengths on the studs match the threads in the engine block. They should not bottom out, but they do want to utilize most of the thread available in the block. ARP studs should be fitted by hand using an Allen key. Do not over-tighten!

CRANKSHAFT

Rover V8 crankshafts are usually very strong and without issues, unless they are being run at very high engine speeds or with large amounts of boost in forced induction applications. The slight exception here is with the TVR-spec 5-litre Rover V8 crankshaft, with its long 90mm stroke. These crankshafts do occasionally suffer breakages when revved much beyond 6,000rpm, so if you have a TVR-spec 5-litre it is well worth limiting the engine speed to a maximum of 6,000rpm.

Stronger EN24 billet steel crankshafts are available, which are capable of operating at higher engine speeds and with more boost in forced induction applications. Crankshafts are also available with a range of alternative stroke lengths, including an 86.26mm stroke for short-stroke 5-litre engines, and a 92mm stroke for 5.2-litre engines. As previously mentioned, it is particularly important to work out the maximum allowable engine speed with the longer stroke crankshafts.

A number of other features should be considered when purchasing a crankshaft for your engine. One is the keyway in the front of the crankshaft, and another is the length of the front of the crankshaft (called the nose). Earlier pre-Serpentine Rover V8 engines are fitted with a short-nose crankshaft and a short keyway. The first Serpentine engines, known as the interim type, are fitted

Pre-Serpentine crankshaft – short nose and short keyway.

Serpentine interim crankshaft – short nose and long keyway.

with short-nose crankshafts, but with a long keyway. This longer keyway is to run the crank-driven oil pump, fitted to all Serpentine engines. The later 38A Serpentine engines use long-nose crankshafts with a long keyway.

The other features to consider are the main bearing and big-end bearing diameters, with the 38A block having larger main bearings (2.5in diameter) and larger big ends (2.185in diameter), for example. It is also worth noting that the 38A crankshafts will not fit the earlier engine blocks without the blocks being modified for clearance – this is due to the larger counterweights on the 38A crankshaft.

If there is any scoring or wear present on the crankshaft bearing faces, these faces need to be

Serpentine 38A crankshaft – long nose and long keyway.

reground and fitted with different size bearings to suit. If using a second-hand crankshaft for an engine build, it is important to check the diameters of the various crankshaft bearing faces to see whether they have been reground before, and to ensure that the correct size bearings are fitted.

CRANK PULLEY ASSEMBLY

A wide variety of crank pulley assemblies have been fitted as standard to Rover V8 engines over the years.

All pre-Serpentine engines have pulleys that accommodate a traditional V-type belt. These engines also usually use more than one V-type pulley on the crank when running additional ancillaries such as power steering and air conditioning. The crank pulleys are bolted to a vibration damper via three or six $5/16$ UNF bolts. There is also often a balancing rim located at the rear of the crank pulley assembly, which is used to balance dynamically the entire crank pulley assembly. The vibration damper has a keyway that locates on to the crankshaft key, and is bolted to the crankshaft via a large $3/4$ UNF bolt with a $15/16$in (23.8mm) hex head. This bolt is technically reusable, but must be inspected before reuse for signs of stretching. It is also worth applying a drop of thread-lock during assembly. Some early Rover V8s fitted to Land Rovers used a crank pulley bolt that had a 'starting dog' as part of the bolt head instead, so that the engine could be cranked over with a starting handle.

Interim-type Serpentine engines have a similar type of vibration damper, but with a seven-groove serpentine pulley (to suit a 7PK serpentine auxiliary belt). On both pre-Serpentine and the interim-type Serpentine engines, the vibration damper has the timing marks located on the outside edge. It is possible for the outer section to separate and rotate around the inner damper section, so that the timing marks are no longer correct. For this reason it is always important to verify that the TDC marking on the damper correlates with when piston no. 1 is at TDC. Once this has been checked, it is then worth marking the damper across both the inner and outer

Crank pulley bolt with 'starting dog' for starting handle.

sections so that if they do separate and rotate it will be easily spotted.

The 38A Serpentine engines are fitted with a vibration damper that has the serpentine pulley grooves machined into the outer section, effectively forming a one-piece crank pulley assembly.

38A front crank pulley.

FLYWHEEL

We will not go into too much detail here – also, many Rover V8 applications are fitted with an automatic

gearbox, so this section is not applicable in those cases.

With regard to flywheels on Rover V8 engines, the only thing worth mentioning is that most standard OEM flywheels are primarily suited to heavier vehicles, such as Land Rovers. For this reason, lighter-weight vehicles fitted with Rover V8 engines will usually benefit from having a lighter-weight flywheel, although it is possible to go too far and reduce the drivability of the car. A lighter-weight flywheel will allow the *engine* to accelerate more quickly due to the reduced mass effectively reducing the inertia. If the flywheel is too light for the vehicle or application, the lack of inertia will mean that more engine speed will be required to pull away from standstill, or the engine will stall. This characteristic is obviously very undesirable for road cars, and could still be an inconvenience for some competition applications.

Lightening flywheels is potentially risky, and for this reason we would recommend purchasing a lightweight flywheel specific for the purpose instead. From experience, a 6.85kg steel billet lightweight flywheel will work very well with a 1,100kg two-wheel-drive sports car – such as a TVR – with no noticeable downsides in drivability.

It is worth noting here that some Rover V8 engines – for example, TVR-spec 5-litre engines – are externally balanced via the flywheel. In this case, if the flywheel is replaced, then the new flywheel would need to be rebalanced as part of the entire crankshaft rotating assembly.

Lightweight Rover V8 flywheel.

DISASSEMBLING, INSPECTING AND ASSEMBLING A SHORT ENGINE

The two main factors when it comes to a successful strip-down and rebuild of a short engine are cleanliness and organization, and the importance of this cannot be overemphasized. To this end it is recommended to clean the exterior of the engine prior to disassembly, then clean and inspect each component as it is removed. Any components that have been inspected and are deemed fit for use should be cleaned again, this time to ensure that they are ready for refitment. These components should then be placed into your clean assembly area, away from the disassembly and inspection areas.

Where there are several components – such as pistons and rods – these should be numbered or marked in a manner that makes it clear where they should be located within the engine. It is always highly recommended that these components are refitted in exactly the same location from which they originated – thus the piston for cylinder no. 1 should go back in cylinder no. 1. It is also worth noting and marking the correct orientation of any components, where relevant.

When rebuilding the short engine, all seals, bearings and piston rings should be replaced regardless of condition.

Individual Component Inspection

Pistons

Clean carbon from the pistons, including in the piston-ring grooves. A piece of old piston ring is useful for cleaning the grooves. Visually inspect pistons for damage and wear, particularly on the piston crown (top) and skirts. If you have any doubts about the pistons, replace them.

Using a micrometer, measure the piston diameter at 90 degrees to the gudgeon pin as well as at 10mm from the bottom of the piston skirt. The correct diameter depends on which particular type or grade of piston is fitted. As an example, the grade 'A' piston fitted to a P38A engine should have a diameter of 3.700in to 3.702in. A slightly larger, grade 'B' piston is available for the same application, with a diameter of 3.701in to 3.703in.

If replacing the pistons, it is very important to make sure that the correct pistons are fitted, to ensure the correct piston-to-bore clearance, gudgeon pin height, compression ratio, and so on. If you are planning on reusing your existing pistons, then trial-fit the new piston rings, and check that the ring-to-groove and ring gap clearances are correct and within tolerance for each piston ring.

Gudgeon Pins

Measure the overall length, the diameter at each end, and the clearance between the pin and the pin locating bore on the corresponding piston. If either of these dimensions is out of tolerance, replace the gudgeon pins.

Connecting Rods

Visually inspect the con-rods for signs of damage, measure their lengths to ensure that they are within tolerance, and inspect the bearing location areas. Visually inspecting the wear present on the old big-end bearings and pistons can help you work out whether or not the con-rods are likely to be bent or twisted, and whether or not they will require further inspection or replacement. The rod bolts/studs should also be inspected and replaced if there is any doubt about their condition. Both the big-end and small-end bores should be inspected and measured for size and circularity on each con-rod.

Crankshaft

The first check is to measure the run-out of the centre bearing journal. This is done by locating the crankshaft on a pair of V-blocks on the front and rear bearing journals, and measuring the run-out of the centre bearing journal, using a dial test indicator (*aka* DTI or 'clock'). If this run-out is more than 0.003in, then the crankshaft is not suitable for a regrind and will need to be scrapped.

If the crankshaft passes this first check, then each bearing journal must be measured thoroughly to ensure that it is within tolerance for diameter, circularity (roundness), radius and width. The relevant workshop manual will give you two figures for each of these measurements – one that dictates whether the crankshaft can be used as is, or if it requires a regrind, and the other whether or not the crankshaft can be reground, or needs to be scrapped.

Once the crankshaft has been fitted to the engine block with new bearings, the crankshaft end float then needs to be measured. This is the amount of axial movement that the crankshaft is able to undergo, measured with a DTI. The fitment of over-size main bearings can sometimes necessitate the machining of the centre main bearing thrust faces to achieve the correct end float.

Cylinder Liners/Bores

Visually inspect the cylinder liners. If there is any sign of liner movement, bore damage or wear, rectify these issues by replacing or reboring the cylinder liners. If visually they appear to be alright, measure the piston-to-bore clearance using the correct piston and a set of feeler gauges. If excessive piston-to-bore clearance is present, you will need to rebore the cylinders and fit larger diameter pistons.

Camshaft Follower Bores

Follower-to-bore clearance should be between 0.0008in and 0.0015in as a minimum. If you have 0.003in or more, the engine block would need to be replaced or the follower bores to be sleeved.

Engine Block

Check the block deck for flatness with a straight-edge and feeler gauges. If the deck is not completely flat, this will need to be machined flat, ensuring that the deck height is the same for each cylinder. If your engine is suffering from coolant loss, get it carefully inspected for cracks and liner movement. If no issues are revealed during that inspection, it is worth getting the engine block pressure tested to ensure that you are not putting your valuable time and money into a faulty engine block.

Once the individual components have been cleaned and are ready for refitment, it is advisable to coat them with a suitable water-dispersant oil such as WD40 to prevent them from corroding.

Assembly

During engine assembly your entire work area should be clean and free from any form of debris.

All components that form part of the rotating and reciprocating assembly should be fully balanced by a reputable engine builder with the correct equipment. Most Rover V8 engines are internally balanced,

Engine block being machined. ROLAND MARLOW, AUTOMOTIVE COMPONENT REMANUFACTURING LTD

Rotating assembly of aftermarket 5-litre engine, viewed from underneath.

meaning that the rotating crankshaft assembly is balanced via the crankshaft counterweights. In these cases the flywheel and crank pulley assembly can be replaced or changed without any negative impact on the balance of the rotating crankshaft assembly, as long as they are dynamically balanced themselves.

Some Rover V8 engines – for example, some aftermarket or TVR-spec 5-litre engines – are externally balanced via the flywheel. This means that the rotating crankshaft assembly is actually balanced via the flywheel. In this case, if the flywheel had to be replaced, it would need to be rebalanced as part of the entire crankshaft rotating assembly. Internal balancing is preferable, particularly for high-revving applications, as this method reduces the bending stresses on the crankshaft.

Be observant and methodical when assembling your short engine. Also, use the correct lubricants for the relevant components – for example, molybdenum disulphide/ ZDDP for camshaft lobes and lifters.

Working Out the True Static Compression Ratio

Once the short engine has been assembled, it is a good time to check the volume above the top piston ring and below the deck face, so that you can work out the true static compression ratio. Although many builders simply calculate the volume above the piston, based on the cylinder bore diameter, we prefer to measure it with a burette and base our compression ratio calculations on actual volume measurements. Done like this, we have found that the true static compression ratios are typically 0.5:1

lower than the stated compression ratio. So a Rover V8 with a stated 9.35:1 might actually be 8.85:1 when measured to include the swept volume between the top piston ring and the top of the piston.

We usually measure the volume on top of the piston with the piston between 0.100in and 0.200in down from TDC. By measuring how far down from TDC the piston is, we can calculate the volume when the piston is at TDC, but will not encounter any issues from trying to measure the volume on top of the piston when it is close to, or even above the deck face.

In order finally to calculate the actual static compression ratio, or to achieve the desired compression ratio, we will also need to measure and/or modify the corresponding combustion volume in the cylinder head.

Burette being used to measure volume above the piston.

Once the short engine is assembled, it is a good time to check where top-dead-centre (TDC) is on cylinder 1, and ensure that it is marked accurately on the front pulley. This is best done using a dial test indicator (DTI) gauge on the top of piston no. 1, and TDC should be marked as the centre of the piston dwell at the top of its stroke. Once the front pulley has been accurately marked, the cylinder heads can be fitted and the rest of the engine can be assembled.

Piston-to-Valve Clearances

The other important check to carry out during final assembly is piston-to-valve clearances. On

Checking top dead centre (TDC) using a DTI gauge.

$$\text{Static Compression Ratio} = \frac{\text{Uncompressed Volume}}{\text{Compressed Volume}}$$

$$\text{Uncompressed Volume} = \text{Compressed Volume} + \text{Cylinder Displacement}$$

$$\text{Compressed Volume} = \text{Volume above Piston @ TDC} + \text{Cyl. Head Combustion Chamber Volume} + \text{Head Gasket Volume}$$

'Volume above piston @ TDC' is calculated based on your volume measurement above the piston with the piston down the bore. So as an example, if we measured the volume with the piston 0.150in (0.381cm) down the cylinder bore to be 40cc:

$$\text{Volume at TDC} = \text{Measured Volume} - \left(\pi \times \left(\frac{\text{Bore}}{2} \right)^2 \times \text{Piston Distance from TDC} \right)$$

$$\text{e.g. } 40\text{cc} - \left(\pi \times \left(9 \cdot \frac{4\text{cm}}{2} \right)^2 \times 0.381\,\text{cm} \right) = 13.56\text{cc}$$

Volume in the cylinder-head combustion chamber is simply measured with a burette.

$$\text{Head Gasket Volume} = \left(\pi \times \left(\frac{\text{Gasket Bore}}{2} \right)^2 \times \text{Compressed Gasket Thickness} \right)$$

So if you had a compressed volume of 58cc and a cylinder displacement of 500cc, giving you an uncompressed volume of 558cc:

$$\frac{558}{58} = 9.62$$

Therefore in this example the engine has a true static compression ratio of 9.62:1.

a standard specification engine with a standard camshaft this check is not necessarily required, but on a modified engine with an aftermarket camshaft or different pistons, these clearance checks are very important. There are two ways of checking piston-to-valve clearance, but with both methods we always recommend checking at least one intake valve and one exhaust valve on each bank. You will need the required camshaft fitted, and will preferably have at least a few solid followers with suitable length pushrods to ensure that you get no complications arising from hydraulic followers changing the true position of the valve. If you only have hydraulic followers to hand, then you will need to locate a DTI gauge on the outer edge of the valve spring retainer to ensure that you are getting the correct lift values at the valve for that particular camshaft (taking the rocker arm ratio into account).

Both methods are quite tricky and time-consuming to get right, but it is worth doing one of these to ensure that your custom engine build does not end with piston-to-valve collision!

The first method is the Plasticene method: this involves placing some Plasticene or something similar – for example Blu-tack – on the top of the piston, in the area that corresponds with the intake and exhaust valves. Then fit the cylinder head and gently nip it down using the head bolts or studs, ensuring that it is properly located by using a torque wrench set to approximately 15lb-ft. Assemble the valvetrain (pushrods, rocker arms, and so on) and carefully rotate the engine through at least four complete revolutions. Remove the valvetrain and cylinder head: you should now see an imprint of an intake and/or exhaust valve in the Plasticene on the top of the piston. Measure the depth of the imprints at multiple points, making a note of the minimum depth for both the intake and exhaust valves. Repeat this test so that you have these values for an intake and exhaust valve on both banks.

Using a DTI gauge to check piston-to-valve clearance when using adjustable rocker gear.

The second method is only relevant if you have rocker arms with built-in adjusters. Assemble the long engine with cylinder heads fully torqued down, and the valvetrain fitted and set up correctly (including setting the rocker adjusters). Locate a DTI gauge on the outer edge of the valve spring retainer, preferably a digital DTI gauge so that it is easy to reset or zero the displayed values. Fit a timing disc to the front of the crank nose and ensure that it is correctly set up to match when that particular piston is at TDC.

Work out where peak valve lift occurs on both the intake and exhaust valves, in terms of crankshaft rotation. Rotate the engine until you reach one of these peak lift points, and zero the DTI gauge at this point. Then use the rocker adjuster to very carefully open the valve further, until you can feel the valve just touch the piston, and then record the value displayed on the DTI gauge, along with the corresponding crankshaft angle. Carefully wind the rocker adjuster back until the value is back at zero, and you are back to the original starting position.

Carefully repeat this process at 5-degree intervals from this maximum valve lift point, going up to 30 degrees both before and after the maximum valve lift point. Once you have established where the minimum clearance occurs, you can then carry out further checks at 1- or 2-degree intervals from that point. Once you have established what the minimum clearance is, record this value.

Repeat this entire process for the other three valves that are to be tested, so that at least one intake valve and one exhaust valve on each bank have been checked. Note that at no point should there be any real force applied to the adjuster: you will need to be very careful, as we don't want to bend a valve in the process of these checks!

Once you have worked out what the minimum piston-to-valve clearance is on the intake and exhaust valves, what is considered to be an acceptable clearance? These tests are carried out with a cold engine and at extremely low engine speeds, so the clearance needs to take into account the maximum engine speeds and operating temperatures.

The Rover V8 long engine grows or expands by approximately 0.040in when it gets to full operating temperature, theoretically increasing the piston-to-valve clearance, but the engine rotating at speed will naturally reduce the piston-to-valve clearance, with a higher maximum engine speed leading to a smaller piston-to-valve clearance. As a guide we recommend a minimum cold clearance of 0.060in on the intake valves, and 0.100in on the exhaust valves.

Timing disc bolted to crankshaft nose.

CHAPTER 3

OIL SYSTEM

The oil system is one of the most critical aspects of any engine build. Without sufficient lubrication the engine will not last more than a few minutes. It is worth paying great attention to this aspect of any engine build, performance or standard. It should be understood that the oil system actually performs two functions: lubrication and cooling. Failure of the oil system in some way is the most common cause of engine failures.

The Rover V8 benefits from regular oil changes, and by regular we mean every 3,000–6,000 miles (4,800–9,650km), depending upon oil type. This may seem excessive, but engines serviced this regularly will repay the owner in greatly increased service life. Engines that are subject to infrequent oil changes will acquire the 'black death', where the engine internals sludge up with carbon and soot. This sludge blocks oil passages and results in accelerated wear.

We would recommend following factory guidelines on lubricants in most engines. These engines have relatively large clearances and generally prefer oils of slightly heavier weight, particularly engines with distributor-driven oil-pump gears. A good quality 20w50 mineral oil is usually recommended in earlier engines, and a 10w40 synthetic oil for later engines with crank-driven oil pumps. Fully synthetic types such as 5w50 Mobil 1 are often recommended for some of the performance variants, such as the TVR units. Synthetic oil has a greater tolerance to heat and is less likely to break down under high temperature conditions. Also, engines run with synthetic oils usually stay cleaner internally for longer. Although these oils last longer, we would still recommend changing them every 6,000 miles (9,650km) as a maximum. Frequent oil changes of a good quality mineral oil are better than less frequent changes of a synthetic type.

For new or freshly rebuilt engines we use a good quality running-in oil with a high ZDDP content. The ZDDP content has been significantly reduced in many engine oils, but is essential for helping prevent excessive wear with flat tappet lifters, especially during the initial bedding-in process. Look for oils that have a ZDDP content of around 1,200ppm.

OIL TEMPERATURE AND OIL COOLERS

Engine oil needs to be maintained at the correct temperature to lubricate properly. A great deal of engine wear can be prevented by ensuring that the engine is operating at the correct oil temperature for as much time as possible.

Oil temperature gauge.

Oil cooler.

Oil temperature should ideally be maintained at between 95 and 110°C. The engine should not be run hard until the oil has attained a temperature of 70–75°C. If you suspect that you have high oil temperatures, then this can be monitored using an oil-temperature gauge. If oil temps are found to be regularly exceeding 120°C, and it is not due to an underlying problem, an oil cooler should be fitted. Any engine fitted with an oil cooler should incorporate an oil thermostat to ensure that the oil is only cooled when required, to prevent excessive engine wear through overcooling. Cold oil is equally as damaging as overheated oil, and will also cost us power due to the increased viscosity and pumping losses.

DISTRIBUTOR-DRIVEN OIL PUMPS

The earlier Rover V8 engines, built between 1967 and 1993, used an oil pump that was driven from the end of the distributor driveshaft. This driveshaft is in turn driven from a skew gear on the camshaft. Some of the newer 3.5-litre engines also retained this arrangement.

The weakness in this design is the pump drive where it comes off the camshaft. The teeth on these skew gears can wear away rapidly if the oil pressure is increased too much; this issue is compounded in racing engines by high engine speeds. This is a well documented issue that plagued many early racing engines. One patch that was used during the Rover SD1 racing era was to take an oil feed line from the

oil pump and route this to a jet in the front cover, which sprays oil on to these gears to increase the lubrication and therefore reduce gear wear. This was partially successful, but did not eliminate the problem entirely.

This is not necessarily an issue on well built road engines, provided the oil pressure is not increased to more than 55–60psi maximum, and the engine is not regularly revved in excess of 6,000rpm. The ultimate solution is to upgrade to the later crankshaft-driven oil pump. To do this you will need the 'interim' front cover with integral crank-driven oil pump, crankshaft damper, and matching (longer) woodruff key. In addition to these parts, you will need to have the slot on your existing crankshaft machined to match the extra length on the new woodruff key. Alternatively, you can fit a crankshaft that already has the longer keyway.

If you cannot justify or afford this conversion, then there are some effective modifications that you can make to improve the efficiency of your existing lubrication system.

First, you need to ensure that the existing system is in perfect condition and running optimum clearances. The first step is to make sure that the lubrication system is in perfect condition with at least factory oil pressure. This may sound obvious, but even rebuilt engines will often have wear in the front

Oil-pump gears for post-1976, pre-Serpentine Rover V8.

cover's oil-pump housing. Despite being immersed in oil, these parts do wear quite badly due to pumping unfiltered oil. Any small particles and debris that are subsequently filtered out by the oil filter will still pass through the pump and pump housing. The oil-pump housing should be carefully inspected for scoring. Any front cover that has scoring should be replaced with new, or one in better condition. If the pump gears are worn, these can be easily and cheaply replaced. With new gears fitted in a new front cover, there should be approximately 0.05mm (0.002in) clearance between the tips of the gears and the housing/front cover.

A used cover with no visual wear and new gears will often have at least double this clearance, with 0.1–0.15mm (0.004–0.006in) being fairly normal. Even this acceptable level of wear will measurably reduce oil pressure by a few psi. More clearance than this indicates that you should replace the front cover with one showing less wear.

The next job is to check the pump end float. This is done by fitting the new gears in the pump housing and measuring the height of the gears above the mating face of the gear housing. The ideal distance is 0.15mm (0.006in). We can subtract this from the thickness of the oil-pump cover gasket (approximately 0.20mm (0.008in)) to check the minimum end float between the pump gears and pump housing. On a new engine this would give an end float of 0.06mm (0.002in). It is not uncommon to see

Measuring the oil-pump end float on a pre-Serpentine Rover V8.

end-float measurements closer to 0.13–0.30mm (0.005–0.012in). This is not acceptable, and should be rectified so that end float is at a maximum of 0.08mm (0.003in).

Finally the oil-pump bottom cover should be inspected and discarded if it is showing any signs of visible wear. The cover can be remachined, but it should be noted that this is anodized to reduce wear and would need to be re-anodized after any machining work.

The second option to improve the efficiency of your existing lubrication system is to fit the larger pump gears from post-1976 engines to pre-1976 engines. The early 1967–1976 oil pumps have shorter gears than the later ones (1976–1993). These early engines can be upgraded with the later gears and front cover, or be upgraded with a kit that consists of the longer gears and a spacer. This is a straightforward and cost-effective upgrade that instantly boosts oil flow by approximately 40 per cent for the same oil pressure. This should be considered an essential modification for early engines.

CRANKSHAFT-DRIVEN OIL PUMPS

The weaknesses of the original distributor shaft-driven oil pumps were overcome with the introduction of the 'interim' and later front timing covers that were first produced in 1994. These later 'interim' or 'serpentine' front covers deliver approximately 25

Measuring the oil-pump clearance on a pre-Serpentine Rover V8.

per cent more volume of oil. The pump gears are directly driven from the nose of the crankshaft, eliminating the distributor drive-gear wear problems that are experienced with the earlier set-ups at high oil pressures and higher engine speeds. Earlier engines can be upgraded to this later set-up, as detailed in the previous section.

There are now aftermarket front covers available from John Eales for those that require a distributor drive and are unable to source a good 'interim' timing cover. The P38A-type front covers are relatively common and easy to source, but have no provision for a distributor drive. Furthermore, they must use a 'short-nose' camshaft rather than the 'long-nose' camshaft of the interim and earlier engines, as the front cover is shorter. This is not a problem, with most camshaft manufacturers now offering their cams in both types. The availability of aftermarket distributor-less ignition systems has made the use of P38A front covers a reasonably straightforward proposition.

To do this, you must have the crankshaft keyway remachined, as with the interim front cover conversion. A P38A front cover set-up not only allows the use of the later crankshaft-driven oil pump, but also makes the overall length of the engine approximately 75mm shorter, improving packaging in tight engine bays.

Crankshaft-Driven Oil-Pump Inspection and Checking for Wear

Any new or rebuilt engine should have the oil-pump gears replaced as a matter of course. It is acceptable to refit an oil pump on an engine that has been stripped for repairs or inspection, provided it shows no signs of wear and the internal clearances are within tolerance, as outlined below.

Crankshaft-driven oil pump cover.

With the timing cover removed, undo the seven screws and the bolt securing the steel oil-pump cover plate, and remove the plate. Before removing the oil pump itself, make scribe marks on the inner and outer pump gears to ensure they are refitted in the correct alignment. Carefully remove the oil-pump gears, and inspect the aluminium housing and steel cover plate for scoring and wear. Any scoring of the housing or cover plate will require a replacement timing cover and/or cover plate. Do

Measuring Serpentine oil-pump clearances – measurement between rotors (maximum clearance 0.25mm).

Crankshaft-driven oil pump.

not be tempted to reuse a front cover that is showing signs of scoring, as this will reduce pumping volume and pressure. Visually inspect pump rotors and oil-pump drive gear, and check the depth of any wear steps on the oil-pump drive-gear teeth: these steps should not exceed 0.006in (0.15mm). If these parts are in perfect condition, then reinstall the pump with reference to the scribe marks made earlier.

Using a feeler gauge, check the clearance between the teeth of the inner and outer gears, and ensure that this does not exceed 0.01in (0.25mm). Place a straight-edge across the mating face to which the pump cover plate screws, and measure between this and the pump gears: the clearance here should not exceed 0.004in (0.1mm).

If any of these clearances are exceeded then the pump should be replaced, and the clearances rechecked. If these clearances are still found to be excessive, then the timing cover should be replaced.

OIL-PUMP PRIMING

Any engine that has been fully disassembled, or even stood up for a considerable amount of time, should have its oil pump primed before starting. Failure to do this may result in oil starvation and catastrophic wear on first start-up. The oil pump in a Rover V8 is located above the oil level, and for this reason they do not self-prime adequately. The exact method of priming can vary depending on the type of oil pump.

Priming the Oil Pump on Distributor-Driven Oil Pumps (1967–1993)

The first method involves manually packing the pump gears with petroleum jelly (for example Vaseline). The oil-pump gears and pump housing should be filled with petroleum jelly, ensuring it is completely filled with no empty gaps or cavities. This provides the necessary lubrication and sealing between the gear faces to ensure the initial pumping that is required to draw oil from the sump. The second (preferred) method requires the engine to be fully assembled with oil up to the correct level.

Measuring Serpentine oil-pump clearances – axial measurement (maximum clearance 0.1mm).

Pre-Serpentine oil-pump drive tool.

A bar is fabricated that has a slot on one end to engage with the drive peg of the oil pump, and the other end is turned down to fit in the chuck of a drill. The distributor is removed and the bar inserted into the distributor drive hole until it engages with the oil-pump drive peg. The other end of the bar is inserted into a high-speed electric drill. Use the drill to drive the oil pump in a clockwise direction until the oil-pressure light goes out.

Priming the Oil Pump on Crankshaft-Driven Oil Pumps

The simplest way to prime these engines is to remove the oil-cooler outlet pipe, blanking bung or oil-pressure sender from the bottom of the timing cover, and insert a length of pipe with the correct fitting to match this outlet. The other end of this pipe is connected to a bottle full of engine oil and raised above the engine level. This bottle is gently squeezed at the same time as the engine is rotated counter clockwise. This rotates the pump backwards and draws oil from the outlet through the pump rotors/gears and backwards through the oil pick-up into the sump. The engine is then filled with the correct grade oil and cranked on the starter, with spark plugs removed, until the oil-pressure light goes out.

Oil pressure gauge.

CAUTION: If the oil-pressure light fails to go out after following these priming steps, then do not be tempted to start the engine in the hope that it will attain oil pressure itself. Simply repeat until the light goes out, or investigate. If you do start the engine and the oil-pressure light remains on, then shut down within a few seconds or catastrophic damage will occur.

OIL-PRESSURE AND PRESSURE-RELIEF VALVES

Before discussing or analysing oil pressures, we should ensure that the oil pressure is being checked with a new or known matched gauge and sender. Electronic sender and gauges, particularly as fitted on many TVR engines, can vary in accuracy. A good quality mechanical gauge offers the most reliable check.

Standard Engines

Oil pressure is often alarmingly low at idle on the 1967–1993 engines with the distributor-driven oil pump. Pressures of 5psi at idle, when hot, are not uncommon on these standard early engines. With a standard engine this is not necessarily a cause for concern, provided the oil pressure is no less than 35psi at 5,000rpm. A new or factory rebuilt engine would have a range of oil pressures from 10psi at 1,000rpm, to approximately 40psi at 5,000rpm. With the later crankshaft-driven oil pump we can expect higher pressures of around 15–30psi at idle when hot, rising to 45psi at 5,000rpm.

Modified Engines

As a general rule of thumb, modified engines with a greater power output than standard should ideally have 8–10psi of oil pressure per 1,000rpm. However, we do not want to exceed 60psi maximum on distributor-driven oil pumps or the drive gear will wear at a very rapid rate. Crankshaft-driven oil pumps do not suffer with this issue, and oil pressure should have at least 8–10psi of oil pressure per 1,000rpm. For an engine regularly revving to 7,000rpm we want an absolute minimum of 55psi oil pressure. Oil pressures in excess of 70psi are not necessary or desirable as they will increase parasitic losses and increase the oil temperature.

Oil-Pressure Relief Valves

The standard oil-pressure relief consists of a small steel cylinder-shaped relief valve, relief spring and cap, or threaded plug. The pressure relief valve should be carefully inspected for scoring or wear, both on the valve itself and inside the valve bore. The valve must move freely inside its bore with no tight spots.

Aftermarket relief valves are available with a ball end to help prevent seizing or sticking. These types of relief valve are commonly referred to as 'tadpole' relief valves due to their appearance. The valve is a ball with a small shaft on which the relief spring locates. The ball shape is far less likely to jam or stick than the standard cylinder shape. These 'tadpole' relief valves do have different flow characteristics to a standard relief valve: the oil pressure will drop much faster on initial opening than the standard valve, due to its shape exposing more flow area for a given opening. The disadvantage of these valves is that they do not necessarily seat as well in the relief bore, leading to oil draining back into the sump over time. This disadvantage can be

Serpentine and pre-Serpentine oil-pressure relief valves.

largely resolved by gently lapping the valve into its seat using a fine lapping paste.

Increasing Oil Pressure

The first step is to make sure everything is in perfect condition and that there are no underlying issues or engine wear causing a reduction in oil pressure. We do not want to mask an underlying issue. Oil pressure should be within standard tolerances before attempting to use any of the methods discussed to increase it any further. Furthermore you should have good reasons for wishing to increase the pressure, such as prolonged high engine speeds in competition engines. Most engine builds will not require an increase in pressure beyond standard values. It is worth pointing out here that increased oil pressure will cause hydraulic lifters to pump up at lower engine speeds than would otherwise be the case. Possible reasons for low oil pressure include:

- worn oil-pump gears
- worn oil-pump housing and/or front cover
- worn bearing shells/ crankshaft journals
- worn camshaft bearings
- worn rocker gear
- worn lifter bores
- worn pressure relief valve/ weak spring

Oil-Pressure Relief Valve Springs

There are a few methods of increasing oil pressure on a healthy engine, including stronger oil relief valve springs and adjustable oil-pressure relief valves. There are no adjustable pressure relief valves available for the crankshaft-driven oil pumps at the time of writing, although they are available for the distributor-driven oil pumps fitted to pre-Serpentine engines. Stronger oil-pressure relief valve springs are available that increase peak oil pressure by approximately 10psi.

Attempting to increase oil pressure on a worn engine using an adjustable oil-pressure relief valve or stronger relief spring will not work. The standard oil-pressure relief valve might begin to open at 30psi and be fully open by 40psi, with an up-rated one

Oil pressure versus engine speed with standard and up-rated oil-pressure relief springs.

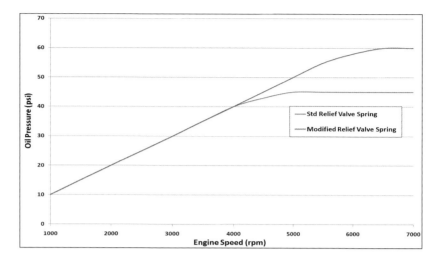

opening at 40 to 50psi. If an engine is only able to generate, say, 10psi oil pressure at idle, the relief valve will be fully shut anyway and increasing the strength of the spring will have no effect on the idle pressure whatsoever.

Restricting the Oil Feed to the Rocker Shafts

This is a worthwhile modification for higher revving engines that will boost hot oil pressure at all engine speeds, including idle, by approximately 3–5psi. The Rover V8 retains a lot of oil in the upper part of the engine at higher engine speeds, and this modification keeps more of the oil where it is needed most – at the bottom of the engine. There is a limit

Restricted oil-feed modification in the cylinder head using a grub screw.

to how far we can take this, however, as oil is not only used to lubricate the valve gear but also to cool the valve springs, particularly on the exhaust valves.

There are two 4.76mm (³⁄₁₆in) oil feeds in each cylinder head that feed the rocker shafts/rockers with oil. Only one of these feeds is used in each head, but both are drilled as the heads are not handed. These feeds are larger than strictly necessary, so they can be drilled and tapped to accept a grub screw. This grub screw should be drilled down its centre with a 1–2mm drill to create an oil jet. The size of this oil jet depends on the engine specification; typically we would use a 1–1.5mm hole on engines fitted with roller rockers, and 1.5–2mm on engines fitted with conventional rocker gear. This oil restrictor or jet can be installed in the cylinder head or cylinder block feed. If it is installed in the heads, ensure that the heads are fitted in the intended orientation, with the restricted oil feed being the one facing the front of the engine block.

This work obviously necessitates removal of the cylinder heads at the very least, and any drilling or tapping operations should only be carried out on a bare block. It is possible to carry out a similar but slightly less effective modification on an otherwise assembled engine by removing the rocker gear and gently inserting a small length of ³⁄₁₆in brake pipe tubing into each feed in the head. This pipe is a tight fit and can be gently tapped into place taking great care not to burr the hole in the pipe or cylinder head.

This method is not quite as effective as the drilled grub screw, as the hole is approximately 2.5mm. Hot oil pressure is typically improved by 2–3psi with this method, or more if the rocker gear is a little worn.

Restricted oil-feed modification in the cylinder head using 3/16in copper brake pipe.

Restricting the Oil Feed to the Camshaft Bearings

This modification is sometimes employed in racing engines. The original oil-feed hole in each camshaft bearing is approximately 4.76mm (0.188in). 1.5mm (0.060in) oil-feed holes can be drilled into the new camshaft bearings at 180 degrees to the original feed holes. The camshaft bearings are then installed into the cylinder block with the new smaller holes aligned with the oil-feed holes in the block. The oil supply is now restricted to the maximum amount of oil that a 1.5mm hole can flow. This is still sufficient for most engines, particularly for racing applications. With the supply to the camshaft bearings restricted, there is more oil delivered to the main and con-rod bearings.

Chevy-Type Valvetrain Oiling System

Another modification is to completely block both rocker-shaft oil feeds in the cylinder heads with undrilled grub screws, and convert to the Chevy-type oiling system for the rockers. This system feeds oil via the centre of the followers and hollow pushrods to the rocker gear. In this set-up, each rocker arm has its own independent oil feed.

CRANKCASE VENTILATION AND PREVENTION OF OIL LEAKS

This is one area that is often overlooked or lacking in many modified engines. The standard engine uses vacuum from the intake manifold to draw gases and excess pressure from the crankcase. Fresh air is

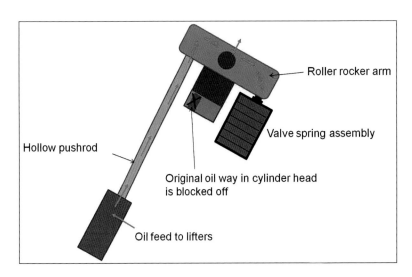

Chevy-type oiling system on a Rover V8.

drawn in from a small breather filter or hose connection on one of the rocker covers, sucked through the crankcase, and then drawn up through the opposite rocker cover via an oil separator or flame trap into the intake manifold.

The vacuum connection to the intake manifold is via a restricted hole to control the level of vacuum and prevent oil being drawn out of the engine under high vacuum conditions (for example, on deceleration with the throttle plates shut). Reducing the pressure in the crankcase to slightly below atmospheric not only helps prevent oil leaks, but also aids piston ring sealing by creating a greater pressure differential across the piston rings.

Helping the piston rings to seal better not only helps prevent further crankcase pressurization, but also has a positive effect on power output by ensuring that more combustion pressure is utilized in the cylinder, rather than being wasted, blowing past the rings into the crankcase. A faulty or ineffective crankcase ventilation system will result in oil leaks that seem impossible to seal, particularly from the rear main and front main seals. If you notice leaks in these areas, we would recommend carefully inspecting the crankcase ventilation system for issues before replacing any seals or gaskets.

Any modification that results in increased engine speeds, greater cylinder displacement or higher cylinder pressures will create greater crankcase pressurization and will therefore require a more effective ventilation system. It should be remembered that an engine that has a 5000cc cylinder displacement is going to displace a similar amount of air in the crankcase as in the cylinders. An engine turning at higher speeds will also be pumping more air around the crankcase. Extra cylinder pressure (more torque) also increases crankcase pressure.

Unfortunately, many modified engines have a crankcase ventilation system that is less effective than the standard one. The positive crankcase ventilation system is often removed and replaced with an oil-catch can and a few breather filters at best. With

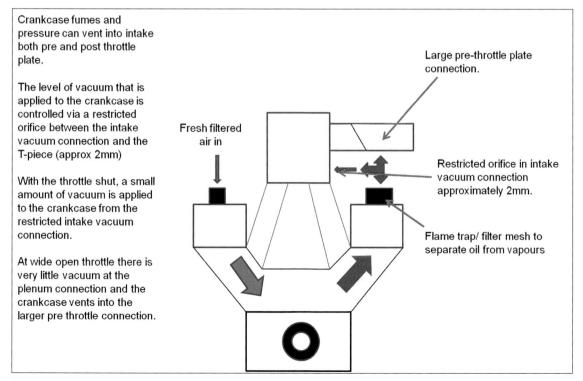

Crankcase fumes and pressure can vent into intake both pre and post throttle plate.

The level of vacuum that is applied to the crankcase is controlled via a restricted orifice between the intake vacuum connection and the T-piece (approx 2mm)

With the throttle shut, a small amount of vacuum is applied to the crankcase from the restricted intake vacuum connection.

At wide open throttle there is very little vacuum at the plenum connection and the crankcase vents into the larger pre throttle connection.

Large pre-throttle plate connection.

Fresh filtered air in

Restricted orifice in intake vacuum connection approximately 2mm.

Flame trap/ filter mesh to separate oil from vapours

Diagram of standard crankcase ventilation system.

this set-up the crankcase has no vacuum applied, and relies on atmospheric ventilation. However, the breather outlets on the engine need to be significantly larger if we are going to rely on atmospheric ventilation. The standard breather connections on the Rover V8 rocker covers are not adequate for this. A far more effective crankcase ventilation system would be one modelled around the original set-up, but with extra capacity to suit the modifications.

Forced induction set-ups require a slightly different approach. We cannot connect directly to the intake manifold, as the intake becomes pressurized when the engine is on boost. However, we can still benefit from a positive crankcase ventilation system by using two one-way valves, or PCV valves and a T-piece, as shown in the diagram.

On some competition engines, or forced induction engines running high levels of boost, it can be undesirable to route the crankcase ventilation through the air intake, as the intake can draw in oil mist or vapour. This oil mist can lower the fuel octane and potentially contribute to detonation on highly stressed engines. In this case we recommend using a minimum of two ¾in breathers routed to an oil-catch tank that is vented to atmosphere.

SUMPS

Due to its long production life and the large number of variants, a wide range of different sumps is available for the Rover V8. It should be remembered that the oil pick-up pipe should also match the sump. These include:

- early sumps (Rover P5B, P6B, early Range Rover), where the oil pick-up is central in the sump
- the Rover SD1: shallow front, oil pick-up pipe at the rear with separate windage tray for oil control and to separate the oil from the spinning crankshaft

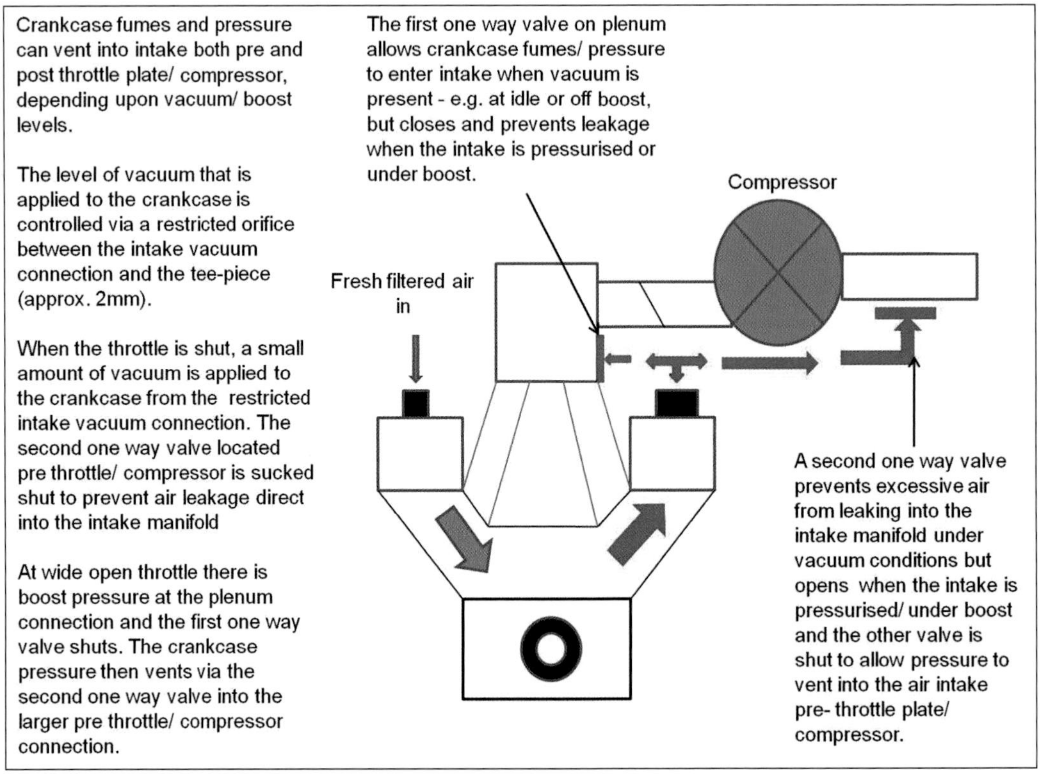

Crankcase fumes and pressure can vent into intake both pre and post throttle plate/ compressor, depending upon vacuum/ boost levels.

The level of vacuum that is applied to the crankcase is controlled via a restricted orifice between the intake vacuum connection and the tee-piece (approx. 2mm).

When the throttle is shut, a small amount of vacuum is applied to the crankcase from the restricted intake vacuum connection. The second one way valve located pre throttle/ compressor is sucked shut to prevent air leakage direct into the intake manifold

At wide open throttle there is boost pressure at the plenum connection and the first one way valve shuts. The crankcase pressure then vents via the second one way valve into the larger pre throttle/ compressor connection.

The first one way valve on plenum allows crankcase fumes/ pressure to enter intake when vacuum is present - e.g. at idle or off boost, but closes and prevents leakage when the intake is pressurised or under boost.

Compressor

Fresh filtered air in

A second one way valve prevents excessive air from leaking into the intake manifold under vacuum conditions but opens when the intake is pressurised/ under boost and the other valve is shut to allow pressure to vent into the air intake pre- throttle plate/ compressor.

Diagram of modified crankcase ventilation system, suitable for forced induction.

Different types of Rover V8 sump.

| Rover P5B & P6 | Range Rover Classic & TVR | Range Rover P38A GEMS |

*Note that this particular sump has been modified for extra clearance around the crank for a 5 litre conversion.

- the later Range Rover Classic: similar to the Rover SD1 – with a shorter, shallow area at the front and welded horizontal baffle
- Range Rover P38A GEMS: pressed steel; oil pipe from the front cover to the rear of the engine
- Range Rover P38A THOR: aluminium cast sump

Sumps can be cut and modified to increase oil capacity or create additional clearance, but you should take great care when doing this to avoid creating oil surge issues during hard cornering or acceleration, which could expose the oil pick-up pipe. Extra sump baffling may also be needed, particularly if the engine is to be used in competition.

The sump gasket is a common source of oil leaks with these engines, and obtaining adequate sealing can be difficult. Our solution is to use oil-resistant RTV sealant in place of the gasket, and a clamp plate at the rear of the sump. This clamp plate was used as standard on earlier engines but omitted later in production. It can be obtained under part number 603943. Two longer bolts, part number HU857, will also be required. The method we employ is as follows: remove the sump, clean all traces of sealant from both flange faces, and degrease thoroughly using brake cleaner. Apply oil-resistant RTV sealant to the sump face, refit the sump, and install the clamp plate at the rear of the sump. Refit all the sump bolts finger-tight, and allow the sealant to go tacky for five to ten minutes. Torque the sump bolts to 12lb-ft. Leave the sealant to cure overnight before refilling with oil.

CHAPTER 4

CYLINDER HEADS

There is no other component in an engine that has more of an impact on its performance than the cylinder head. An effective cylinder head not only has to allow as much airflow as is required for the engine capacity and maximum engine speed, it also has to mix this air thoroughly with fuel and burn it as efficiently as possible within its combustion chamber.

It is easy to look at the standard head castings for the Rover V8 and wonder what the designers were thinking. However, if you consider the design criteria of a fairly wide power-band, good fuel efficiency and low emissions, it makes sense. Small ports and valves give good torque at low engine speeds due to high air velocity at low engine speeds, offset ports give high swirl for good fuel atomization, and offset valves enable the spark plug to be placed in the centre of the cylinder for good combustion efficiency. These same small valves and ports that give good torque at low engine speeds will restrict airflow and reduce torque at higher engine speeds. The bends in the port reduce peak flow capabil-ity, and the offset valves reduce cylinder flow by increasing valve shrouding.

It is important to understand that every aspect of the cylinder head is a compromise between the vari-ous design criteria. Whilst the cylinder head repre-sents the ultimate bottleneck to intake and exhaust flow, it is only part of a package of components that must work in harmony together.

With respect to tuning the Rover V8 engine for more performance, the cylinder heads are the most significant restriction. For this reason, it is worth establishing which cylinder heads or head modifica-tions are to be used first, and then design the rest of the engine to make them work to the best of their ability for your chosen application.

STANDARD CYLINDER HEADS

Considering the Rover V8 engine enjoyed a long production life, there is surprisingly little variation between standard cylinder head types, although one should be aware of a few key types:

Rover V8 cylinder heads, showing valve and port positions.

- Buick and Oldsmobile heads
- Rover 1967–1976
- Rover 1976–1982
- Rover 1982–1994
- Rover 1994–2004

Buick and Oldsmobile Heads

There are key differences between the Buick and Oldsmobile heads. The Buick has the familiar five-bolt pattern around each cylinder, whilst the Oldsmobile has six bolts. There are distinct differences in the combustion chamber, too, with the Buick head having a relatively shallow chamber and valves that are offset from the centreline of the cylinder bore in the same way as the Rover head. The spark plug has a central location.

The Oldsmobile uses a much deeper combustion chamber in combination with flat top pistons. The valves are located much closer to the centreline of the cylinder than the Buick/Rover types, with the spark plug in an offset location. The valves are slightly larger in the Oldsmobile heads. There are actually two different types of Oldsmobile head: one low compression type with a 51cc chamber, and a high compression version with a 38cc chamber. The Oldsmobile engine has steel rockers located on rocker-shaft bolts that tie down through the cylinder head and into the block. Due to the extra head bolt, the Oldsmobile heads will not fit on the Buick or Rover cylinder blocks.

Buick 300 Heads

The Buick 300 was a larger capacity, cast-iron version of the Buick 215. For the 1964 model only, this engine was fitted with aluminium cylinder heads. These heads have four bolts around each cylinder, much like the later Rover four-bolt heads, and due to a common design ancestry will fit the Rover V8. These cylinder heads have slightly larger intake valves, at 41.5mm. These heads used to be highly sought after in aftermarket Rover V8 tuning circles as a performance upgrade, due to the slightly larger ports and valves. The standard Rover head can be easily modified with porting and larger aftermarket valves to exceed the performance capability of these unmodified Buick heads. This, combined with the rarity and cost of these heads, makes their use far less common today.

Rover 1967–1976

These are the original Rover V8 heads, and were essentially the same as the Buick 215 heads. They have a 36cc combustion chamber. Valve sizes are 38mm on the intake, and 33mm on the exhaust with three angle valve seats. These early heads use the shorter reach (12.7mm) spark plug. These heads have slightly less flow than the later versions, although they can be successfully modified in the same way as the later heads with larger valves and porting, to yield reasonable results.

Rover 1976–1982

The Rover V8 head design received a few alterations for the introduction of the Rover SD1 in 1976. The most obvious is the change from a short reach (12.7mm) plug to a long reach (19mm) plug. The intake and exhaust valves were increased in size from 38mm on the intake to 40mm, and the exhaust from 33mm to 34mm; interestingly the valve-seat width remained the same at 38mm on the intake despite the larger 40mm valve width. These small changes slightly improved cylinder head flow over the earlier heads.

Rover 1982–1994

These heads are commonly referred to as 'Vitesse' or 'EFI' heads, and are basically the same as the above, with a few small detail differences. The main difference is a larger minimum port area achieved through machining the valve throat 1mm wider, and utilizing waisted stem intake valves. These valves are waisted down from the full 8mm stem width, to approximately 7mm just behind the valve head. The combination of a narrower stem and wider throat increases the minimum port area and therefore improves full lift cylinder head flow. All heads from this date are suitable for unleaded fuel, as they are fitted with very hard valve seats as standard.

Rover V8 cylinder head 1982–94, in stage four format with big valves.

Rover 1994–2004

These are commonly referred to as 'four-bolt' or '28cc' heads, and are easily identified by the four-bolt cylinder head bolt pattern. The fifth head bolt, beneath the exhaust manifold, was found to aggravate cylinder head sealing issues as it 'tilts' or pulls the cylinder head, reducing the clamping force on the opposite face, so it was deleted for the 1994 model onwards. The combustion chamber volume was reduced from 36cc to 28–30cc by machining the deck face. This was done to compensate for the larger volume of the new composite head gasket that was introduced to replace the tin head gasket type used on all earlier engines. Overall compression remained the same. However, the later 28cc heads can be fitted with the thinner tin gasket to yield an increase in compression ratio (by approximately 0.6:1 on a standard 3.9).

Ports are slightly larger on these heads, and there is more area around the bend in the port, resulting in a flow improvement of approximately 5 per cent over the earlier heads. The common availability of these later heads makes them an ideal basis for modified engines. However, the earlier heads do have more material left in the ports, particularly around the short side turn, allowing for more freedom when carrying out extensive porting.

CYLINDER HEAD MODIFICATIONS

We must carefully consider our intended usage and design criteria before modifying or selecting

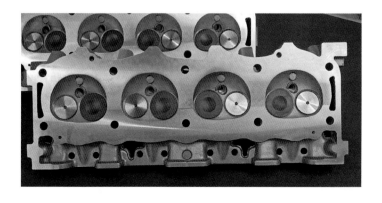

Rover V8 cylinder head 1994–04.

modified cylinder heads. The cylinder head should be the centre point of a package of well thought out modifications that work together. The cylinder head represents the major impediment to performance, so getting good horsepower from this engine is all about effective cylinder head modifications. These engines often struggle to make 60bhp per litre, yet equivalent 2-valve pushrod engines (such as the modern GM LS engines) can easily make in excess of 75bhp per litre in standard form, and 90bhp per litre in modified form. The fundamental difference between these engines is the cylinder head design.

There are a number of different suppliers providing modified Rover V8 head castings in various forms. Very few of these suppliers provide any quantifiable information, such as an airflow chart for their products. Furthermore, many suppliers commonly use the designation 'stage one', 'stage two', 'stage three', and so on, with no clear definition of what these stages mean. For this reason it is worth finding out exactly what has been done when comparing different heads, and not assuming that one supplier's designation (for example, stage two) is the same as another supplier's. Despite this confusion, there is a generally accepted stage of modifications that most suppliers' products conform to, listed below.

Home-Brewed Heads

The Rover V8 head is certainly not a high performance component, and even relatively simple modifications can yield noticeable improvements. In order to develop and produce our own cylinder heads, ideally we would have both the specialist tools and knowledge not only to create but also to test the efficacy of any modifications. This equipment includes a cylinder head flow bench, velocity probes and dynamometer, as well as the more basic porting tools such as an air compressor and die grinder. Fortunately for the knowledgeable enthusiast, we provide detailed step-by-step instructions and pictures of the various stages of modification to enable them to modify their own cylinder heads without any of the expensive test equipment.

Essential Porting Tools

The following equipment is essential for anyone contemplating their own cylinder head modifications:

- Air compressor, ideally one that can keep up with your die grinder running continuously without slowing – this means at least 10cfm and ideally 14cfm or more
- Die grinder – these are relatively inexpensive, and even a cheap one will get the job done

Table 7: Valve and throat dimensions for different stages of head modification

Cylinder head modifications	Valve diameters (intake/exhaust)	Valve seat diameters (intake/exhaust)	Valve throat diameters (intake/exhaust)
Standard	40mm/34mm	38mm/33mm	34mm/29mm
Stage one	40mm/34mm	38mm/33mm	35mm/29mm
Stage two	40mm/34mm	39.5mm/33mm	36mm/29mm
Stage three	41.5mm/35.5mm	41mm/34.5mm	37mm/31mm
Stage four	43mm/37mm	42.5mm/36mm	38mm/32mm

Table 8: Port dimensions for different stages of head modification

Cylinder-head modifications	Intake port dimensions	Exhaust port dimensions
Standard	Standard: 41 × 25mm	Standard: 34 × 23mm
Stage one	Standard: 41 × 25mm	Standard: 34 × 23mm
Stage two	44 × 26 × 7.5mm rad. corners	Standard: 34 × 23mm
Stage three	44 × 27 × 7.5mm rad. corners	35 × 25mm
Stage four	44 × 28 × 7.5mm rad. corners	40 × 28mm

Testing exhaust port flow on a flow bench.

Testing on a chassis dynamometer.

- An assortment of tungsten carbide burrs – the oval and flame-shaped burrs are the most commonly used. We prefer the double-cut burrs for the ports, and a flame- or cylinder-shaped diamond-cut pattern for the throats
- A tapered mandrel to fit a 6mm collet or chuck, and assorted cartridge rolls. The most useful cartridge rolls are the 13 × 25mm and 10 × 25mm cylinder types (60 grit)
- Internal calipers – these are used to measure the internal dimensions of ports and valve throats
- Metal rule and sharp metal scribe, to measure and mark out port faces
- An assortment of flap wheels – between 34 and 38mm are most useful for cleaning and opening up round openings, such as the throat
- Air belt sander, useful for finishing straight port edges

Porting: An Introduction

Before we start grinding away at our heads, we really need an insight into what we are trying to achieve. The goal is to identify the greatest bottleneck to airflow, and work on that first. We have broken the port down into individual sections in the diagram opposite, and have measured the flow rate of each section (at 25in pressure drop) to illustrate where our efforts should be focused.

From this diagram, it should become clear that the major bottleneck to airflow is the intake valve and throat. This should always be the case, as we want maximum velocity to occur at the back of the valve, not out in the port somewhere. We could

A selection of porting tools.

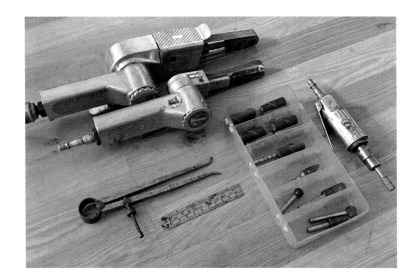

easily enlarge the main port body by opening it up to the full gasket diameter, but the overall gas flow will remain the same as the bottleneck is still at the valve. Clearly, what is needed is more airflow through the valve throat and valve area. This brings us nicely on to the first stage of modification: opening the valve seat to full valve diameter, and enlarging the valve throat.

Stage One

This stage of modification means different things to different specialists or suppliers. Many 'stage one' heads seem to have had very little in the way of modification – perhaps a light clean-up of the valve throat and port areas. For ourselves and the purpose of this book, stage one modification means one thing: removing the primary bottleneck by opening the valve seat up to full valve seat diameter and enlarging the valve throat.

All post-1976 Rover V8 cylinder heads used a 40mm diameter intake valve as opposed to the 38mm intake valve of earlier heads. Despite having a 40mm valve, these later heads still used a 38mm diameter valve seat.

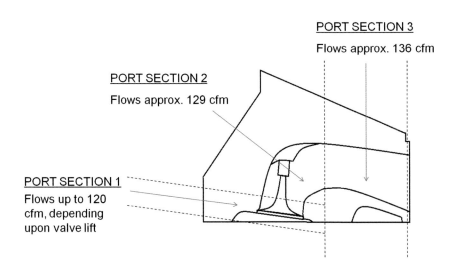

PORT SECTION 3
Flows approx. 136 cfm

PORT SECTION 2
Flows approx. 129 cfm

PORT SECTION 1
Flows up to 120 cfm, depending upon valve lift

Standard intake port, showing flow rates of different sections.

Intake valve and throat.

Valve seat being machined. ROLAND MARLOW,
AUTOMOTIVE COMPONENT REMANUFACTURING LTD

1. Open up the intake valve throat to approximately 36mm, carefully using a carbide burr in a die grinder. This can be done by a number of specialists with CNC tooling if you are not confident. It can be quite tricky to make sure this stays round, so keep moving the tool in a circular motion. It helps to define the valve seat clearly so you have a visual reference. The throat includes the hard valve seat insert and the aluminium for approximately 20mm past the insert itself.

2. Recut the intake valve seat to full valve diameter. You must ensure that the valve seat in the head is smaller than the seat on the valve by at least 0.5–0.8mm. This is because the valve is an interference fit in the head. For example, we would cut the seat at 39.5mm for a 40mm diameter valve. It is easiest to get this done by a company

Valve throat being enlarged.

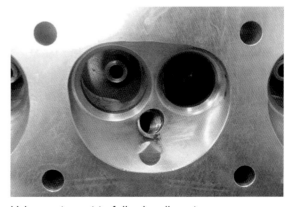

Valve seat recut to full valve diameter.

The standard valve has a 45-degree seating face right up to its full 40mm diameter. All that is required is to recut the existing valve seat in the heads to 39.5mm (allowing at least a 0.5mm interference between valve seat and valve). This single modification improves flow up to approximately 0.300in of valve lift where the valve is in close proximity to the valve seat.

The next step is opening up the valve throat diameter by 2mm to approximately 36mm diameter. This improves flow from 0.300in of valve lift and up when the valve is no longer in close proximity to the valve seat, and the nozzle formed by the throat and valve stem becomes the main bottleneck. This throat modification should ideally be done before the valve seats are recut, as a slip with a carbide burr here could ruin your valve seat face.

with the necessary equipment to cut the three angle seats in one go. However, it is possible for the determined enthusiast to do this themselves by hand with some practice and patience, using the excellent Neway-type valve seat cutting tools.

Table 9: Valve seat dimensions

Valve seat angle	Valve seat width
30-degree top cut	Approx. 1.2mm
45-degree seat face	1.5mm
60-degree bottom cut	Blend into throat

These simple steps will improve peak flow by approximately 7 per cent, but more importantly we gain flow throughout the upper lift range without unduly sacrificing port velocity. An engine modified in this manner will still produce good low engine speed torque and fuel economy. But what is this worth in terms of extra torque and horsepower? These modifications are worth approximately 10–20bhp on the later P38A-type cylinder heads, and approximately 15–30bhp on the earlier type heads.

Stage Two

With the first stage of modifications we removed the primary bottleneck by improving the gas flow through the intake valve seat and throat. If we refer to the relative port flow diagram on page 58, we can see that the first port section now flows almost as efficiently as the second port section. We do not want to improve the flow of the valve seat and throat further, without first improving the flow in the rest of the port. Remember, we always want maximum velocity to occur at the back of the valve. If we improve the flow any more in section one, without improving the flow in section two, then we will end up with maximum velocity occurring in the port bend, and very little or no flow improvement at full lift, as the primary bottleneck is no longer in section one. With this in mind, our second stage of modifications is all about improving the flow in port section two/three (*see* overleaf).

1. Carry out the throat and valve seat modifications described for stage one.
2. Scribe the port faces to match a standard intake gasket using a sharp scribe and ruler. This should be approximately 44 × 26mm with a 7.5mm radius in each corner.
3. Use a 13mm diameter round burr on a die grinder to open up each corner to the scribed line you made in step 2.
4. Use a belt sander or round burr to open up the flat sides of the port to the radiused corners.
5. Use a 13mm cartridge roll to smooth this port face into the rest of the port. Getting a good radius on the corners of the rectangular port improves the coefficient of discharge (C_d) without massively increasing the port volume. Blend the round, curved part of the port (section two) into port section one and into port section three.
6. Make sure there is a smooth radius on the short side turn of the port into the valve throat. Do not remove too much material here! We want as large a radius as possible without any sharp edges, steps or lips. A small strip of emery cloth on your finger can be useful for this smoothing work. We can use our cartridge roll and belt sander to remove a little material from the roof of the port where it begins to bend (long side turn). Many people like to remove the valve guides at this point and grind away the valve guide boss. However, it is possible to streamline the valve guide boss with the guides still in situ, rather than remove it altogether. There is very little difference in flow between a streamlined boss and one that is removed altogether, and this choice is largely dictated by whether or not you are replacing the guides. It should be understood that we are refining the existing port contours and shape rather than wildly reshaping them. It is worth noting here that knowing where the waterways are located within the cylinder head is very important when carrying out porting work.

Stage Three

The third stage of modification involves fitting larger intake and exhaust valves to the standard valve

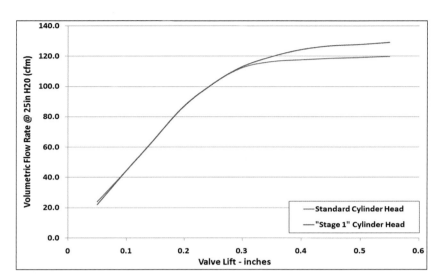

Flow graph comparing standard P38A and stage one intake.

Stage one intake port, showing flow rates of different sections.

PORT SECTION 3
Flows approx. 136 cfm

PORT SECTION 2
Flows approx. 129 cfm

PORT SECTION 1
Flows up to 128 cfm
depending upon valve lift

PORT SECTION 3
Flows approx. 148 cfm

PORT SECTION 2
Flows approx. 139 cfm

PORT SECTION 1
Flows up to 130 cfm
depending upon valve lift

Stage two intake port, showing flow rates of different sections.

seat inserts, as well as opening up the round throat and port bend from 37mm to approximately 38mm. Valve sizes are increased from the standard 40mm intake and 34mm exhaust, to 41.5mm and 35.5mm respectively. The porting modifications described under stage two increased the flow capability of sections two and three far beyond the flow potential of section one. The installation of larger valves seeks to further improve the flow capability of section one. The larger valves will increase the low lift flow due to the greater valve area. Larger valves and valve seats allow us to open up the valve throat, increasing the high lift flow. This is a very popular stage of modification as it yields good results for a relatively modest investment.

1. Open up the intake valve throat to approximately 37mm. This can be done at the same time the valve seats are recut if being done on a Bridgeport mill, cylinder head machine, or similar. Alternatively, you can open up the throat carefully using a carbide burr in a die grinder. It can be quite tricky to make sure this stays round, so keep the tool moving in a circular motion. It helps to define the valve seat clearly so you have a visual reference.

2. Recut the original valve seats to suit the larger valves, allowing a minimum 0.5mm interference between valve seat and valve. For example, for a 41.5mm valve we would cut the seat to 40.8–41mm to allow for a 0.7–0.5mm interference fit between valve and seat.

3. Open up section two carefully, to match the diameter of the throat. Use your tungsten carbide initially, followed by a cartridge roll for the final blending. There should be a smooth transition between sections with no sharp lips or sudden changes in area.

4. Scribe the port faces to match a standard intake gasket using a sharp scribe and ruler. This should be approximately 44 × 26mm with a 7.5mm radius in each corner.

5. Use a 13mm diameter round burr on a die grinder to open up each corner to the scribed line you made in step 4.

6. Use a belt sander or round burr to open up the flat sides of the port to the radiused corners.

7. Use a 13mm cartridge roll to smooth the port face into the rest of the port. Getting a good radius on the corners of the rectangular port improves the coefficient of discharge (C_d) without massively increasing the port volume. Blend the round curved part of the port (section two) into port section three.

Make sure there is a smooth radius on the short side turn of the port into the valve throat.

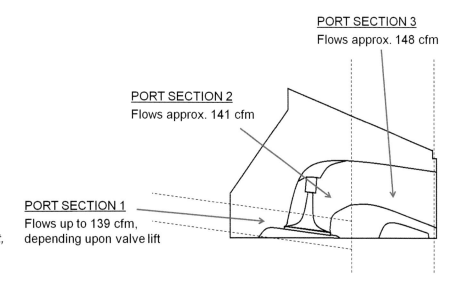

PORT SECTION 3
Flows approx. 148 cfm

PORT SECTION 2
Flows approx. 141 cfm

PORT SECTION 1
Flows up to 139 cfm, depending upon valve lift

Stage three intake port, showing flow rates of different sections.

Do not remove too much material here! We want as large a radius as possible without any sharp edges, steps or lips. A small strip of emery on your finger can be useful for this smoothing work. We can use our cartridge roll and belt sander to remove a little material from the roof of the port where it begins to bend (long side turn).

Stage Four

This stage of modification is generally considered the limit of the standard Rover V8 head casting without going to the great expense of welding up ports, fitting larger valve seat inserts and fitting offset guides for even larger valves. Stage four involves fitting larger 43mm intake and 37mm exhaust valves. Full lift flow improves slightly, but is still ultimately limited by the valve throat size. Low lift flow is considerably improved due to the larger valve and therefore larger curtain area. This has the net effect of increasing the average flow across the entire valve lift range.

1. Open up the intake valve throat to approximately 38mm. This can be done at the same time the valve seats are recut if being done on a Bridgeport mill, cylinder head machine or similar. Alternatively, you can open up the throat carefully using a carbide burr in a die grinder. It can be quite tricky to make sure this stays round, so keep moving the tool in a circular motion. It helps to define the valve seat clearly so you have a visual reference.

2. Recut the original valve seats to suit the larger valves, allowing a minimum 0.5mm interference between valve seat and valve. It is just about possible to do this on the standard seats, but we will often use a 0.7 to 1mm interference to ensure there is sufficient room on the original seat to allow for a small 60-degree bottom cut and blend between the 45-degree seat and the throat.

3. Open up section two (the round curved part) carefully to match the diameter of the throat using your tungsten carbide burr initially, followed by a cartridge roll for the final blending. There should be a smooth transition between sections with no sharp lips or sudden changes in area.

4. Scribe the port faces using a sharp scribe and ruler to approximately 44 × 27mm with a 7.5mm radius in each corner.

5. Use a 13mm diameter round burr on a die grinder to open up each corner to the scribed line you made in step 4.

6. Use a belt sander or round burr to open up the flat sides of the port to the radiused corners.

7. Use a 13mm cartridge roll to smooth the port face into the rest of the port. Getting a good radius on the corners of the rectangular port improves the coefficient of discharge (C_d) without massively increasing the port volume. Blend the

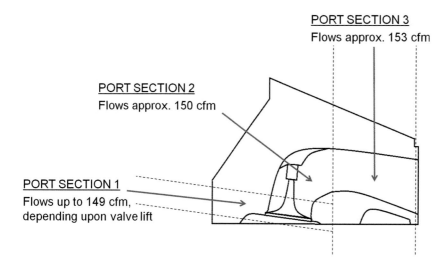

PORT SECTION 3
Flows approx. 153 cfm

PORT SECTION 2
Flows approx. 150 cfm

PORT SECTION 1
Flows up to 149 cfm,
depending upon valve lift

*Stage four intake port,
showing flow rates of
different sections.*

round, curved part of the port (section two) into port section three.

Make sure there is a smooth radius on the short side turn of the port into the valve throat. Don't remove too much material here! We want as large a radius as possible without any sharp edges, steps or lips. A small strip of emery on your finger can be useful for this smoothing work. We can use our cartridge roll and belt sander to remove a little material from the roof of the port where it begins to bend (long side turn).

Custom Modifications

With extensive work it is possible to gain even more flow from the original Rover V8 head castings, but this work is very time-consuming and usually only used for one-off racing applications. Relocating the valve seats and valve guides allows the fitment of even larger valves (for example, a 47mm intake valve) but this can conversely lead to increased valve shrouding, which reduces the overall gains that could be made with this extensive modification.

Changing the port angle by filling the port floor and raising the port roof is another extensive modification that yields further improvements in flow rate. By doing this we have gained an additional 12cfm at 0.500in of valve lift over a stage four big valve cylinder head. This large gain over a stage four head demonstrates that the standard port bend is one of

the major impediments with the original Rover V8 head casting.

AFTERMARKET CYLINDER HEADS

The relatively recent availability of high-performance aftermarket cylinder heads is a very exciting development in Rover V8 evolution. These aftermarket cylinder heads are completely different castings, designed to bolt on to the Rover V8 short engine, but utilizing valvetrain components from existing pushrod V6 or V8 engines (such as Buick and Chevy). They usually necessitate a different intake system, and sometimes a different exhaust system as part of their overall installation.

At the time of writing there are three options available if you want to extract some serious performance from a naturally aspirated Rover V8:

- Merlin F85: with 1.73in intake and 1.45in exhaust valves, as well as slightly larger ports as standard
- TA Performance: with up to 2.02in intake and 1.6in exhaust valves, larger ports, valves moved to the centre line of the bore, and raised exhaust ports
- Wildcat: with 1.94in and 1.6in exhaust valves, larger ports, valves moved to the centre line of the bore, and raised intake and exhaust ports

We have tested these different cylinder heads on our flow bench, along with the various standard Rover

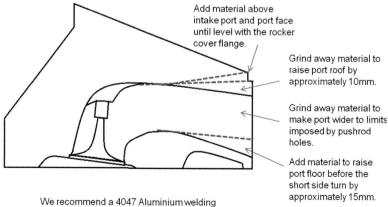

Raised intake port modifications.

Add material above intake port and port face until level with the rocker cover flange.

Grind away material to raise port roof by approximately 10mm.

Grind away material to make port wider to limits imposed by pushrod holes.

Add material to raise port floor before the short side turn by approximately 15mm.

We recommend a 4047 Aluminium welding rod for all filling and welding operations.

Example of raised port welding.

V8 options. The results were very interesting, showing that these aftermarket heads are not always the best solution for every application. Naturally this depends on where you want peak torque to occur, as well as the available budget for the rest of the engine build. You will probably require a different intake system, exhaust system and engine management to ensure that the gains are worthwhile with these aftermarket heads.

As can be seen, up to 0.400in of valve lift in the Merlin F85 and TA Performance heads offers no gain in terms of volumetric flow rate over the stage three or stage four modified Rover V8 cylinder heads. This means that if your application is using a low lift camshaft and you are looking for performance gains at lower engine speeds, these aftermarket cylinder heads would not represent a good investment. It is worth noting here, however, that these aftermarket heads were tested in their standard 'unported' condition. In other words, there is a lot more material left to be removed if required, whereas the stage four Rover V8 cylinder head has been extensively ported and has little or no material left to remove.

The Wildcat cylinder heads yield phenomenal gains in terms of volumetric flow rate, in their standard 'unported' condition. This is due to the significantly improved intake port shape with the Wildcat

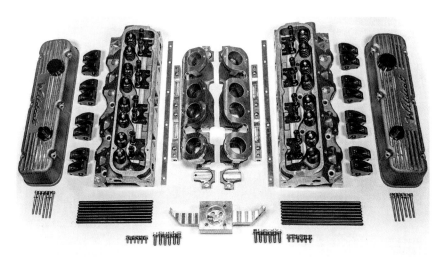

Wildcat cylinder head and valvetrain.

Aftermarket cylinder-head flow-bench test results.

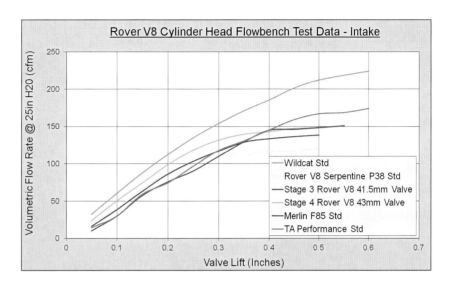

Rover V8 Cylinder Head Flowbench Test Data - Intake

- Wildcat Std
- Rover V8 Serpentine P38 Std
- Stage 3 Rover V8 41.5mm Valve
- Stage 4 Rover V8 43mm Valve
- Merlin F85 Std
- TA Performance Std

Merlin F85 cylinder heads fitted to a 4.8-litre Rover V8.

heads, with the intake valve-to-port face angle providing a virtually down-draught design.

So what sort of gains would we typically expect to see with a set of aftermarket cylinder heads? This naturally depends on the rest of the engine specification, but we have personally seen a 4.8-litre Rover V8 with Merlin F85 heads producing 370bhp, a 5-litre engine with TA Performance

TA Performance cylinder head on the flow bench.

heads producing over 400bhp, and 5-litre engines with Wildcat heads producing over 450bhp. These engines were all built for competition use – with solid camshafts, individual throttle bodies, and so on – but with careful attention to the rest of the engine specification these aftermarket heads can also be used for a very powerful road-car engine.

As an example, we have built ourselves a road-going 4.1-litre Rover V8 with Wildcat cylinder heads and a Kent M238 camshaft. This engine was put in our TVR Chimaera and produced a very impressive 382bhp, equating to over 93bhp per litre! This set-up also utilized a dual-plane exhaust manifold and single-plane tunnel-ram intake manifold.

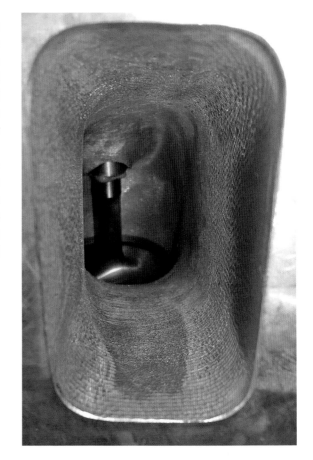

RIGHT: *Wildcat intake port.*

Wildcat set-up in a TVR Chimaera.

CHAPTER 5

CAMSHAFT

The most widely used terms when discussing camshafts are lift and duration, often to the complete exclusion of all other factors. This is a gross simplification of the camshaft's function. There are other important considerations, such as valve overlap, lobe centre angle (LCA), and, perhaps most significantly of all, valve event timing. We will break down these areas below, but it is important to note that these factors are intrinsically linked.

VALVE EVENT TIMING

Valve event timing describes the situation when the valves open and close in relation to crankshaft position; it is measured in degrees of crankshaft rotation. The most common method for listing valve event timing is to state the inlet opening point first, followed by the inlet closing point, and then the exhaust opening point, followed by the exhaust closing point. An example might be a Piper 270 camshaft with a 26-66-66-26 valve timing. This means that the intake valve opens 26 degrees before top-dead-centre (BTDC), and closes 66 degrees after bottom-dead-centre (ABDC). The exhaust valve opens 66 degrees before bottom-dead-centre (BBDC) and closes 26 degrees after top-dead-centre (ATDC).

Valve event timing is the most fundamental aspect of camshaft design. However, it is also the most complex and difficult method to apply when

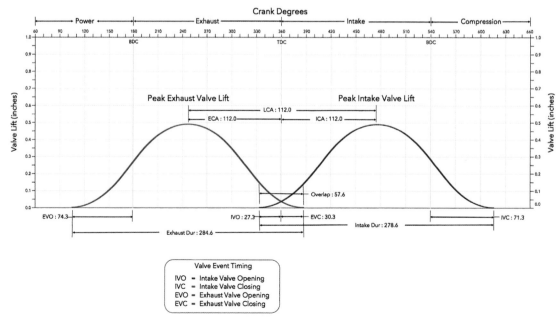

Camshaft timing diagram.

choosing a cam. The vast majority of tuning compa-nies and individuals do not have the resources or understanding to choose a camshaft based on valve event timing as the central parameter. Further-more, some camshaft manufacturers do not supply valve event timing information for fear of competi-tors copying their designs. Unfortunately this makes it very difficult to assess those profiles or test their compatibility using engine simulation software.

There are a number of variables attributed to valve event timing that are much easier to apply to camshaft selection.

LOBE CENTRE ANGLE

The lobe centre angle is simply the angle formed between the full lift position of the inlet lobe and the full lift position of the exhaust lobe. Lobe centre angle is widely misunderstood, and is often neglected in many textbook explanations of camshaft function.

The first thing to understand is that there is usually a small range of lobe centre angles (plus or minus 2 degrees) that will produce the widest power-band for a particular engine specification. If you have to widen the lobe centre angle on a camshaft more than 1 or 2 degrees to reduce overlap and produce the characteristics you want, then the chances are it has too much overlap and duration. Therefore you are simply fixing one cam selection error with

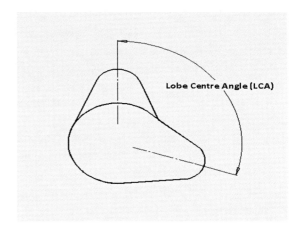

Lobe centre angle.

another! This will reduce performance throughout the engine's entire power-band.

There are several factors that affect the optimum lobe centre angle, the main one being the amount of intake flow in relation to the capacity of the cylinder it has to feed. For a given cylinder head flow, smaller capacity engines will require a wider LCA and larger engines will require a narrower LCA. From this state-ment we can see that increasing the cylinder head flow for a given cylinder capacity will require a wider lobe centre angle (LCA).

Other factors that affect optimum lobe centre angle include compression ratio and valve acceleration (that is, camshaft ramp rate or rocker ratio). Increasing the

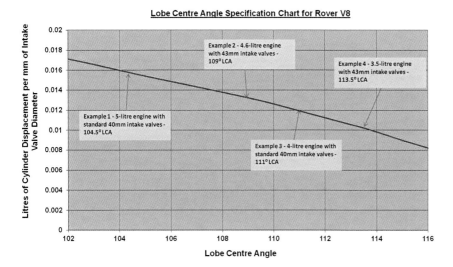

LCA selection graph.

static compression ratio beyond 11:1 will likely require a widening of the LCA, and lowering the compression much below 9:1 will require the reverse.

Please refer to the lobe centre angle chart on page 67 to help you focus on the ideal LCA for your specification of engine. This is a simplified analysis of lobe centre angle (LCA) based on valve size rather than intake flow, but it is accurate enough to get us to within a few degrees of the ideal, and avoids the inclusion of heavy mathematics!

VALVE OVERLAP

Valve overlap describes the amount of time that both the intake and exhaust valves are open at the same time, and is expressed in degrees of crankshaft rotation. The ideal amount of valve overlap used when specifying a cam is entirely dependent on the engine's intended use. Engines requiring good idle and low engine speed characteristics should not use more valve overlap than is necessary. Conversely, engines required to deliver good high speed performance will need significantly more overlap to achieve the performance desired.

The effect of valve overlap on engine performance can be understood when we consider that there can be significant intake flow on the overlap period when the piston is at TDC, the exhaust valve is closing, and the intake is just beginning to open. With an effective exhaust design, at certain engine speeds

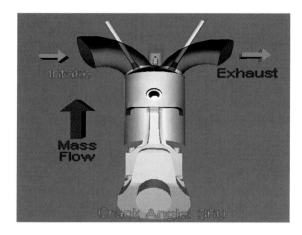

Intake and exhaust interaction.

a positive pressure pulse will have travelled down the primary pipe until it opens into the collector. At this point a negative pressure wave is reflected and will ideally reach the exhaust valve just as the intake valve is opening and the exhaust valve is closing, creating a significant vacuum to help draw more air and fuel into the cylinder.

At higher engine speeds we can effectively use the interaction between the exhaust and intake to initiate intake flow, before the piston begins to descend on its induction stroke. Clearly the more overlap, the larger the window there is for this interaction to occur. The downside of this interaction is that it reduces low engine speed performance in the same manner that it increases higher engine speed performance.

Valve overlap triangle.

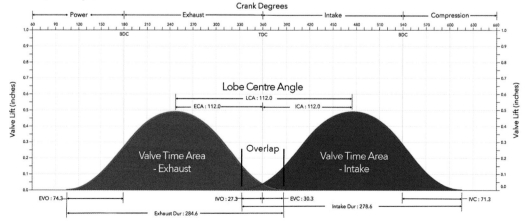

At low engine speeds, gas velocity is considerably lower, and exhaust gases can literally flow backwards from the exhaust into the intake, contaminating the cylinder with hot gases, reducing charge density and therefore torque output. This situation is made much worse in the case of a 90-degree V8 such as the Rover unit, particularly when fitted with the standard EFI single-plane intake, where all cylinders feed from a common plenum. When one cylinder is at TDC on the overlap period, another is beginning its induction stroke. The cylinder beginning its induction stroke can suck straight through the intake and exhaust of the cylinder in the overlap phase, contaminating the intake manifold with exhaust gases, and significantly reducing manifold vacuum. This can be understood as having a large unwanted hole from the exhaust into the intake manifold.

This reduction in vacuum and loss of charge density is compounded by the need for more idle bypass or throttle opening to maintain the same idle speed, thus further reducing manifold vacuum. The negative effects of an excess of valve overlap can be reduced by the use of a dual plane or 180-degree intake manifold, as this divides the overlap and induction phases of the cylinders into two separate intakes or plenums. This can improve manifold vacuum by as much as 50 per cent! Throttle bodies can also reduce the negative effects of valve overlap by ensuring that all cylinders effectively have their own intake with no interaction possible between cylinders.

For further discussion on this, as well as the pros and cons of different manifold types, please refer to chapter 7, 'Intake System'.

Table 10: Overlap versus intake manifold pressure at idle

Valve overlap	Typical pressure with single-plane manifold
30–45 degrees	20–35kPa
50–60 degrees	35–45kPa
60–70 degrees	45–60kPa
70–90 degrees	60–75kPa

To help you determine the overlap range suitable for your requirements, we have produced an overlap selection guide based on both real-world experience and computer modelling of many different camshaft types. This will help your understanding of the concept. Notice that the suggested amount of overlap for certain characteristics will vary, as it will depend not only on the type of intake manifold used, but also on the engine capacity and valve size. It is true that for a given amount of cylinder head flow, the larger capacity engines can tolerate more overlap whilst still providing good idle and low engine speed performance.

The important point here is for a 'given amount of cylinder head flow'. An example of this would be if you wished to maintain the same idle and low speed characteristics of your engine but chose to fit ported big-valve cylinder heads. A reduction in valve overlap would be necessary to maintain the same idle characteristics. Conversely, if the cylinder head flow was sub-optimal not only could we get away with more overlap, but we would need more overlap to produce the flow required.

Overlap Selection Guide

30–45-Degree Overlap Camshafts

Camshafts in this overlap range typically have smooth idle characteristics. They provide excellent torque and response at low engine speeds, making them ideal for vehicles that require good low to mid-range performance, such as heavy 4×4s. These camshafts generally give good throttle response and fuel economy from idle to 4,000–5,000rpm. They are ideal for anyone who does not operate the engine outside the standard 1,000–5,000rpm power-band, and who requires maximum low rpm torque output.

The standard Range Rover P38a 4.6 camshaft falls into this category, with only 34 degrees of valve overlap, 14/70/64/20 valve event timing, and 264-degree duration. This gives a very smooth idle, good fuel efficiency, and low exhaust emissions. This camshaft has a very wide lobe centre angle of 115 degrees. This camshaft represents the mildest of the camshafts available for the Rover V8, but this does not mean that it does not have a place in an engine build. Whilst this camshaft would restrict engine breathing above 4,000rpm, it would still be a good choice for someone who requires a combination of maximum low speed torque output and good fuel efficiency.

The Kent H180 is a good example of an aftermarket camshaft in this overlap range, with 46 degrees of valve overlap, 23/59/59/23 valve event timing, and 262 degrees of duration. This would make a good upgrade for the OEM camshaft mentioned above. The H180 has a relatively narrow lobe separation angle of 108 degrees, making it ideally suited to the larger capacity engines that are intake flow restricted, such as the standard 4.6. This camshaft has a modest amount of overlap and less duration than any of the standard camshafts, yet still gives a good performance gain over these standard offerings. This is due to its higher ramp rate and valve lift, meaning that this camshaft offers the largest possible window of flow within this conservative amount of overlap and duration.

50–60-Degree Overlap Camshafts

These camshafts typically give a good spread of power from just above idle to 5,000/5,500rpm. Idle quality and low speed torque output are slightly reduced when compared to camshafts in the 35–45-degree range, but the mid-range and top-end power is correspondingly increased. This really is the largest overlap range to consider if you have a heavy vehicle or automatic transmission, and need to maintain acceptable low speed torque and a good idle quality. Any more overlap than this and the idle begins to suffer noticeably, and low speed torque output drops off markedly.

The TVR51 camshaft, as fitted to a standard TVR Chimaera 400, deserves a mention in this category with just 51 degrees of overlap, a 272/ 278-degree duration, and a 112-degree lobe separation angle. The combination of relatively wide duration and low overlap gives a good balance between reasonable idle quality, bottom end response, and good high rpm performance.

The Piper 270i is another example of an aftermarket camshaft in this category, with 52 degrees

overlap, valve event timing of 26/66/66/26, and 272-degree duration. This camshaft has a lobe separation angle of 110 degrees.

The Kent H200 also falls in this category, with 57 degrees of overlap, 270-degree intake/ 282-degree exhaust duration, and valve event timing of 23/67/68/34. The lobe separation angle is 109.5 degrees. This camshaft can still be considered to have a reasonably smooth idle and provides a relatively wide torque band, so therefore makes a good road camshaft for a vehicle that is used daily.

60–70-Degree Overlap Camshafts

This can be considered the start of the high performance camshafts. Idle quality and low speed torque will be down when compared to camshafts with less overlap. Camshafts in this overlap range are generally biased towards mid- and top-end power output, depending on the amount of duration.

One example from the lower end of this overlap range includes the unusual TVR885, with 60 degrees of overlap, a wide lobe separation angle of 115 degrees, and 284-intake/300-degree exhaust duration. This camshaft has a valve event timing of 26/78/86/34. This is a hybrid profile, combining a large duration and lift with a wide lobe separation angle and, therefore, a relatively low amount of overlap. The fairly large duration of this camshaft will ensure that peak torque occurs higher up in the engine's speed range, whilst the relatively low amount of valve overlap maintains reasonable idle qualities and fuel efficiency. All these are major considerations for a road-going sports car.

A more conventional performance camshaft in this overlap range is the Piper 285, with 62 degrees of overlap, and 276-degree duration. This camshaft is ground on a narrow 107-degree lobe separation angle, making it an ideal choice for those who require a higher power output on the larger capacity and, consequently, more valve-restricted engines.

70–90-Degree Overlap Camshafts

The lower end of this overlap range can still just about be considered street drivable, whilst the upper end is usually reserved for competition vehicles that do not have to be driven on the road. Cam profiles in the 70–90-degree overlap range are heavily biased towards top end power output and have a significantly reduced idle quality and fuel efficiency, and low speed output when compared to camshafts with less valve overlap. As the overlap period is increased, the dynamic compression at lower engine speeds is reduced, so more static compression and/or greater low speed ignition advance is not only desirable, but often necessary to maintain acceptable part throttle manners.

The importance of an efficient exhaust system from exhaust valve to tailpipe cannot be overstressed when using high overlap camshafts. The scavenging effect that occurs during the overlap period relies on an exhaust system that creates a vacuum or sucks on the exhaust port. If the exhaust system has any noticeable degree of back pressure, exhaust reversion will result, exacerbating the side effects of these high overlap cams and negating any power advantage that might be gained. If you intend to use camshafts in this overlap range it may be worth considering using a dual plane or individual throttle body manifold, to maintain manifold vacuum by ensuring that minimal undesirable interaction occurs between cylinders, during the overlap phase.

At the lower end of this overlap range we have the Kent H214, with 71 degrees of overlap, a 110-degree LCA, and a 284/298-degree duration. This camshaft has a respectable amount of valve lift at 11.9mm/12.44mm for the intake/ exhaust, and valve event timing of 31/73/78/40. This camshaft offers a very good spread of power whilst retaining a reasonable idle quality and low speed output, and really represents the upper end of the road-going cams.

The Kent H224 is the next step up in the Kent range of cams, with 85 degrees of overlap, a 111-degree LCA, and 304/ 310-degree duration. The high overlap ensures excellent high speed scavenging, whilst the long duration ensures the torque peak occurs high up in the engine's powerband. These two factors ensure excellent top-end horsepower. The cost of this is significantly reduced low speed output, poor idle quality, increased emissions output, and increased fuel consumption.

At the extreme end of this range we have the Piper 320, with 98 degrees of valve overlap, a 104-degree lobe centre angle, and 306-degree valve duration. This has the greatest valve lift of any of the cams discussed, at 13.64mm/13.59mm. Valve event timing is 47/79/75/51. This camshaft is only for high rpm competition use, and reduces the effective power-band of the engine considerably.

Summary of Valve Overlap
- Changes in valve overlap can significantly affect peak torque values
- More overlap = more high rpm output, but with a reduction in low rpm output and idle quality
- Less overlap = less high rpm output but with a better idle and low rpm output
- Larger capacity engines tolerate more overlap for a given cylinder head flow
- Dual plane intake manifolds or individual throttle bodies will tolerate more overlap
- With an effective exhaust system, the negative pressure exhaust pulse will generate significant vacuum on the intake during the valve overlap phase. This increases power output within a particular engine speed range

DURATION

Duration is the number of degrees the valves are open for, expressed in degrees of crankshaft rotation, in a complete four-stroke cycle (720 degrees). There are different ways of measuring duration, the most commonly used being seat-to-seat and 0.050in lift timing methods. Seat-to-seat duration is the number of crankshaft degrees from the valve lifting off the seat until the valve closes. Measuring duration at 0.050in simply involves measuring the duration between the cam follower lifting from 0.050in and returning to 0.050in of lift.

Duration can be measured at any number of different lifter heights, including, but not limited to, 0.050in, making cam duration comparisons potentially tricky.

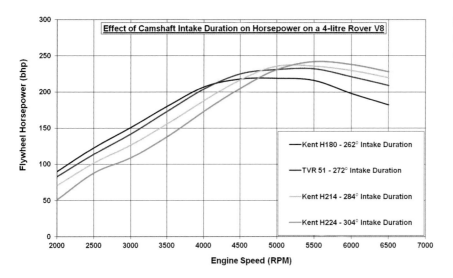

Effect of camshaft intake duration on a 4-litre Rover V8.

However, most camshaft manufacturers clearly state the measuring methods used – for example seat-to-seat or 0.050in, 0.030in, and so on. When describing camshafts in this book, we are referring to seat-to-seat duration as this is currently the most commonly used method in the UK. The majority of performance-orientated camshafts available for the Rover V8 have seat-to-seat durations of between 260 and 310 degrees.

Note that the camshafts shown in the graph do also have different timing values (LCA, overlap and so on), as well as different amounts of lift. This is used broadly to illustrate the typical effect of increasing the intake duration. The amount of duration specified for a camshaft is almost always a compromise. Extra duration does not significantly affect peak torque in the same manner as increased valve overlap. It simply moves the torque peak higher up the rev range, and therefore allows the production of more horsepower due to the fact that horsepower is a function of torque and engine speed.

LIFT

Lift is the distance that the valve is raised from the valve seat. It is worth noting that the peak lift figures given in most camshaft catalogues and in our own camshaft table are theoretical valve lift figures. Theoretical lift is worked out by multiply-

ing the camshaft lobe lift by the rocker arm ratio. Theoretical lift differs from true lift for a number of reasons, including clearances and flex in the valve-train itself, or any changes in rocker geometry.

Most camshafts, standard or aftermarket, have a peak valve lift in the range of 0.390in to 0.550in. The standard production camshafts have a peak valve lift of 0.390in. It is important to observe that the most a Rover V8 with standard cylinder heads and valve springs can safely accommodate is 0.430in of lift. This is to ensure that there is a minimum clearance of 0.050in between the valve spring coils at full lift. Any less than this 0.050in and we are in danger of the spring becoming coil-bound, putting massive stress on the entire valvetrain and potentially breaking the valve spring, retainer or rocker arm, with disastrous consequences.

Direct replacement valve springs with fewer coils are commonly available from aftermarket camshaft suppliers, to allow increased valve lift whilst still maintaining a safe amount of coil clearance. Examples of such springs include Kent Cams VS44 single valve springs, which can safely accommodate 0.465in of lift, and the Piper VSSV8, which allows up to 0.550in lift.

Valve spring bind is not the only mechanical factor that affects the amount of valve lift we can safely use. The amount of clearance between the underside of the valve spring retainer and the top of the valve guide/stem seal is also limited, depending on the production age of the cylinder head you are using. Piston-to-valve clearance also needs to be considered on heavily modified engines with valve lifts of over 0.490in. If in doubt, this should be checked carefully. Refer to the table below to check standard valve clearances of the different production cylinder head types.

There are exceptions to the examples given in the table. Engines that have already been modified may have more clearance than is specified. TVR engines are one example of this, and the only way to be sure with such a non-production engine is to partially disassemble the cylinder heads and measure the clearance yourself.

Mechanical considerations excepted, how much lift should we use? This depends largely on the specification of the rest of the engine. A standard Rover V8 cylinder head will become port and throat restricted by approximately 0.390in of lift. That is to say that lifting the valve any further from the seat will not result in any more peak flow, as the valve throat and/or port itself is now the greatest restriction, and not the area between the valve and valve seat. A typically modified head with a larger throat area, increased valve size and port modifications, will show flow gains when we continue to lift the valve as high as 0.500in.

The modified cylinder head will clearly respond more favourably to increased valve lift than the standard one. Does this mean that there is no point in using camshafts with any more lift than the heads will flow? This is not necessarily the case if you consider that the camshaft only lifts the valves to their peak lift momentarily, spending as little as 2 degrees at peak lift and the rest of the time below this. If we increase the valve lift beyond optimum for peak flow we can improve the average flow or flow area 'under the curve', increasing the total flow in and out of the cylinder.

A major consideration for a road engine, when specifying cam lift, should be reliability and longevity. The Rover V8 has small diameter, narrow cam lobes – and there is no doubt that increased lift results in reduced camshaft longevity. If your engine has modifications that justify the use of a particularly high lift camshaft, and you are happy to change these components more often than standard, then these are compromises you may choose to live with. If, however, your engine is relatively standard, there is less to be gained from increased lift and you may wish to stick with cams giving less than 0.450in lift and enjoy the ease of installation and increased service life.

To summarize camshaft lift:

- The maximum valve lift a standard Rover V8 head can accommodate is 0.430–450in, depending upon the production age of the head
- Camshafts for this engine commonly have peak valve lifts in the range of 0.390–0.550in
- Increased lift results in reduced camshaft longevity
- Piston-to-valve clearance should be checked very carefully on engines with peak valve lifts above 0.490in

Table 11: Standard spring and valve guide clearances

Cylinder-head type	Valve lift before coil bind occurs with standard springs	Valve lift before valve retainers touch valve guide/ valve stem seal
Pre-1976 cylinder heads (short reach plug)	0.450in	0.500in
1976–1993 cylinder heads (rubber washer stem seals)	0.430in	0.500in
Post-1993 cylinder heads (neoprene-type valve stem seals)	0.430in	0.430in (with neoprene stem seals fitted)

Measuring valve retainer to valve guide clearance.

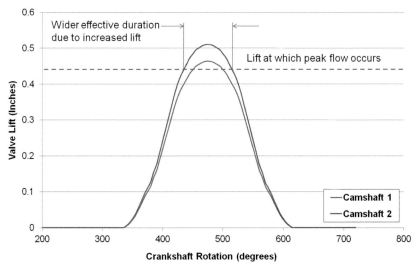

Intake flow versus valve lift.

RAMP RATE

Ramp rate is the rate at which the camshaft lifts the valve from its closed position. A camshaft with less duration and higher peak lift will usually have a higher ramp rate as a consequence. A higher ramp rate will always lead to the valve being open for longer, and will therefore usually produce higher peak power. However, a higher ramp rate also puts more load on the valvetrain, and will therefore reduce its longevity and reliability. Increased ramp rate opens and closes the valves much more rapidly, leading to an increased chance of valve control issues.

HYDRAULIC VERSUS SOLID CAM PROFILES

Although the various factors discussed here apply to both hydraulic and solid camshaft profiles, there are some differences it is worth being aware of. Solid camshafts have a long ramp so that the valvetrain can take up the clearances smoothly, whereas hydraulic camshafts have a short ramp because the clearances are taken up by the hydraulic followers instead. For this reason, it is not usually a good idea to use a hydraulic camshaft with solid lifters, or vice versa. A hydraulic camshaft profile with solid

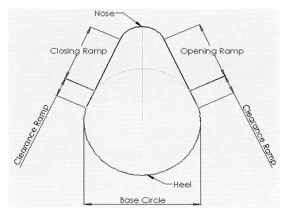

Camshaft lobe diagram, showing 'ramps'.

followers will generally not last as long as a solid camshaft profile, and a close eye will need to be kept on the valve clearances. A solid camshaft profile with hydraulic followers will not be as responsive as the same set-up with solid followers, or the equivalent hydraulic profile with hydraulic followers.

A solid camshaft set-up usually gives slightly faster engine response and slightly more power than the equivalent hydraulic set-up, but is noisier and will require periodic adjustment of the valve clearances.

Roller camshafts are now starting to become available for the Rover V8 engine. These are available in both solid and hydraulic formats. Roller set-ups can reduce wear on camshafts and lifters, particularly when higher valve spring rates are employed for high engine speeds.

CAMSHAFT SELECTION EXAMPLES

Now, let us try some example engine builds, using the guidelines above to specify a camshaft to match.

3.5-litre Road Engine in a Rover SD1 Vitesse

Our first example is a 3.5-litre fast road engine in a classic Rover SD1 Vitesse. This engine has standard internals, but has had 10.5:1 compression pistons fitted, and the cylinder heads have been modified to the stage one specification outlined in Chapter 4, 'Cylinder Heads'. The engine is running a standard single-plane EFI intake manifold, and

tubular exhaust manifolds with a 4-2-1 configuration. The owner wants a good overall performance improvement, but insists that the car must remain driveable, be moderately fuel efficient and maintain a reasonably smooth idle. Furthermore he does not want to have to remove the cylinder heads again for any valve lift modifications. This will limit valve lift to 0.430in or less.

This car has a 3.528-litre capacity engine (0.441ltr per cylinder) and 1.575in-diameter intake valves. This gives 0.441/1.575 = 0.28ltr per inch of valve diameter. If we look this up on our LCA selection graph it suggests a 112-degree lobe centre angle. Now that we know our optimum LCA we can look at how much valve overlap we require. If we look at our valve overlap guide we can see that a 3.5-litre engine with a single-plane intake needs something in the range of 35–55 degrees to produce the performance required, whilst still maintaining a good idle quality with its single-plane intake manifold.

So far we have the following specifications:

- 112-degree LCA
- 30–55-degree valve overlap
- 0.390–0.430in valve lift

At the lower end of this range the Piper 255 would match the owner's criteria admirably, with a lobe centre angle of 112 degrees, 48 degrees of overlap and 272-degree valve duration. With only 0.420in (10.67mm) of valve lift, this camshaft would bolt straight in, requiring no head modifications. Another possibility would be the Kent TVR51. This would give a little more top end performance whilst still staying within our original criteria, with a 112-degree lobe centre angle, 51 degrees of valve overlap and a 272/278-degree valve duration. This is still a 'bolt-in' modification with a valve lift of only 0.425in (10.8mm). Either of these camshafts will give the owner a significant performance improvement with no other modifications required.

Land Rover Fitted with a 4.6 GEMS Engine

Our second example is a Land Rover that is fitted with a 4.6 GEMS engine. The engine has been rebuilt to standard specification, and the owner wants to choose a camshaft that will give a good performance improvement without losing the low speed torque or engine response that is essential for towing their 3.5-ton livestock trailer. The owner uses the vehicle as a daily driver, clocking up high miles driving to jobs up and down the country. He therefore requires good road performance and fuel efficiency, combined with the widest possible spread of torque for towing.

This engine has a 4554cc cylinder capacity (0.569ltr per cylinder) and 1.575in-diameter intake valves. This gives us 0.569/1.575 = 0.361ltr per inch of valve diameter. If we look at our lobe centre angle chart, 0.361ltr per inch of valve diameter gives us an ideal LCA of around 108 degrees. Now we take a look at our valve overlap guide, and can see that we require a camshaft with around 30–45 degrees of overlap to produce the maximum low speed torque output. The duration should be on the low side for this application as we want to tilt or bias the torque curve in favour of low speed running. Valve lift is open as the owner has not yet fitted the cylinder heads and does not mind making minor modifications for clearance, if necessary.

So far we have arrived at the following specifications:

- 108-degree LCA
- 30–50 degrees overlap
- 0.390-0.550in valve lift

The first candidate that meets all these requirements is the Kent H180, with a 108-degree lobe centre angle, making it an ideal choice for this valve-restricted engine. This camshaft has 46 degrees of valve overlap, maintaining excellent idle and low speed torque characteristics. It has reasonably high lift at 0.440in (11.2mm), ensuring good flow within its conservative amount of overlap. Clearances will need checking carefully with this amount of lift, as this is at the limit on many production heads. Valve duration is a mild 262 degrees on both intake and exhaust, ensuring that its torque is biased towards the lower end of the engine's power-band.

The Piper 270 or 270i is another possibility, although the valve overlap is greater than required. The Piper 270 has a 108-degree LCA, 56 degrees of valve overlap, and 10.67mm of lift. The 270i is virtually the same camshaft, but the LCA has been widened to 110 degrees, reducing valve overlap to 52 degrees. This move was made to maintain idle quality on fuel-injected cars, with their single-plane EFI intake. Duration is quoted as 272 degrees. Either of these cams would produce a good spread of torque with this engine, although the reduced lift and increased valve overlap/duration means the power would be produced a little higher in the engine's power-band than with the Kent H180.

A large range of camshaft specifications is shown in the camshaft specification table in the Appendix at the back of this book. These specifications are as complete as we could possibly make them, but any that do not have their valve event timing shown should be regarded as incomplete and cannot be accurately modelled.

CAMSHAFT THRUST PLATES AND THRUST BOLTS

As standard, the camshaft is held in place during operation by the way that the lifters and camshaft lobes are ground, as well as the presence of the timing chain. The camshaft lobes have a slight angle ground on them. The slightly convex face on the lifters means that the lifters rotate as they are pushed up and down. The combination of this lifter rotating action along with the slight angle on the lobes means that the camshaft is constantly being pushed towards the back of the engine, keeping it in place.

When the camshaft, lifters and timing chain start to wear, the camshaft is no longer being held in place properly and starts to move axially (called camshaft 'walk'). When this wear gets worse, the camshaft nose will start to knock against the inside of the timing cover and can even wear a groove into the timing cover as a consequence.

The fact that the camshaft is not always located axially by any other method means that any camshaft, lifter and timing chain wear is accelerated. There are

Wear on the inside timing cover from axial camshaft movement.

Camshaft retaining collar being fitted.

Camshaft retaining collar and camshaft thrust plate.

a number of methods available that can be used to properly locate the camshaft; these are as follows:

Camshaft thrust bolt/button: This is a teflon piece on the end of the bolt that is threaded into the camshaft nose. This small cylindrical teflon piece usually has about 0.1mm clearance from the timing cover, limiting axial movement of the camshaft.

Cam retaining collar: Part number ERR5926. This was fitted to some late interim Rover V8 engines as standard. This collar bolts to the block and prevents the camshaft moving axially.

Camshaft thrust plate: Part number ERR2609. This was fitted to the 38A engines as standard. It is very similar to the retaining collar, and also bolts to the block to prevent the camshaft moving axially.

INSTALLING AND TIMING YOUR CAMSHAFT

Correct installation and bedding in is essential to get the best performance and reliability from your new camshaft. Do not be tempted simply to slot the camshaft in, line up the factory timing marks and hope for the best: the engine will run, but you could be losing anything from 10–100bhp by not ensuring that the camshaft is timed correctly. Worse still, if the clearances are not carefully checked, you could experience a catastrophic breakage in the valvetrain. Remember that if a rocker or pushrod fails you will lose all oil pressure instantly as the camshaft follower can come out of the block, uncovering the oil galleries and destroying your engine!

Checking the cam timing and valvetrain clearances is not difficult, nor is it particularly time-consuming to do, and it ensures you are getting the best performance and reliability out of your chosen camshaft profile.

This guide is not intended to replace the factory workshop manual, but to supplement it where necessary.

1. Before installing the camshaft, inspect the camshaft bearings carefully. If there is any doubt about their condition, get them replaced.
2. Lubricate the camshaft journals thoroughly with the correct camshaft lubricant and carefully insert the camshaft into the cylinder block. Take care not to damage the camshaft bearings.
3. Fit the camshaft thrust plate or retaining collar. Note that there are two different types depending on the engine. Some engines are not fitted with a collar or thrust plate. These should be fitted with a collar, plate or thrust button. This should be considered an essential upgrade to prevent excessive camshaft axial movement.
4. Turn the camshaft by hand and check that it rotates freely in its bearings with no binding or tight spots.
5. Fit the camshaft sprocket key to the cam, ensuring that the key is parallel to the shaft. (Failure to ensure that the key is parallel can reduce lubrication to the camshaft drive gear.)
6. Turn the crankshaft carefully to bring number one piston to top-dead-centre (TDC).
7. Temporarily fit the camshaft sprocket to the cam, ensuring that the marks 'F' or 'Front' are facing outwards.
8. Rotate the cam until the timing mark on the sprocket is in the six o'clock position, aligned with the timing mark on the crankshaft sprocket.
9. Fit the chain around the sprockets, keeping timing marks aligned. Fit chain and sprockets to the crankshaft and cam, ensuring that the timing marks are still aligned.
10. Fit a cam timing disk to the crankshaft nose, securing it loosely with the crankshaft damper bolt.
11. Make a small pointer using a piece of welding rod, a bolt sharpened to a point, or similar. Set the timing disc at zero with number one cylinder at TDC, securing it in place with the crankshaft damper bolt.
12. Temporarily insert a camshaft inlet follower into its follower bore. Position a dial test indicator (DTI) gauge on to the follower, and zero the gauge. We use a bar with the correct thread for the intake manifold bolt or intake gasket clamp bolt, and clamp the DTI gauge to this. If you do not have a dial test gauge you can, at a push, check full lift carefully using a vernier calliper or depth micrometer.
13. Rotate the crankshaft clockwise until you reach the specified peak lift position – for instance, 108 degrees after TDC. Check that the inlet valve has

Checking the camshaft timing.

Using a dial test indicator to check valve lift.

achieved maximum lift and is in the middle of its dwell period. Rotate the crankshaft further, and make sure the follower is definitely at peak lift and does not continue to rise.

14. If full lift is achieved before or after the specified position, then you will need to adjust the cam timing using a multi-keyway pulley or vernier adjustment pulley. Multi-position pulleys usually allow standard (0-degree) and plus 2- or minus 2-degree adjustment. Some allow standard (0) and plus 4-degree or minus 4-degree adjustment. The vernier types are easiest to use as they allow infinite adjustment.

15. Note that if you are using a multi keyway pulley and only have a choice between setting the cam timing slightly advanced or slightly retarded, then it would be better to set it slightly advanced as you will lose less power than running retarded cam timing, and the cam timing will naturally retard as the chain stretches. Timing really needs to be within 1 degree of the specified figure. Of course it is better to use a vernier pulley and set it correctly.

16. Once you are satisfied that the cam timing is correct, rotate the engine twice and re-check it again. Adjust if required.

17. Fit the camshaft spacer with the flange to the front, and re-fit the distributor drive gear (only relevant on distributor-ignition engines).

18. Fit the camshaft pulley bolt and washer, and tighten to 60Nm.

Before your engine is run you will need to do some basic clearance checks. Check the following carefully:

1. Check the valve retainer to valve guide clearance.
2. Check the piston to valve head clearance.

Change the engine oil and filter if you are replacing the camshaft on a used engine.

Running in Your New Camshaft

Running in your camshaft properly is not difficult and does not take much time, but it can make a massive difference to the longevity of your freshly installed camshaft and followers. The first twenty minutes running is critical for any camshaft.

1. Before attempting to start the engine, rotate the engine by hand and ensure it all rotates freely.
2. Prime the oil system, and make sure that everything is ready for the engine to start immediately without excessive cranking. The aim is for the engine to start as soon as possible.
3. Start the engine, and immediately raise the revs to 2,500rpm. Ensure there is adequate oil pressure at all times.
4. Do not let the engine idle below 2,000rpm during the first twenty minutes of running, but vary the speed gently between 2,500 to 3,500rpm. This reduces the load on the valvetrain and ensures the camshaft and followers have sufficient lubrication during this critical running-in period.
5. Change the engine oil and oil filter.

AVOIDING PROBLEMS

On engines with particularly high valve spring pressures (280lb nose pressure or more), it is worth bedding in the camshaft on a lighter set of springs. Although this seems time-consuming it can save the camshaft and followers from premature failure, as most problems will occur during the initial bedding-in process.

CHAPTER 6

VALVETRAIN

The valvetrain on a Rover V8 engine consists of lifters (also known as followers), pushrods, rocker gear, valve springs, retainers and valves. The function of the valvetrain is to translate the motion of the camshaft to the intake and exhaust valves. The Rover V8 is a 2-valve per cylinder pushrod engine. This type of valvetrain design was very common in the 1950s to 1980s – for example American V8s, A-series, B-series – and is still used in the Chevy LS V8 engines today.

When designing or assembling a valvetrain system for your Rover V8, you need to take the following factors into consideration:

- maximum engine speed
- maintenance and longevity
- noise level
- valve lift
- camshaft ramp rate
- valvetrain weight
- oil-system type

LIFTERS

Lifters translate the motion of the camshaft lobes to the pushrods. There are two main types of lifter: hydraulic and solid. Lifters are also known as followers and tappets. The Rover V8 lifter is a 'flat tappet' design, as opposed to a roller-type design. Although described as flat, this type of lifter is not actually flat, it has a convex face with a large radius. These Rover V8 lifters are designed to be used with a flat tappet camshaft that has a taper ground – by approximately 0.025mm – on to the camshaft lobes; this design means that the lifters rotate in their bores as the camshaft rotates. This also ensures that the

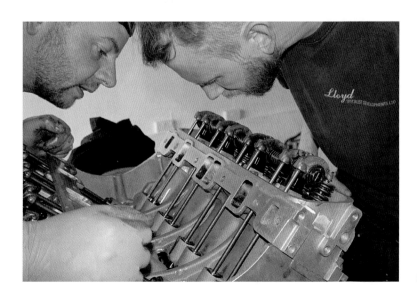

Rover V8 pushrod valvetrain.

wear on the lifter face is distributed evenly across the face. The lifters must be free to rotate in the lifter bores, and this can be observed when rotating the engine with the lifters, pushrods and rocker gear installed. If the lifters do not rotate, the camshaft and lifters will wear out extremely quickly.

The Rover V8 is fitted with hydraulic lifters as standard. This is because most original applications for the engine require component longevity, as well as very low maintenance and low noise levels. A hydraulic lifter is a fairly complex component — it works by taking up the clearance using an internal piston controlled via oilways in the lifter.

The hydraulic lifter will also act as a rev limiter, by holding the valve open for longer at higher engine speeds. This immediately reduces cylinder pressure and will effectively stop the engine from passing a particular rpm point. The particular engine speed (rpm) at which this occurs is a function of the valvetrain harmonics; this is affected by camshaft profile, hydraulic lifter design, valvetrain weight and valve-spring pressures. On a standard Rover V8, this usually occurs at between 5,200rpm and 6,200rpm, depending on camshaft and valvetrain specification as well as preload setting and oil pressure.

The hydraulic lifter is set up with the lifter plunger depressed slightly, with the lifter on the heel of the corresponding cam lobe – this is called 'setting the pre-load'. With a standard hydraulic lifter, this is usually between 0.5mm and 1.25mm, with the minimum amount reducing the likelihood of lifter pump up. This is done at the same time as checking and adjusting the rocker-arm geometry, using shims under the rocker-shaft pedestals. It is well worth noting here that it is possible to fit some rocker shims incorrectly, blocking the oilways in the cylinder head in the process. If your rocker shims only have one oilway hole in them, then particular attention must be paid at this stage of the build to ensure that this does not happen. These shims are also available with two oilway holes so that this mistake cannot occur.

Lifter preload should be checked with the valvetrain fully assembled and the lifter on the heel of the cam. The lifter preload can be difficult to measure, as you need to try and measure between the inner piston and the retaining clip. This can be done by taking a piece of wire, bending the last 5mm at 90 degrees, and flattening the end to your desired

Worn lifter that has not been rotating.

Hydraulic lifter disassembled.

Rocker pedestal shim fitment.

Rocker pedestal shim in place.

preload setting, using a vice. You can then use this as a gauge when setting the preload on each lifter. You may even find it beneficial to make two gauges, one smaller and one larger than the required preload setting, as a set of go and no-go gauges.

In some instances it is not possible to get enough lifter preload, even though no rocker pedestal shims are fitted. In this case it will be necessary either to machine some material off the bottom of the rocker pedestals by the required amount, or to fit adjustable pushrods or adjustable rocker arms.

Hydraulic lifters can become problematic if there are any issues with the oil supply, if the lifters are poor quality, if the valve springs are too weak, or if the valve springs are too strong. If the valve springs are too weak and the valves 'float' at any point, the hydraulic lifter will take up the slack and prevent the valve from closing properly. This is known as lifter 'pump-up'. If the valve springs are too strong – the spring poundage is too high – then this can lead to lifter collapse, where the oil bleeds out of the lifter, rather than overcoming the spring force. This leads to reduced valve lift and, therefore, reduced engine performance.

As well as the standard Rover V8 lifter, there are a number of alternative lifters available. These followers can be sourced from an American V8 with a 0.842in outside diameter – such as a Chevy – and include lifters that are designed for a higher rpm limit. At the time of writing, manufacturers of such hydraulic followers include Crane, Crower, Federal Mogul, Isky Racing, Rhoads. We have successfully used 'hi-rev' hydraulic lifters on Rover V8s revving up to 7,000rpm. These lifters usually have different recommended preload settings, with the 'hi-rev' lifters sometimes requiring very little preload (for example 0.05mm) and including a heavy-duty snap ring to ensure that the hydraulic follower does not break during high rpm use.

When using alternative lifters it is worth checking that the radius of the convex face is compatible with the taper ground into the camshaft lobes. If this is not the case, premature lifter failure is likely to occur.

Solid lifters are often fitted to competition-spec Rover V8s, where outright engine performance is more important than longevity, low maintenance and low noise levels. This type of lifter needs to leave a small clearance (known as valve clearance) to allow for thermal expansion and the required camshaft

Hydraulic lifter, showing the gap between the retaining clip and the inner piston.

Standard hydraulic, hi-rev hydraulic and solid lifters.

lobe ramp clearance. This valve clearance needs to be checked and adjusted periodically. Typical cold clearance values when using solid lifters with the Rover V8 are between 0.006in and 0.012in on the intake, and 0.007in to 0.015in on the exhaust, depending on camshaft and valvetrain specification.

Solid lifters improve engine performance by virtue of their dynamic response; they are generally lighter than their hydraulic counterparts and impose no natural rev limit on the engine speed. This means that an electronic rev limit must be used with solid lifters on a Rover V8, either in the form of an electronic fuel or ignition cut.

PUSHRODS

The pushrod translates the motion of the lifter to the rocker gear. The standard Rover V8 pushrod is a steel rod with a ball formed on each end. It has a stem diameter of ¼in, with a ³⁄₁₆in radius ball on both ends. It is 8in in length. Heavy duty and adjustable pushrods are readily available from a number of different suppliers.

When using aftermarket pushrods or camshafts with more than 0.480in of lift, sometimes it is necessary to enlarge the pushrod clearance holes in the cylinder heads. With the cylinder heads removed, this can be done using either a drill or a carbide burr with a die-grinder.

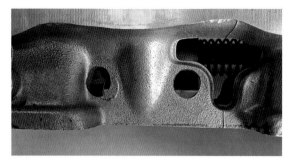

Enlarged pushrod clearance holes.

With the correct roller rockers and lifters, Chevy hollow pushrods can be used as part of the oil system to lubricate the rocker gear.

Some of these aftermarket pushrods are available with a ⁵⁄₃₂in radius ball on the lifter end, making them suitable for a number of aftermarket lifters (such as Federal Mogul, Crane, Rhoads, Crower). These usually have a ⁵⁄₁₆in stem, and often require the pushrod holes in the cylinder head to be enlarged, particularly if you are using a high-lift camshaft.

ROCKER GEAR ASSEMBLY

The rocker arm translates the motion of the pushrod to the tip end of the valve.

The standard rocker gear assembly consists of aluminium rocker arms running on a steel rocker shaft. The rocker shaft is mounted to the cylinder head with four aluminium pedestals and corresponding bolts. The standard rocker assembly is generally

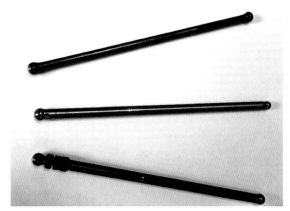

Standard, adjustable and Chevy-type hollow pushrods.

Standard rocker-gear assembly.

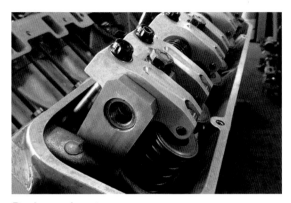

Rocker end post.

Standard and roller rocker arms.

regarded to have a safe engine speed limit of approximately 5,800–6,200rpm, depending on the camshaft used. If you are planning on exceeding this limit, then you will require rocker end posts to prevent rocker-shaft breakage, as well as better rocker arms that are less prone to breakage at elevated engine speeds.

Standard rocker arms have an aluminium body with a steel pad that contacts the valve tip. These steel pads are prone to breaking at higher engine speeds and valve lifts, particularly with less than ideal rocker geometry. All-steel rocker arms are available – such as Federal Mogul – and these are significantly stronger, but they come with a valvetrain weight penalty that can negate any high speed advantages if used with

hydraulic lifters. The ideal rocker arm set-up is roller rocker gear – for example Yella Terra. This features a steel roller instead of a pad, which reduces valve-train friction and load, and usually reduces valvetrain weight – which in turn improves engine response, engine speed capability and longevity.

When assembling the rocker gear, particular attention needs to be paid to the geometry between the rocker arm and valve tip at both closed and full lift positions, to ensure that the rocker arm or valve tip is not overloaded. Overloading the rocker arm or valve tip exacerbates valvetrain wear, and at high speeds can lead to valvetrain failure. Rocker arm geometry is primarily adjusted by placing shims

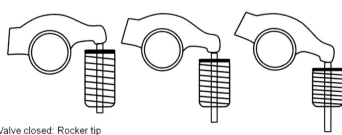

Valve closed: Rocker tip contact is slightly behind the centreline of the valve.

Valve at half lift: Rocker tip contact is ideally on the centreline of the valve. The valve-train is rapidly accelerating and overcoming increasing spring pressure. We want the valve-train to be at it's strongest point here.

Valve at full lift: Rocker tip contact is slightly beyond the centreline of the valve. Although the spring is most compressed, valve-train loading is actually less due to inertia and the fact that the valve mass is no longer rapidly accelerating.

Rocker arm geometry.

of different thickness under the rocker pedestals, but adjustable pushrods and/or adjustable rocker arms can also be used to help optimize it. If you are using hydraulic lifters, this is done at the same time as setting the lifter preload.

The standard Rover V8 rocker arms have a rocker ratio of 1.6:1: this means that 0.3in of lift at the camshaft translates to 0.48in of lift at the valve. If you are planning on using non-standard rocker arms, the rocker ratio will need to be checked as it will obviously affect the valve lift. As an example, if Volvo adjustable rocker arms are used with a rocker ratio of 1.5:1, then the same 0.3in of camshaft lobe lift will translate to only 0.45in of lift at the valve.

VALVE SPRINGS

Valve springs retain the valves in the cylinder head via the valve-spring retainers and collets. These springs also govern the force within the valvetrain, which affects the acceleration, speed capability and longevity of the valvetrain system. The correct selection and installation of the valve springs and related components is essential in producing a reliable and well performing valvetrain. When installing different camshafts or valvetrain components, you need to ensure that the valve springs are of a suitable specification. The valve springs must be able to keep the valvetrain under full control over its entire operating range, whilst at the same time not putting more stress on the valvetrain than is absolutely necessary.

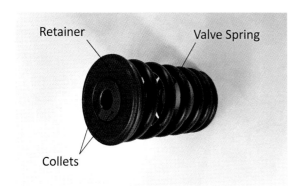

Valve spring, retainer and collets.

You must first ensure that the valve spring is rated correctly for your application, and that you can install that valve spring at its correct install height. Each type of valve spring is rated in terms of its spring load at its particular install height, as well as its spring rate or stiffness. The spring rate is usually expressed in pounds of load per inch of travel, or the load required to compress the spring by a given distance. For example, the standard single valve spring on a Rover V8 has a spring rate of about 250lb per inch. This means that the spring requires 250lb of load to compress it by 1in, or, more usefully, it requires 125lb of load to compress it by ½in. Camshaft manufacturers sometimes specify a maximum 'nose poundage': this is basically the maximum spring load at full lift. Exceeding the maximum peak spring load for a particular camshaft will significantly reduce the life of the camshaft and followers.

The install height is the length of the valve spring when installed on the cylinder head. So, as an example, the standard single valve spring on a Rover V8 has a spring preload of about 75lb, at an install height of 40mm (1.575in). The spring load of this same valve spring increases in proportion to the valve lift, so the spring load at 9.9mm of valve lift is about 170lb.

When purchasing valve springs you will also receive information regarding their correct install height, as they must be installed at their correct install height. This is usually measured using a set of vernier callipers, taking into account the valve-spring seat recess in the cylinder head. This measurement can be taken without fitting the valve springs, as long as the retainer, collets and valve are fitted, with the valve making full contact with the valve seat. You may find that you do not have the correct spring install height, in which case you may have to either fit valve-spring seat shims to shorten the spring install height, or you will need to machine the valve-spring seats deeper into the cylinder head to lengthen the spring install height.

The next check that needs to be carried out is that the valve springs cannot become coil bound. This is where the coils in the valve springs make contact with

Measuring the valve-spring platform recess on the cylinder head.

Single, double and triple valve springs.

each other, effectively making the spring solid at the moment coil contact is made. This situation can be very destructive to the valvetrain. When assembling the valvetrain, the cold static clearance between each valve-spring coil at peak valve lift must be at least 1.25mm. This can usually be calculated without having to fit the valve springs, based on the correct install height, the gap between the coils at the correct install height, and the peak valve lift. Standard single valve springs are usually alright for valve lifts up to 10.9mm (0.430in). If your application has more valve lift than this, it will require different valve springs that will not become coil bound at peak valve lift. Direct replacement single valve springs are available – for example Piper VSSV8 – that have a slightly higher spring rate but with more coil clearance, allowing peak valve lifts of more than 12.7mm (0.500in).

Although Rover V8 engines are usually fitted with single valve springs, many TVR applications are fitted with double valve springs as standard. These double valve springs also have a slightly higher spring rate and more coil clearance, again allowing peak valve lifts of more than 12.7mm (0.500in).

An added advantage of double or even triple valve springs is that the different coils will have different resonant frequencies. This means that only one spring within the spring pack will suffer from resonance at a time, and the slight contact friction between the different coils will reduce these resonant frequencies.

When a valve spring does hit its resonant frequency it will momentarily lose control of the valve, which can lose a significant amount of engine power. This loss of control of the intake or exhaust valve can exhibit itself in one of two ways: valve bounce and valve float. Valve bounce occurs as the valve closes on to the valve seat but the spring does not have sufficient control to keep it shut, literally causing it to 'bounce' off the valve seat. This causes the valve to temporarily open again when it should be closed, losing engine power. This often sounds like an ignition cut rev-limiter at high engine speeds.

Valve float occurs as the valve reaches, and then exceeds, peak lift. Although in some cases this might actually momentarily increase engine performance, loss of valve control in this manner can also lead to piston-to-valve collision and should generally be regarded as undesirable.

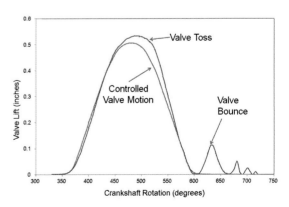

Valve bounce and valve toss.

It is preferable, where possible, to build a valvetrain that does not suffer from resonant frequencies within the engine's operating range. This is usually only a problem for Rover V8 engines operating at higher than standard speeds. To calculate the different natural frequencies of the various valvetrain components (including frequencies caused by the camshaft lobe motion) is beyond most automotive professionals, let alone the amateur enthusiast. So the best approach we can take is to try and push the valvetrain component frequencies well outside the engine's operating range. We can do this by simply ensuring that the valvetrain components are as light as possible, including the valve springs, rocker arms and so on. Lighter weight valvetrain components will have a higher natural frequency, and therefore should not suffer from resonance within the engine's operating engine speed.

Another valve spring option is to use beehive valve springs. The spring rate of this type of spring changes as it is compressed, and the resonant frequency also changes as it is compressed, decreasing the likelihood of resonant frequency being an issue, and improving the control of the valve. These springs are particularly beneficial with hydraulic lifters, reducing the chance of lifter collapse or pump-up. Beehive valve springs are set up slightly differently to more conventional valve springs, with less cold static clearance required between spring coils at full lift.

Another seemingly obvious but occasionally overlooked point is that the valve spring must locate properly within the spring seat on the cylinder head and on the valve-spring retainer, both on the outside diameter and inside diameter of the valve spring. Sometimes the spring seats on the cylinder heads need to be machined to accommodate different valve springs (for example, double or triple valve springs). When mixing and matching different valvetrain components, it is also possible to fit the valve springs with the incorrect retainers, so a thorough visual check is required to ensure that the retainers locate properly on the valve springs.

The next check to be carried out is the full valve lift clearance between the top of the valve guide and the bottom of the valve-spring retainer. Again this can be calculated without having to fit the valve

Measuring the valve retainer to valve guide clearance.

Beehive valve spring.

springs, by measuring the clearance at the correct install height and subtracting your peak valve lift. The minimum cold static clearance required is 1.25mm at peak valve lift.

VALVE-SPRING RETAINERS AND COLLETS

The standard retainers on most Rover V8 engines from 1980 onwards (part number ERC573A) are made from sintered iron, and should only be used up to 5,800rpm. Stronger steel retainers were previously fitted to production engines up to 1980. High-tensile steel retainers are available from specialist suppliers, and these are highly recommended if the engine speed is going to exceed 5,800rpm. TVR-spec Rover V8 engines fitted with double valve springs are usually fitted with stronger steel retainers as standard – these can be used up to approximately 7,000rpm. Titanium retainers are also available if you are planning on using your engine at particularly high engine speeds.

Valve-spring retainer.

Collet and valve stem location.

The collets are used to secure the retainer to the valve – the valve has a collet locating section on a section of valve stem just below the valve tip.

The correct collets must be used for the particular retainers and valves that you are using. Collets can appear to be correct, particularly if the mismatch is between the collet and retainer due to a different degree of taper or major/minor diameter, but the use of incorrect collets can lead to dropping a valve, so it is important to check carefully.

VALVES

We have already looked closely at valves in Chapter 4, 'Cylinder Heads', but it is also worth mentioning again in this chapter. The first thing to consider here is valvetrain weight. The weight of the intake and exhaust valves affects the dynamic behaviour of the valvetrain and its ability to maintain control of the valves at higher engine speeds. A heavier valvetrain will require stronger valve springs to maintain control of the valves, but this increases the load on the valvetrain, reducing the longevity and performance. There are a number of different valves available for the Rover V8, with waisted stems and larger diameter heads. Both intake and exhaust valves are available with waisted stems as standard. The later 40mm intake valves (part no. ERC9088) have waisted stems, as do the earlier 34mm exhaust valves (part no. 614089).

The other consideration is the valve diameter in relation to valve lift, and its effect on the piston-to-

Table 12: Intake and exhaust valve weights

Valve type	Valve weight
Inlet 49.3mm Wildcat	111g
Inlet 43mm big valve (TVR BV)	92g
Inlet 41.5mm big valve (DW500)	86g
Inlet 40mm EFI waisted stem	83g
Inlet 40mm pre-EFI non-waisted stem	91g
Exhaust 40.6mm Wildcat	96g
Exhaust 37mm big valve (TVR BV)	85g
Exhaust 34mm EFI non-waisted stem	86g
Exhaust 34mm pre-EFI waisted stem	84g

valve clearance. The valves on a Rover V8 are not parallel to the piston, and therefore a larger diameter valve will have less piston-to-valve clearance than a smaller diameter valve for the same amount of lift.

Piston-to-valve clearance should be considered when assembling the long engine, with piston deck clearance, camshaft lift and valve deck clearance being just a few of the factors to be established here. Then, once the valvetrain has been 'dry assembled', the piston-to-valve clearance should be checked; this can be done in a number of different ways, although it is always more difficult with hydraulic followers.

One method is to put a piece of Plasticine or Playdoh on the top of the piston in the area where the valve would theoretically meet the piston, fit the cylinder head, and then turn the engine over through two complete revolutions by hand. The thickness of the compressed plasticine can then be measured to see what cold clearance is left.

Another method is to use an adjustable valvetrain, adjusted correctly and then brought to peak lift with the aid of a DTI (dial test indicator) on the valve tip or retainer. This crank and cam timing point is then recorded, and the DTI reset to zero. With the engine crankshaft in this same position, the valvetrain is then carefully adjusted until the valve touches the piston – the reading on the DTI being the cold clearance. The valvetrain is then readjusted to bring the DTI back to zero, before carrying out any further checks. The minimum piston-to-valve clearance often occurs in a different position to TDC, so this procedure must then be repeated in 5-degree steps of crankshaft rotation, to establish where the minimum clearance occurs.

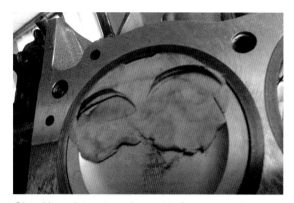

Checking piston-to-valve cold clearance using Playdoh.

Once you have identified where this point occurs, you can repeat this at 1-degree intervals around the minimum point, if required. This minimum point depends on camshaft specification and long engine dimensions (for example deck clearances, valve diameters).

The exact amount of required cold clearance needs to allow for the fact that there will be less clearance when the engine is at maximum speed. It also assumes that the valvetrain will maintain control of the valve throughout operation. We generally recommend an absolute minimum of 0.060in cold clearance on the intake valves, and 0.100in clearance on the exhaust valves, although the exact amount required will depend on the engine specification and engine speed requirements. If maximum reliability and longevity is of paramount importance, rather than maximum performance, it is probably best to regard 0.100in on the intake and 0.120in on the exhaust as your minimum cold clearances instead.

CHAPTER 7

INTAKE SYSTEM

The intake system is the means by which the engine takes in air, prior to the cylinder heads. The intake system as a whole includes the air filter(s), intake pipework, airflow meter (if fitted), throttle body(s) or carburettor(s), and intake manifold. The intake ports and valves of the cylinder heads are also part of the intake system, and whilst this is dealt with in Chapter 4, 'Cylinder Heads', the design of an effective intake system needs to take them into account. When designing an intake system, we start at the intake valve and work outwards to the air filter(s). A good intake design should not reduce the flow rate over a bare cylinder head – a well-designed intake manifold can actually boost the flow over a bare cylinder head.

Whichever type of intake manifold you choose, you will want to ensure that it is port-matched to the cylinder heads. It is worth bearing in mind here that, whilst theoretically you want to be constantly tapering down towards the back of the valve, practically it is important that there is not an impeding flange lip anywhere in the direction of flow. For this reason we recommend that the dimensions of the port in the intake manifold at the cylinder head are marginally smaller than the dimensions of the corresponding port face in the cylinder head. This approach can also reduce the effects of reversion. Our own experience has demonstrated that exact port matching is time-consuming and unnecessary, provided there is no lip in the direction of flow, and no abrupt or large changes in the port area.

There are a few standard intake manifolds available for the Rover V8 engine, as well as a wide range of aftermarket intake manifolds. Here we will first look at the carburettor manifolds available, followed

Port opening at cylinder head face is slightly larger than opening at intake manifold face. This ensures there is no lip in direction of flow.

Cylinder head port face should be approx 1mm larger than the intake manifold port face. The port in the head is only larger than the intake manifold port for the first few mm.

Intake manifold port matching.

by fuel-injection manifolds, and individual throttle bodies. Then we will look at how to analyse and select the right intake manifold for your application.

CARBURETTOR INTAKE MANIFOLDS

There are numerous carburettor manifolds available for this engine. Although fuel injection is now the mainstay, the Rover V8 was running on carburettors for approximately half of its production life. Despite carburettor set-ups often being associated with simplicity, a carburettor manifold is trickier to design than an EFI manifold, and subject to a great many conflicting requirements.

Most manifolds on a fuel-injected set-up are 'dry' manifolds, in that they only have to deal with air. The fuel source (injector) is typically mounted close to the cylinder head and intake valve. All carburettor manifolds are 'wet' manifolds because they have to deal with both air and fuel. Unfortunately air and fuel have very different molecular weights, and do not behave in the same manner. A gently sweeping, mandrel-bent tube will offer little restriction to airflow, but can cause a 'wet' mix of air and fuel to separate. The fuel is much heavier and readily separates from the air. A sweeping curve will often cause the fuel to centrifuge out of the air, resulting in the air reaching the cylinder first, and the fuel dribbling in as liquid afterwards. This creates poor engine response, reduced fuel economy, high HC emissions, and a loss of power. An ideal 'dry' manifold usually makes a terrible wet manifold for these reasons.

It is very difficult to design an effective 'wet' manifold that both flows air effectively and considers the fluid dynamics of fuel. This is one of the reasons that a good fuel injection system will almost always produce more power, with lower emissions and fuel consumption, than an equivalent carburettor set-up. Modern computational fluid dynamics (CFD) and wet flow testing have helped produce more effective carburettor intakes in recent times. However, these are mainly limited to a few American companies such as Edelbrock.

Twin SU/Stromberg Manifold

This was the standard configuration, originally designed by Rover to mount twin SU or Stromberg carburettors, and was used for many years.

This manifold is a dual plane design with two separate manifolds combined into one. There are slight production variations of this same manifold, but they are essentially the same design. One half of the manifold or 'plane' is connected to the right-hand carburettor, and feeds cylinders 1, 7, 4 and 6, while the other half is connected to the left-hand carburettor, and feeds cylinders 2, 8, 3 and 5. The induction pulses alternate between manifold halves or planes. This phasing ensures that neither manifold half or carburettor receives two consecutive induction pulses. The induction pulses are equally divided so there is 180 degrees of crankshaft rotation between pulses, which is why this type of intake manifold is sometimes referred to as a '180-degree manifold'.

These manifolds are restrictive to airflow for many higher output engines, due to their compact nature and the complex routing of the intake runners. There are many sharp bends and changes in cross-sectional area that serve to restrict airflow. That said, this does not mean that these manifolds have no place in certain applications. They were originally designed for good cylinder filling at lower engine speeds and reduced emissions with carburettors. The tortuous intake ports with their sharp bends help to ensure that a homogeneous mix of air and fuel is delivered to each cylinder, delivering improved fuel efficiency. The small ports keep air velocity high for more torque at lower engine

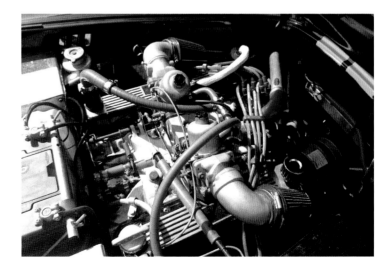

Twin SU carburettor manifold.

speeds, and the dual plane or 180-degree phasing ensures excellent throttle response.

If originality must be preserved, and this manifold is to be retained on a performance V8, then there are a number of steps we can take to improve the airflow. The castings are not particularly accurate so these manifolds do respond to minor porting work, such as opening up the ports to closely match the cylinder head port and gasket profile dimensions, as well as equalizing the size and shape of the individual intake runners as much as possible. Even with all these modifications, these manifolds struggle to flow enough air to produce more than 250bhp.

Four-Barrel Carburettor Manifolds

There are comparatively few new manifolds available today to mount American four-barrel carburettors, such as those made by Holley and Edelbrock. Of those few that are available, they can be divided into two types: single plane and dual plane. These are commonly referred to as 360-degree and 180-degree manifolds respectively.

360-Degree/Single Plane Manifolds

These are the simplest of the two design types, with all cylinders connected and drawing from a single central plenum below the carburettor. All four barrels open into the same central plenum, and the individual runners can all be relatively straight and close to equal length. These manifolds offer the advantage of improved airflow at higher engine speeds, due to the short and free-flowing intake runners. In addition, the flow of all of the four barrels (chokes) of the carburettor are available to any of the cylinders, unlike a dual-plane manifold where only half the carburettor can be 'seen' by one half of the engine. Another major advantage of this type of manifold is their extremely compact nature. These carburettor manifolds have a low install height compared to many other induction set-ups.

One disadvantage of this type of manifold is having consecutively firing cylinders drawing from the same plenum area, resulting in an inconsistent air-fuel mix between cylinders. High overlap performance camshafts worsen this situation because one cylinder on the overlap phase, with both intake and exhaust valves open, can effectively leak air and exhaust gases into the common plenum area. This reduces the manifold vacuum and contaminates the next cylinder with exhaust gas.

180-Degree/Dual-Plane Manifolds

These are essentially the same in concept as the original twin SU/Stromberg set-up, with two separate manifolds stacked into one unit. One half or plane feeds cylinders 1, 7, 4 and 6, while the other half feeds cylinders 2, 8, 3 and 5. Each half is fed by two barrels of the carburettor. Each half only sees an induction pulse every 180 degrees of crankshaft rotation, unlike the single-plane or 360-degree manifold that sees an induction pulse every 90 degrees of rotation. There is no overlap of intake cycles. This keeps consecutive firing cylinders isolated from each other, helping to reduce the negative effects of high overlap camshafts.

These manifolds can be subdivided into low and high rise types. Due to the way these manifolds are stacked, low rise types typically have a sharper entry bend from the intake runner into the intake port and therefore have lower airflow rates, so become restrictive at higher engine speeds. The low rise types are more compact with a lower installation height, giving more bonnet clearance. The

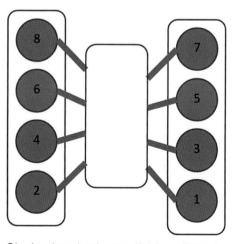

Single-plane intake manifold configuration.

original twin SU/Stromberg manifold is an example of a low rise manifold. High rise types, such as the Edelbrock Performer, have a much less severe entry bend from the intake runner to intake port and are therefore less restrictive at higher engine speeds. The increased height is also their main disadvantage, reducing bonnet clearance.

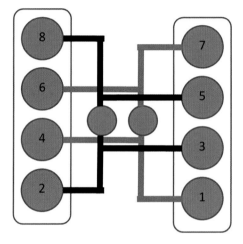

Dual-plane intake manifold configuration.

Quad Carburettor Manifolds

Undoubtedly, the best performing carburettor manifolds available for this engine are the individual runner manifolds, designed to suit four Weber or Dell'Orto twin-choke carburettors. These manifolds have an individual isolated runner and throttle per cylinder. This set-up does not make use of energy in the other runners to boost low end torque in the same manner the other designs can, but is virtually immune from the negative effects of cylinder to cylinder interaction, making them ideal for high performance engines with large overlap camshafts. Airflow is typically excellent, with few sharp bends. There are quite a few variations of this manifold type, including ones with very short runner lengths and crossover types, such as that produced by John Eales, which offer a longer tuned runner length. These are available to suit side-draught and down-draught versions of carburettor. Due to the recent proliferation of Weber/Dell'Orto pattern EFI throttle bodies, these intakes are now considered universal in that they can be used to mount either carburettors or throttle bodies.

Boxer Quad SU Carburettor Manifold

This once popular set-up is no longer in production, although it is worth a mention as it is still occasionally seen on some older engines, and for sale second-hand. This manifold is fabricated in steel, and mounts four SU carburettors with one carburettor feeding each pair of cylinders. Its long, straight runners have relatively consistent port volume and

Boxer Quad SU intake manifold.

Rover V8 EFI intake manifold.

give good flow. All the runners should be connected via small diameter balance pipes to equalize manifold vacuum between carburettors. These manifolds can yield good results, particularly with regard to torque at low engine speeds. The main disadvantage with this set-up is the fact that consecutive firing cylinders 5 and 7 are paired together. This can result in intake charge robbing and therefore reduced flow to these cylinders.

FUEL-INJECTION MANIFOLDS

The main advantage of the EFI manifolds is that the fuel is injected at the cylinder head face by individual injectors, so the intake manifold only has to deal with the requirements of air rather than the conflicting requirements of a 'wet' air-fuel mix. This results in much more consistent air-fuel ratios between individual cylinders, which improves performance, fuel efficiency and emissions. There are a number of OEM fuel injection manifolds available. One of the earliest was the 'Federal' injection system fitted to Rover V8s for certain export markets that had particularly stringent emissions requirements, such as California. This intake system is more suited to low emissions than performance, and is sufficiently rare that it will get little more than a brief mention here.

Rover Vitesse and Land Rover EFI Intake 1984–1999

Without doubt, the most common and popular EFI manifold for the Rover V8 is the unit designed by Land Rover engineer Richard Twist, first fitted to the Rover SD1 Vitesse and subsequently in Land Rover engines (3.5/3.9/4.0/4.2 and 4.6), up to the introduction of the 'Thor' unit in 1999. This basic design was used with the Lucas 4CU, 14CU, 14CUX and GEMS engine-management systems. This intake manifold is divided into three parts: the intake base that is bolted between the cylinder heads, a centre section with unequal length bell-mouthed runners, and the plenum with side-mounted throttle body. This is a well designed intake manifold that can be modified to make a fairly effective induction set-up on a performance engine. This manifold is a single-plane design with all runners drawing from a common plenum, limiting its usefulness for engines with particularly high overlap, wide duration camshafts.

Interestingly, the manifold base itself is designed so that some of the inlet runners cross over, placing all the runners for cylinders 1, 7, 4 and 6 on one side and all the runners for cylinders 2, 8, 3 and 5 on the other side.

This creates unequal runner lengths in the manifold base that are corrected to equal length by the length differences in the bell-mouthed intake runners in the upper half. Why Rover engineers

Rover V8 Firing Order = 1-8-4-3-6-5-7-2

Intake runner paths in EFI intake base.

went to such efforts when they could have made the runners in the base of equal length in the first place is unclear. It is possible that the manifold was originally intended to be a dual-plane design with consecutive firing cylinders kept separate in much the same way as the carburettor dual-plane intake. This was the reasoning behind the design of our Lloyd Dual Plane intake manifold.

Modifications

The first place to start with any modifications is to port match the intake port faces to your selected cylinder heads. It is far easier, and just as effective, to make the port faces at the cylinder head face 1mm smaller than the corresponding cylinder head ports, than it is to port match exactly. Do not forget to ensure that the manifold gasket does not protrude into the port. We have pulled apart many engines that have nicely ported heads and intake, with a standard intake gasket that protrudes into the port, negating the advantages of port matching.

The next point of modification really depends upon the cylinder heads you have selected. Any cylinder head that flows more than 140cfm @ 25in pressure drop will ideally have the severe bend or 'dog-leg'

Lloyd Dual Plane EFI intake manifold.

Port matching to intake manifold gasket.

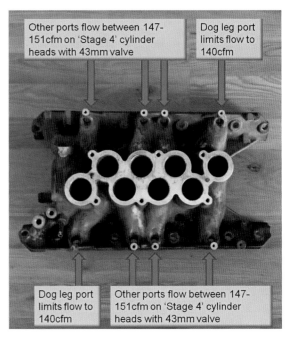

Other ports flow between 147-151cfm on 'Stage 4' cylinder heads with 43mm valve

Dog leg port limits flow to 140cfm

Dog leg port limits flow to 140cfm

Other ports flow between 147-151cfm on 'Stage 4' cylinder heads with 43mm valve

Relative flow rates of intake base runners.

restriction removed from runners for cylinders 1 and 8. This is not an issue on cylinder heads below 'stage three' level of modification (*see* Chapter 4, 'Cylinder Heads'), as even the 'dog-legged' ports can flow more than the cylinder heads themselves. On engines with airflow greater than 140cfm@25in ΔP, the severe bend progressively chokes cylinders 1 and 8, resulting in lost performance and inconsistent air-fuel mixtures between cylinders. Removal of this severe bend involves building up the outside of the 'dog-leg' port with aluminium welding, followed by internal porting to straighten the port. We use a 15 per cent silicone welding rod and an AC TIG process to do this.

The next restriction in this particular manifold occurs at the bend just after the round 38mm section, and just before it blends into the rectangular section of the runner. This section abruptly changes area, and a slight blending to make this transition as smooth as possible should be considered essential on all engines with stage three and up levels of cylinder head modification. A set of internal callipers is a great help here to get a picture of what is happening in terms of changes in the internal area. These modifications are all that is required to get the best out of this particular set-up.

The most popular modification to these intakes is to open up the round 38mm section of the intake runners and fit larger 44mm or even 48mm bell-mouthed runners. Contrary to popular opinion,

Modified intake base.

this can be detrimental to performance, as this creates an even greater port taper between the bell-mouthed runner and the rectangular section of the port. This sudden change in cross-sectional area reduces flow considerably. Unfortunately many of us are still stuck in the 'bigger is better' mindset. Marketing demands also play a part here, because if your competitor is offering 48mm bell-mouths then an offering with 38mm ones appears inferior. Interestingly, a straight 38mm round pipe can outflow an

Using internal callipers to measure port dimensions.

original cast cylinder head's intake port by a significant margin.

This concludes our intake base modifications, and the next area is the plenum itself. The standard 65mm throttle body begins to restrict airflow at approximately 260–270bhp on most engines. A common modification is to machine the throttle opening and install a larger 72mm throttle plate. This is the largest that can be sensibly machined into the existing casting. A 72mm throttle plate will begin to restrict airflow beyond approximately

300bhp. It is also possible to cut and weld on larger or multiple throttle bodies. We have also cut and welded two standard plenums back to back, to provide two 65mm throttles, using the trumpet base as a jig to hold the two halves. Alternatively, there are a number of aftermarket plenums available with multiple throttles – twin or triple – that are a bolt-on fitment.

Remember, larger is not always better, and the smallest throttle body that does not restrict airflow is the correct size. If we go too large, air velocity can drop, reducing performance. Furthermore, large single plates can produce a large change in airflow for a small change in throttle angle, making a vehicle harder to set up and control. A dual-plane manifold requires more throttle area than a single-plane manifold of the same flow rate, as any one cylinder is only able to breathe through or 'see' one half of the throttle area, as compared to a single plane where any cylinder can breathe through all of the throttles.

It is worth noting here that although significantly increasing the throttle area rarely improves engine power on most Rover V8s, largely due to the restrictive cylinder head design, it does have the advantage of improving throttle response. Naturally, more

Larger bell-mouthed runners on the intake base.

Two plenums cut and welded back to back.

throttle area will require some adjustment of the fuel system to suit.

INTAKE MANIFOLD SELECTION

The first thing to consider here are any physical space constraints. This is not likely to be a problem for most 4 × 4 applications, but it is a common problem with sports cars, kit cars and race cars. With confined engine bays, this will rule out a few intake manifolds straightaway.

The next things to consider are the intake port flow and dimensions of the cylinder heads that you are using, as well as your requirements in terms of horsepower, torque and engine speed range. Ideally you would have engine simulation software, flow bench, and a dynamometer at your disposal to establish the optimum intake manifold for your application. Even if you do have this equipment available, the following should be useful in narrowing down what to test. If you do not have access to this equipment, or time to carry out extensive test-

Carbon-fibre plenum.

ing, the following information will be helpful in identifying an intake manifold that is suitable for your application.

Knowing whether or not a particular intake manifold will reduce or add power to a particular engine set-up is obviously important. So we tested a range of different intake manifolds on the same stage four, big-valve Rover V8 cylinder head to see at what point the intake manifold becomes a restriction.

The graph shows that an intake manifold can reduce or even boost the overall flow rate of the cylinder head and intake manifold combination. In our test both carburettor manifolds reduced the overall intake flow from valve lifts of about 0.2in upwards, whereas the fuel injection manifolds all increased the flow rate of the overall assembly. As was to be expected, the fully ported fuel-injection base flowed the most out of all the manifolds tested on the stage four cylinder head.

The flow rate of the intake manifold is ideally closely matched to the flow rate of the cylinder head. A manifold with large ports and intake runners may flow well alone, but when combined with cylinder heads of considerably less flow, will only serve to reduce velocity in the intake system. Reduced

intake velocity will create less flow through the cylinder heads, and will also reduce or negate any positive pulse tuning effects.

INTAKE RUNNER DESIGN

As a rough rule, shorter runner lengths place the point at which peak torque occurs further up the rev range and, conversely, longer runner lengths place peak torque further down the rev range. Whilst to a certain extent this holds true for the Rover V8, the key point here is that it is the relationship with the camshaft timing that is of particular importance. As an example, a common mistake is to use a fairly 'sporty' camshaft – that is, with more camshaft overlap and duration – in conjunction with longer runner lengths. This will reduce the bottom end torque without any gain in peak horsepower, because the runner length is too long for the camshaft and engine specification.

The standard Lucas fuel injection manifold has a total runner length, from the back of the intake valve, of 15.5in. This works well with the standard 3.5-litre engine and camshaft (with 285 degrees of total seat-to-seat intake duration and less than 10mm of lift), placing peak torque at a low usable position

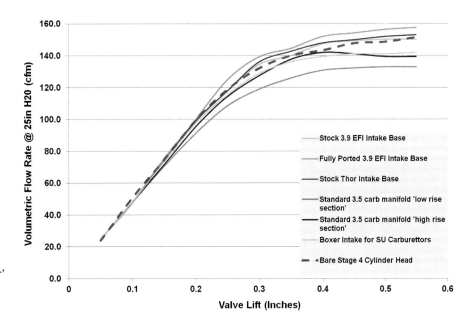

Flow rates of standard intake manifolds tested on the same 'stage four' big valve cylinder head.

Standard EFI trumpet base.

within the rev range (approximately 3,200rpm) whilst providing reasonable horsepower. If you are making any engine modifications from this point, it is well worth remembering this baseline as a reference.

If you want to push the torque further up the rev range and make more horsepower as a result, not only will you require a camshaft with more lift and/ or duration, you will also need to shorten the intake runners to ensure that you do not end up with an engine that makes no more power than standard. If you want to push the torque further down the rev range instead, you will require a camshaft with less overlap (as a consequence of less duration) as well as longer intake runners.

A good real-world example of how this works goes back to when we first fitted our Range Rover Classic with the Lloyd Dual Plane intake manifold, with its longer 17.5in total included runner length.

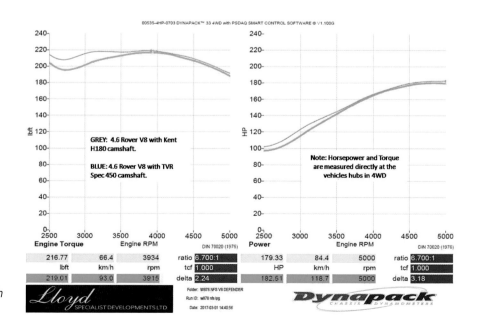

Dyno graph comparing similar 4.6-litre engines with different camshafts.

This Range Rover had a TVR-spec 4.6-litre engine with the relatively aggressive TVR-spec camshaft and produced 180bhp at 5,000rpm and 216lb-ft of torque at 4,000rpm, directly at the hubs on our Dynapack chassis dynamometer. We were then tasked with an engine build on our friend's Land Rover 110. This vehicle was to be used for a great deal of heavy towing, so bottom-end torque was of particular importance. He also wanted to use one of our Lloyd Dual Plane intake manifolds for the improved throttle response.

This particular 4.6-litre engine was built with a Kent H180 camshaft, with 262 degrees of total intake duration and 11.2mm of lift. The cylinder heads were built to the same specification as the TVR-spec 4.6-litre, and the engine management system was optimized to the same standard using the same type of Canems programmable ECU. This engine produced as much horsepower at the hubs as the TVR-spec engine, but with power produced lower down in the rev range, giving a broader spread of torque without any sacrifice in peak horsepower. Both vehicles had the same ZF4HP22 auto-box, and both were running with four-wheel drive on the same chassis dyno. The longer runner length of the intake manifold clearly worked best with the 'milder' camshaft.

When looking at the intake runner diameter on a Rover V8, it is worth reiterating that in most cases this engine is severely cylinder head restricted, and for this reason larger diameter runners are rarely required. Smaller diameter runners will give more intake air velocity, which in turn gives more intake flow right up to the point at which the smaller diameter starts to become a restriction.

The intake valve is going to spend considerably more time at the lower valve lifts. Therefore the larger runner diameters will only be of benefit for the extremely brief moment that the valve lift and cylinder head flow will be a restriction with the smaller diameter runner. And in many cases the valve lift, cylinder head flow and engine speed will rarely reach the point at which the standard intake runner diameter becomes a restriction.

PLENUM DESIGN

The purpose of an intake plenum is to provide a reservoir of air post-throttle and to dampen out any negative effects of pulse tuning. The standard single plenum design on a fuel injected Rover V8 supplies a reservoir of air for all 8 cylinders. The volume of a single plenum ideally needs to be equal to, or greater

GEMS EFI plenum.

than, the total capacity of the engine. The standard fuel injection plenum from the Lucas-based injection systems has a volume of about 3.8ltr, whereas the later GEMS fuel injection plenum has a larger volume of about 4ltr.

Plenum spacers are available that fit between the trumpet base and plenum top, therefore increasing the plenum volume. A typical 15mm spacer will add 0.5 litres to the total plenum volume, as well as increasing the distance between the top of the intake trumpets and plenum lid.

Although it is possible to take advantage of the positive effects of intake pulse tuning with a smaller plenum volume, with a Rover V8 using a common plenum this is not a practical proposition due to the consecutive firing cylinders using the same source of intake air. The only time you would consider trying to take advantage of the positive effects of intake pulse tuning is with two separate plenums arranged in a dual-plane manner, so that consecutively firing cylinders are not sharing a common source of intake air. Even in that case, it is not a straightforward exercise to establish the correct intake system dimensions, requiring sophisticated engine simulation software and an accurate dynamometer to verify the theoretical results.

THROTTLE BODIES

The original 65mm throttle plate tends to pose a restriction at peak horsepower values above 270bhp, at which point it is worth upgrading to a 72mm throttle plate. All things being equal, a larger throttle plate will also improve throttle response by virtue of the increase in throttle area for the same given throttle position. Multiple throttle plates give the same result – an increase in throttle area. Table 13 shows the total throttle area at wide open throttle (WOT) for a number of different throttle plate combinations, so that we can easily compare the various solutions purely in terms of throttle area. Calculated throttle area assumes that all throttle plates have an 8mm throttle spindle.

Although increasing the throttle area will usually improve the throttle response and remove any airflow restriction at that point, if overdone it can

Table 13: Throttle body flow rate calculations

Throttle body configuration	Total airflow (cfm) @1.5in hg
1 × 65mm	587
1 × 72mm	721
1 × 90mm	1,126
2 × 44mm	538
4 × 48mm	1,281
4 × 52mm	1,503
8 × 32mm	1,139
8 × 36mm	1,441
Lucas 5AM air flow meter – 1 × 50mm	464

lead to a jerky and aggressive throttle that can be difficult to drive at low vehicle speeds. If this is the case, a progressive throttle cam can be used to open the throttle more slowly at low throttle pedal positions, and faster at larger throttle pedal positions.

The other solution to this problem is to use electronic throttle control, although this does require a suitable aftermarket ECU and a drive-by-wire throttle pedal. This type of system allows us to map or calibrate the throttle plate to open more or less for a given amount of throttle position, therefore making the throttle more or less aggressive. This set-up can even be changed at the flick of a switch or press of a button, via a switchable 'maps' function on the ECU, to provide different throttle calibration for different weather or road/track conditions.

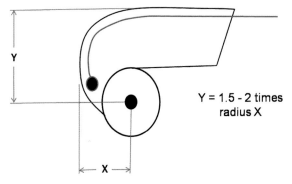

Progressive throttle cam.

Drive-by-wire throttle body on a Rover V8.

INTAKE PIPEWORK AND AIR FILTERS

A good quality air filter should be regarded as an essential component of your engine. It is pointless to spend considerable time, money and effort building or modifying your engine only to risk a significantly reduced engine life, or engine failure, for the sake of a good air filter. In the past it was considered acceptable in racing circles to run engines with a coarse mesh in place of the air filters. A coarse mesh will neither flow well, nor filter adequately. Air-filtration systems have significantly improved in the last forty years. This means that a good quality air filter, such as the ubiquitous K&N, will pose no restriction to your engine, but will undoubtedly provide increased longevity.

K&N air filter.

We always recommend inspecting your air filter or air filters as part of the vehicle's annual service. If the air filter is a disposable item, it is likely to require replacement every 6,000–12,000 miles (9,650–19,300km), whereas a serviceable air filter will benefit from cleaning and re-oiling annually. Serviceable air filters can be drawn into two separate types — the K&N type with the cotton-gauze structure, or the foam exterior type (for example Pipercross). We find that the cotton-gauze type of air filter tends to last longer than the foam exterior type. This is because the foam-type filter tends to degrade over time, and also become blocked more easily than the cotton-gauze type. The folded design of the cotton-gauze filter also provides more surface area and therefore poses less of a restriction, even when full of dust and debris.

Some applications use an air-filter box or case to house the air filter. In many cases these are not restrictive, but in some instances they are. A manometer can be used to measure the pressure drop at any part of the intake system, including the air-filter box and air filter, and therefore see how restrictive it is.

Degraded foam filter.

Air filters are usually rated in terms of horsepower, and we always try to fit air filters that will easily out-flow our horsepower requirements. The published ratings are not always accurate however, so it is always worth testing if you have any doubts.

The location of the air filter or air intake is important. Firstly the temperature of the intake air charge has a direct effect on the output of the engine, so placing the air filter in a cooler location is definitely advantageous. Conversely having the air filter located directly above the engine, or even above the exhaust manifolds, will have a detrimental effect on the output of the engine.

The graph below is an example of an engine that has 245bhp at an intake temperature of 25°C. This clearly illustrates how a change in air tempera-ture affects the power output of the engine, with a temperature range of 40°C giving a difference of 20 horsepower in our example. This assumes that the air pressure remains constant.

Naturally, any improvements in engine torque via a reduction in intake air temperature will require an adjustment in fuelling, particularly if the fuelling is controlled via carburettors.

The next consideration when locating the air filter or intake is environmental ingress, this is of particular importance to off-road applications. In this regard, the air filter or intake needs to be located away from any area that is prone to excessive amounts of dirt or any water. Off-road applications usually utilize intake snorkels to locate the air intake as far away from potential ingress of dirt and water as possible.

The addition of a snorkel can sometimes provide a gain in torque at low engine speeds, due to the longer intake length. Conversely it can also reduce torque (and by extension, horsepower) at higher engine speeds. The best solution in these cases is

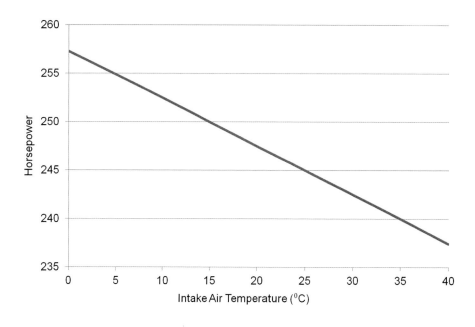

Effect of intake air temperature on horsepower.

to fit two snorkels, which will remove the restriction at higher engine speeds.

The intake pipework between the air filter and throttle plate obviously needs to flow plenty of air, ideally more air than the engine will ever require, effectively acting as a reservoir of air in the same manner as an intake plenum. However, with state-of-the-art instrumentation and an accurate dyno, it is possible to optimize the intake ducting dimensions (length and diameter) to take advantage of positive pulse tuning effects, but for 99.99 per cent of us it is a much safer bet simply to make the intake ducting as large as possible. This ensures that the intake ducting will not provide a restriction, and will also ensure that the intake system is not subjected to negative pulse tuning effects.

It should go without saying that the intake pipework should be sealed to prevent ingress of dirt into the engine. It should also be located away, or insulated from exhaust or engine heat as much as is practically possible. When using an airflow meter, an intake pipe that is not sealed properly can cause engine management calibration issues due to unmetered air being taken in after the airflow meter. Whilst we are on the subject of airflow meters, in most cases they do cause a slight restriction by virtue of their design. High performance applications often benefit from either larger airflow meters,

or from removing the airflow meter altogether by converting to a manifold pressure or throttle position based engine management system.

Ram-air is often used by drag racers to increase the pressure of the air intake, but is rarely beneficial unless the vehicle is regularly driven at speeds well in excess of 100mph (160km/h). To put this into perspective, the improvement in engine performance at 100mph from a well designed ram-air scoop is equivalent to the performance improvement from a 6°C drop in intake air temperature. When you then take into account that the performance improvement from the drop in intake air temperature is available at all vehicle speeds, it is easy to see which gain is the more straightforward!

It is also worth noting that your fuelling system needs to compensate for the increased air supply at the higher vehicle speeds. This is straightforward with a modern EFI system, but a carburettor-based fuel system will require more work, with the float bowls needing to see a modulated version of the same ram-air pressure effect in order to provide adequate fuelling compensation, with increased vehicle speed.

The intake pipework is ideally made from a material that does not readily absorb heat, and it is often beneficial to insulate the intake pipework, again to reduce the intake air temperature.

CHAPTER 8

EXHAUST SYSTEM

The main function of the exhaust system is to extract all the spent exhaust gases from the cylinders of the engine. Another very important function, and one that is not so widely understood, is to help draw in fresh air and fuel. This is more commonly known as scavenging.

When designing or specifying an exhaust system, the three main considerations are performance, packaging and noise levels. An efficient exhaust system will be advantageous not only in terms of performance, but also in terms of fuel efficiency and noise reduction.

As with all other areas of engine tuning, there is a real advantage in considering the design of the exhaust system in conjunction with the other areas, in particular with the camshaft and intake system. Clever design of these three areas can lead to the exhaust system effectively sucking additional intake air into the cylinder during the camshaft overlap period. This can potentially lead to volumetric efficiencies in excess of 100 per cent. In other words, the cylinders are actually being overfilled. The most knowledgeable engine designers or tuners will design these individual systems so that they all coincide at a particular engine speed or speed range.

There are a reasonable number of exhaust manifolds available for the Rover V8, most of which come from production vehicles; they are therefore primarily designed to be cost effective to mass produce, and to be comfortably packaged within the vehicle's engine bay. Applications include the Rover SD1, Range Rover, Land Rover, TVR, Morgan, Marcos, MG RV8 and Triumph TR8.

Cast-iron exhaust manifolds generally last longer as they are much less prone to vibration fatigue

Cast-iron exhaust manifold.

than tubular steel manifolds, and the greater wall thickness means they will take longer to corrode through. They are often a little quieter in terms of engine bay noise, and produce much less under-bonnet heat than the tubular types. This increased heat can often negate the advantages of some tubular designs.

There are two main types of cast-iron manifolds commonly used in Rover V8 OEM applications. These are the highly restrictive single-outlet manifolds used on early vehicles, such as the Rover P6, and the much more efficient dual-outlet manifolds first seen in the Rover SD1. The single-outlet manifolds have no place on a performance engine, whilst the dual-outlet manifolds can form the basis of a very efficient and quiet system. Production cast-iron manifolds do tend to be restrictive for highly modified Rover V8 engines, and there is a massive choice of tubular types that usually flow better than the original cast types.

PRIMARY EXHAUST PIPES

Commonly referred to as the primaries or primary pipes, these are the first exhaust system sections that the exhaust gases enter once they have left the exhaust ports in the cylinder head. Once the exhaust port and exhaust valve dimensions in the cylinder head have been taken into account, we start here when evaluating the exhaust system design.

We will look at the optimum primary exhaust system design for various specification of Rover V8 engines. If designing and building a pair of exhaust manifolds from scratch, this will obviously act as an excellent guide, but it will also allow the reader to make an informed decision when looking to purchase an existing design of Rover V8 exhaust manifold.

There are a number of different exhaust manifold designs used for V8 engines, the most common by far being either 4-into-1, or 4-2-1. Another less common but very effective design is the dual-plane or crossover manifold.

4-into-1 Designs

These designs are, without doubt, the most straight-forward to fabricate, collecting all four primary pipes on one bank and connecting them to a single outlet. The early production single-outlet cast manifolds are a 4-into-1 design. It is worth noting that the advantages and disadvantages of this design differ from those seen with a conventional 4-cylinder engine. With a 4-cylinder engine, the 4-into-1

design commonly achieves best peak horsepower. However, rarely does this design achieve best performance at any engine speed with a 90-degree V8, such as the Rover V8.

The reason for this is the engine's firing order. The exhaust pulses on one bank of a Rover V8 do not occur at neat 180-degree intervals like a 4-cylinder, but have irregular spacing instead. The primary pipe for cylinder 1 will receive a pulse followed 270 degrees later by cylinder 3, with cylinder 5 following 180 degrees after that. Cylinder 7 will then pulse a mere 90 degrees after cylinder 5. These two consecutive pulses appear to the exhaust as one extra-large pulse, restricting gas flow from these cylinders. It is clear from this that the pulses are never going to be synchronized, even if the pipes are all of equal length.

4-into-2-into-1 Designs

The 4-into-2-into-1 designs are also reasonably common and fairly straightforward to fabricate, compared to the more complicated dual-plane or crossover manifold. The standard dual-outlet cast manifolds, first seen on the Rover SD1, are an example of a good 4-into-2-into-1 design. This layout is commonly referred to as 'Tri-Y' in the United States, and is very popular with 90-degree V8 engines, for good reason.

This type of design attempts to sort out the irregular exhaust pulses into a configuration that can aid scavenging and at least remove the negative

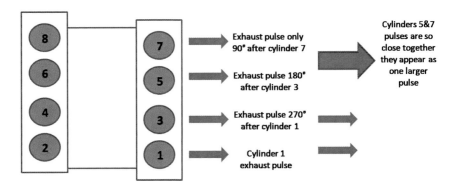

Exhaust pulse timing on left-hand exhaust manifold bank.

Cylinder firing order: 1,8,4,3,6,5,7,2

4-into-1 exhaust manifold for a TVR Chimaera or Griffith.

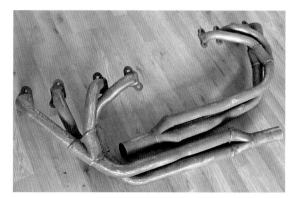

4-2-1 exhaust manifolds for a Rover SD1.

effects of consecutive firing cylinders. In this layout, cylinders 1 and 5 are connected together, and so are cylinders 3 and 7. On the other bank, cylinders 2 and 4 are paired, as are 6 and 8. If we look at the Rover V8 firing order, we can see that we then have a minimum of 180 degrees of crank rotation between exhaust pulses in the secondary pipes, and a maximum of 450 degrees. This design offers a good compromise between complexity of fabrication, installation and performance.

This type of design can be seen fitted as standard on Rover V8-engined vehicles, such as the Rover SD1, some models of Range Rover Classic, and Land Rover Discovery. Some enthusiasts decide that it does not look very 'free flowing' and replace it with a sporty-looking tubular 4-into-1 design. Such an upgrade often results in no increase in performance (sometimes even a loss in midrange torque) due to the less than ideal pulse tuning of a simple 4-into-1 set-up, and the fact that the thin wall tubular manifolds emit a lot of heat into the under-bonnet area, thus increasing air-intake temperatures. This is not to say that a good tubular 4-into-1 design is not worth considering in some cases, just that things are not as simplistic as they first appear.

Dual-Plane or Crossover Designs

The dual-plane or crossover design undoubtedly represents the ultimate manifold design for the Rover V8 engine, or any other 90-degree V8.

However, it is also the most complex to design and install. It can be a major challenge, if not impossible on some cars, to fit such a design in the limited confines of the engine bay. This design joins the eight primary pipes into two main pipes: thus cylinders 3 and 5 from one bank are joined to cylinders 2 and 8 on the opposite bank. Likewise cylinders 4 and 6 are joined to cylinders 1 and 7. If we look again at the firing order we can see that this ensures perfectly equal-spaced exhaust pulses on each main pipe.

An exhaust pulse occurs in each main pipe exactly every 180 degrees. This is exactly the same situation as with a conventional 4-cylinder engine. This layout provides us with the opportunity to get ideal scavenging. For example, imagine cylinder 3 exhaust valve opens, the positive pressure pulse reaches the end of the primary pipe, and then returns as a negative pressure pulse or vacuum along the primaries for cylinders 3 and 5. This negative pulse or vacuum arrives at cylinder 5 just as the exhaust valve is closing and the intake is beginning to open (the overlap period).

This vacuum will literally help draw out the old exhaust gases and provide a significant vacuum on the intake valve, helping to draw fresh air and fuel into the cylinder before the piston has even begun to descend on its induction stroke. This scavenging effect can be surprisingly powerful, and can match, or often exceed, the vacuum applied when the piston descends on an induction stroke.

Dual-plane exhaust manifold on a TVR Chimaera, with equal primary lengths.

Dual-plane exhaust manifold on a TVR Chimaera, with unequal primary lengths.

In our experience, typical peak torque gains with a dual-plane exhaust design are in the order of 10 per cent, so a Rover V8 producing 250lb-ft of torque at the peak would expect to gain approximately 25lb-ft of torque, assuming that there are no other limiting factors. This is obviously a very worthwhile increase, but a dual-plane exhaust is usually very difficult to install in most applications. One notable exception to this is the TVR Chimaera and Griffith, as their forward-facing exhausts and the clearance around the front of the engine provide enough space to fabricate and fit a dual-plane exhaust system.

Primary Pipe Length

With a conventional 4-cylinder engine or a flat-plane (180-degree) V8, the length of the primary exhaust pipe is critical in achieving peak torque at the desired engine speed. However, with the Rover V8, the firing pulses down each exhaust manifold do not occur at regular intervals. This means that the length of the primary exhaust pipes is much less critical. This also means that there is no real performance advantage in making each primary exhaust pipe the same length. It is worth pointing out that when we talk about primary pipe length, we should include the distance from the back of the exhaust valve to the port face in our calculations.

Note that this only applies for 4-1 or 4-2-1 manifold arrangements – the dual-plane exhaust manifold will mean that the firing pulses down each bank will occur at regular intervals. Therefore the system will behave just like two 4-cylinder engines, and conventional primary length exhaust theory will then apply.

Primary Pipe Diameter

This is not simply a case of 'bigger is better'. An excessively large diameter can be just as detrimental to engine performance as a primary pipe diameter that is too small. This is because if the exhaust gas velocity is reduced, then the exhaust gas-flow rate will also be reduced. The beneficial scavenging effect is likewise reduced with a large primary size. In practice, a primary pipe that is marginally smaller in diameter than ideal will offer better overall performance than a primary pipe that is marginally larger than ideal.

To establish the optimum primary exhaust pipe diameter, ideally you would know the exhaust port flow at full valve lift. As this is not usually possible unless you are equipped with a flow bench, we have shown in Table 14 the optimal primary pipe diameter for a given power output.

So as an example, if you have a tuned 4.0 Rover V8 with 260bhp, then a 38mm (1.5in)-diameter primary exhaust pipe would be the optimum.

As a rule of thumb, a reduction in primary pipe diameter will move the torque peak lower down the rev range, and an increase will move the torque peak higher up the rev range.

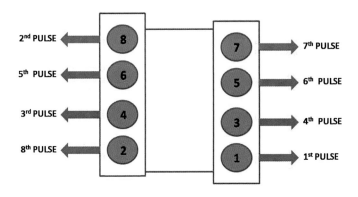

Cylinder firing order: 1,8,4,3,6,5,7,2

Rover V8 firing order.

Table 14: Optimum primary exhaust-pipe diameters

Engine horsepower range	Optimum primary pipe diameter
Up to 200bhp	34mm
Up to 300bhp	38mm
Up to 450bhp	44mm

SECONDARY EXHAUST PIPES AND COLLECTORS

Secondary Pipe Length

Unlike the primary pipe length, the secondary pipe length is critical to achieving optimum performance on the Rover V8. The optimum secondary length will vary depending on engine capacity and camshaft selection. There is really no substitute for practical testing on an engine or chassis dyno to establish the optimum length for your particular application. However, the Rover V8 generally favours longer secondary pipes.

Secondary Pipe Diameter

As with the primary exhaust pipe, there is an optimum diameter where peak exhaust gas flow rate is achieved. This dimension is not as critical as the secondary pipe length, but as with the primary pipes, going too large will cost more power than being slightly too small. Secondary pipe diameter is usually in the range of 44–57mm, with 50mm working reasonably well in most applications.

Table 15: Primary versus secondary exhaust-pipe diameter

Primary pipe diameter	Equivalent secondary pipe diameter
34–38mm	44–50mm
41–50mm	50–57mm

Collectors

The collector is where the primary or secondary pipes join together as one. There are a number of different styles of collector, all with their own characteristics. The main point here is that whichever collector design you use, it can only alter the torque curve below the engine speed at which peak torque occurs. The power curve above peak torque is far more influenced by primary pipe diameter and secondary pipe length.

We will briefly outline each type of collector here, along with their relative advantages and disadvantages.

Baffle Collector

With this basic collector design, the primary or secondary pipes terminate suddenly into an open tapered chamber. The abrupt opening from a primary exhaust pipe into an open collector causes a positive pressure wave that exits into the collector to be reflected as a negative or vacuum pressure wave back up the primary pipe. The upshot of this is that at certain engine speeds this negative pressure wave or vacuum will arrive at the open exhaust valve, helping to draw out the spent exhaust gases and beginning the induction process by scavenging the cylinder.

At other engine speeds, a positive pressure wave will arrive at the closing exhaust valve and help prevent too much air-fuel mixture being drawn into the exhaust during the overlap phase, therefore preventing over-scavenging of the cylinder. The downside of this design is that at some engine

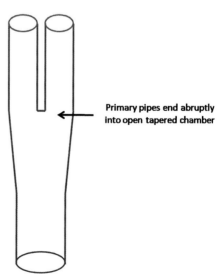

Primary pipes end abruptly into open tapered chamber

Baffle collector.

speeds, the opposite phenomenon will occur, with a positive pressure wave arriving at the open exhaust valve, preventing or obstructing the gas flow and a negative pressure wave arriving when the exhaust valve should shut.

This over-scavenging of the cylinder results in a loss of power and increased fuel consumption, and the longer the valves are held open, the more likely we are to experience these negative effects. For this reason we would recommend this collector design for engines with a relatively low overlap camshaft, and a duration of 285 degrees or less.

Merge Collector

With this design, the primary or secondary pipes do not end suddenly, but rather merge or blend into the main exhaust section. The gradual change in area reduces the strength or intensity of the reflected pressure wave, therefore helping to prevent the negative aspects of pulse tuning that can be experienced with the common baffle collector described above. Of course, we also lose out on some of the positive aspects of pulse tuning. This design is best suited to V8s fitted with a high overlap camshaft and durations above 290 degrees.

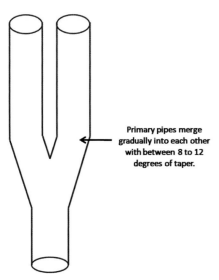

Primary pipes merge gradually into each other with between 8 to 12 degrees of taper.

Merge collector.

Venturi Merge Collector

The venturi merge collector is really just a variant of the merge collector. The primary or secondary pipes merge together before flaring back out again to meet the main exhaust section. This creates a venturi section that increases the gas speed, therefore increasing the scavenging effect of the primary or secondary pipes. This venturi section also reduces the intensity of reflected pressure waves, whilst keeping the velocity of the exhaust gases reasonably high. This design is most suited to maximum effort V8s with high overlap, long duration camshafts, and engines with particularly large main exhaust pipes. We would usually consider this design where an engine has a very large diameter main exhaust pipe, in relation to the diameter of the primary pipes.

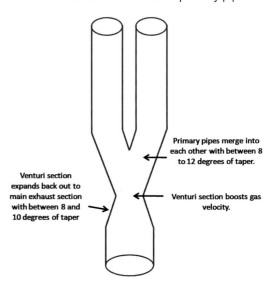

Primary pipes merge into each other with between 8 to 12 degrees of taper.

Venturi section expands back out to main exhaust section with between 8 and 10 degrees of taper

Venturi section boosts gas velocity.

Venturi merge collector.

Split Baffle Collector

The final collector type discussed here is what we refer to as the 'split baffle' collector. It is also referred to as the 'split interference' collector. Externally, the split baffle collector appears much like the basic baffle collector, but puts an internal divider between pairs of primary pipes.

This effectively converts the 4-into-1 baffle collector into a 4-2-1 configuration. The split baffle differs from our usual 4-2-1 configuration in that it offers

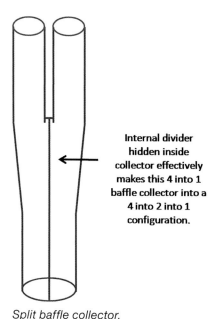

Internal divider hidden inside collector effectively makes this 4 into 1 baffle collector into a 4 into 2 into 1 configuration.

Split baffle collector.

an unusual combination of long primary pipes and short secondary pipes. This hybrid configuration offers some of the benefits of a 4-2-1 system, such as increased mid-range torque, but does not restrict the engine breathing at high speeds with long secondary runners. With this design, primary pipes of cylinders firing 270 degrees and 450 degrees apart are joined together. This unequal phasing means that different cylinders peak at different speeds, producing a broader, flatter torque curve. Another benefit of this divider is that the collector volume is halved, helping to reduce the intensity of reflected pressure waves, and reduce undesirable flow turbulence.

Dynamometer testing with your particular engine set-up is needed to find the optimum collector to divider length. However, a divider around 6–8in long seems to work reasonably well in most applications. This often means the divider will extend out of the collector and slightly into the main exhaust section. This design is sometimes used in competition to disguise from other competitors the fact that effectively a 4-2-1 configuration is being used; it is therefore also called the 'stealth 4-2-1' collector.

MAIN EXHAUST AND BALANCE PIPES

The optimum dimensions of the main exhaust pipe depends on a number of factors, such as manifold design, primary pipe length, main exhaust pipe length, engine capacity, catalyst or non-catalyst, and horsepower output. This is best determined by dynamometer testing, but we have provided a simplistic table below of what works well, based on our own experiences. Please note, you can add ¼–½in extra diameter downstream of the catalytic convertor, if an engine is fitted with one, due to the extra heat that is added.

Table 16: Recommended exhaust-pipe diameters

Horsepower	Exhaust pipe OD single exhaust	Exhaust pipe OD twin exhaust
130–180bhp	2.25in	1.75in
180–220bhp	2.5in	2in
220–270bhp	2.75in	2.25in
270–360bhp	3in	2.5in
360–450bhp	3.5in	2.75in

Balance Pipes

A balance pipe should be considered essential in building an effective performance exhaust system on any Rover V8 that has a separate exhaust pipe for each bank. A balance pipe almost always improves performance at some point in the engine's power curve over individual pipes. This is due to the pulse-tuning effects previously mentioned, and also the fact that any one bank now has the flow capability of both exhausts and silencers. If we have a twin-silencer set-up and each silencer is capable of flowing 250cfm, then with both pipes connected via a balance pipe, any one bank can see the full 500cfm flow of both silencers.

The other important virtue of a balance pipe is that it always creates a quieter exhaust note to the tune of 1–3db less, making it an effective 'zero-loss' silencer. The diameter of the balance pipe does not seem to be critical, and anything from a three-quarter to full exhaust pipe diameter seems to work well in our experience. Ideally the balance pipe would take the form of a sleeve blending the two separate pipes together over an 8–12in length. Unfortunately this is often impossible in many installations, and in this case a straight balance pipe between the main pipes will have to be used. Balance-pipe exhaust sections are also commonly available in the form of an 'X-pipe' or 'H-pipe'.

CATALYTIC CONVERTORS

The legal requirement for catalytic converters to be fitted to many modern vehicles certainly makes creating a free-flowing exhaust system a bit of a challenge. Many people resort to fitting a removable section so that the catalyst can be removed and replaced easily. However, the use of such a modification on the road is illegal in many countries, and you are advised to research the laws in your area regarding this.

If retaining the catalytic convertor is essential, then there are several things we can do to ensure that the back pressure and associated power loss is kept to an absolute minimum.

Choose a Free-Flowing Design

Choose the most free flowing catalytic convertor you can get. This point seems to be stating the obvious, but how do we evaluate what makes an effective catalytic convertor? You will see many aftermarket catalytic convertors graded by CPSI or cells per square inch. Factory catalysts can contain as many as 400 CPSI, whilst aftermarket performance replacements can contain as few as 100 CPSI. Fewer cells typically

Catalytic convertor.

give less back pressure, however fewer cells usually create a catalytic convertor that is less effective at reducing emissions. The aim is to find a catalytic convertor that gives the least back pressure, whilst still meeting the minimum emissions requirements.

We have seen so called 'performance' catalytic convertors that neither flow well, nor meet the minimum emissions requirements. An effective catalytic convertor will contain a reasonable amount of semi-precious metals, so if the aftermarket catalytic convertor seems very cheap, it is likely that it does not contain much in the way of these metals, and is unlikely to be particularly effective at reducing emissions. The CPSI appears to be the main criterion by which an aftermarket catalytic convertor is graded, but is only one aspect of a free-flowing design.

Many catalytic convertors flow poorly as a result of extreme flow turbulence, caused by the exhaust having to expand very rapidly to meet the full diameter of the honeycomb core, and then reducing very abruptly to meet the diameter of the exhaust outlet. It is not unusual for the entry taper between the inlet and outlet of the catalytic convertor and the honeycomb sections to be between 30 and 70 degrees. This is too steep to prevent excessive turbulence. Ideally, we would be looking at an entry/exit angle of 15 degrees or less.

Design the Exhaust System around the Catalytic Convertor

It is common to design the exhaust main section, then add the catalytic convertor as an afterthought. Really we need to design the exhaust around the catalytic convertor. Ideally, the exhaust section would begin to taper gently over a length of at least 5in, before and after the catalytic convertor, to ensure that the transition in diameter between exhaust and the honeycomb core occurs over a reasonable length to minimize flow turbulence and maintain velocity in the exhaust system. Another point worth mentioning again here is that the exhaust system after the catalytic convertor should be slightly larger than the section prior to the catalytic convertor, due to the extra heat expansion.

Monitor the Condition of the Catalytic Convertor

Most catalytic convertors will degrade over time, particularly in tuned engines that are running richer fuel mixtures and experience long periods of full throttle running. Catalytic convertors fare best running under stoichiometric conditions (14.7:1 AFR), where there are no unburnt hydrocarbons or excessive NOX emissions. Under WOT (wide open throttle), the fuel system must be set to run rich (11.8-13.2), but this creates a great deal of work for the catalyst dealing with all the unburnt hydrocarbons. The catalytic reaction creates a great deal of heat, and this heat can easily melt the honeycomb innards, creating a large flow restriction.

The easiest way to monitor the condition of the catalytic convertor is to measure the back pressure before and after the catalytic convertor (preferably when new), using a pressure manometer, and to check this periodically to ensure that the measured back pressure has not increased. This is essential on competition engines that must run a catalytic convertor, as the power loss from a melted catalytic convertor will often get progressively worse, without the vehicle driver or owner noticing immediately. It is worth noting that a partially melted or obstructed catalytic convertor cannot always be seen by looking at the honeycomb from both ends. We have seen catalytic convertors that visually appear fine until we cut them open and find an obstruction in the centre of the honeycomb section.

SILENCERS

Silencer selection is critical in any performance exhaust system that requires some form of noise reduction. There are very few applications that will be able to use 'open' exhausts, with nearly all forms of competition now having reasonably tight noise limits. The good news is that there are some great silencer designs that do not create excess back pressure or reduce engine performance. The bad

Exhaust silencer.

news is that there are also many that are very inefficient, reducing the exhaust flow considerably over the plain pipe, and we cannot tell which designs work based on their size or physical appearance.

Unfortunately, exhaust silencers are commonly rated in terms of their entry and exit size, not their flow rate, but it is really the flow rate we are interested in. What we are looking for is a silencer that can match the flow rate of the plain pipe to which it is connected, whilst reducing the noise to acceptable levels. For example, assuming we have a 3in exhaust pipe, we want a silencer that can match the flow rate of a plain 3in pipe. We would usually establish this on a flow bench, as we can flow-test our plain exhaust pipe and also flow-test our silencer at the same test pressure to ensure the two components of our system are compatible.

One thing we can state with absolute certainty is that back pressure is counter productive to performance. This is not a two-stroke engine! The camshaft timing should determine when the exhaust stops flowing, not the exhaust design. It is outside the scope of this book to describe and evaluate every type of silencer, but suffice to say that flow rate and noise reduction, and not size, should be our primary criteria in selecting a performance silencer.

CHAPTER 9

COOLING SYSTEM

The cooling system of any internal combustion engine performs a vital function: to ensure that the engine gets up to, but does not exceed, normal operating temperature. The Rover V8 engine is water cooled: this means that the heat from the engine is transferred to the coolant in the cooling system, which is in turn cooled by the flow of air passing over and through the radiator. The coolant is pumped around the cooling system via the radiator, using an engine-driven water pump. On the Rover V8 the water pump is driven by the auxiliary belt.

When tuning the Rover V8 it is worth bearing in mind that more performance will correspondingly increase the demand on the cooling system. If you make a 50 per cent improvement in torque or horsepower, you will need a cooling system that will cope with a 50 per cent increase in heat energy.

Normal operating temperature on a Rover V8 depends on what it is being used for – a high performance race engine will perform best at about 80°C,

but a road-going Rover V8 will give better fuel economy and longer oil life if run at 96°C coolant temperature. It is worth noting here that we do not recommend running your Rover V8 at the higher 96°C if it is not fitted with a flange-linered engine block and is in less than perfect condition. As this is at the upper limit of the recommended coolant temperature there is little margin for error, as many owners of the Range Rover P38 will testify! On an engine fitted with conventional liners (without a flange or 'top-hat'), these steel liners can slip when the engine is overheated, requiring an engine rebuild to rectify the problem.

When we refer to 'coolant temperature' here we are referring to the circulating temperature when the engine is running; the temperature is often higher in some parts of the cooling system – for example, near the exhaust valves in the cylinder head.

The coolant consists of both water and antifreeze. The water is used to transfer the heat from the cylinder block and heads to the radiator, while the anti-

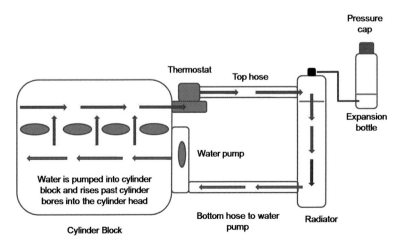

Typical cooling system.

freeze is used to prevent the water from freezing and to inhibit corrosion throughout the cooling system. Without enough antifreeze, oxides can form in all the coolant passageways, including the engine block, cylinder heads, water pump, coolant pipes, vehicle heater matrix and radiator. This corrosion will reduce or even prevent the transfer of heat through the cooling system. An aluminium engine such as the Rover V8 is actually more prone to corrosion within its cooling system, therefore we always recommend a 50:50 mix of water and antifreeze in all weather conditions.

The only exception to this is with all-out race engines, where a weaker mix is required to provide extra cooling by virtue of the higher percentage of water. This should only be done when the cooling system has already been optimized as much as possible, and will require more frequent renewal of coolant than usual. We usually use an ethylene glycol-based antifreeze with the Rover V8 engine; this is blue in colour and is compatible with the standard seals in a Rover V8 engine.

It is worth noting here that the coolant system should be flushed through and replenished with new coolant every two years as part of the vehicle's service schedule, to ensure the correct strength of antifreeze protection and to prevent the build-up of corrosion within the cooling system.

Air is another factor that will reduce or prevent the transfer of heat through the cooling system. Air occurs within the cooling system when there is a leak, when the cooling system is poorly designed, or is difficult to bleed after a coolant flush. If the system is free from leaks and is particularly difficult to bleed, a vacuum pump can be used to remove the remaining pockets of air from the cooling system.

The Rover V8 uses a pressurized cooling system. Pressurizing the coolant raises its boiling point considerably. Water at sea level will boil at 100°C; by raising the pressure of the cooling system to 15psi, the boiling point is raised to approximately 120°C. This helps prevent pockets of steam being trapped within the system, prevents localized boiling (such as near the combustion chamber), and ensures

that the cooling system does not boil over after the engine has been switched off. Any loss of system pressure, such as leaks or a faulty pressure cap, will lower the boiling point of the coolant.

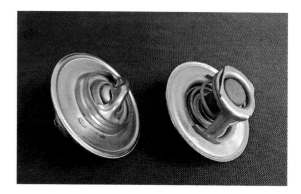

Typical thermostat, showing both sides.

The thermostat is an important part of a pressurized coolant system, as not only does it ensure that the system remains largely closed to the radiator during warm-up, it also maintains coolant pressure in the cylinder block and heads to prevent localized hot-spots. If the water passes through the engine too quickly it will not have sufficient time to absorb heat. For this reason we would always recommend retaining a thermostat or restrictor plate, even on race engines. There is a range of thermostats available for the Rover V8 engine, including 74°C, 82°C, 88°C and 92°C.

In very cold weather you may find that the engine actually struggles to get up to full operating temperature, noticeably reducing the fuel economy. In this case it is sometimes worth installing a higher temperature thermostat. In extreme cases you may have to also fit a cover on the front of the radiator, usually called a radiator muff or blanket.

WATER PUMP

The water pump is a vital part of the cooling system. It helps circulate the coolant around the system via the radiator, and maintain the pressure within the cooling system. A number of different water pumps are available for the Rover V8, depending on the application.

Land Rover fitted with a radiator blanket.

Rover V8 water pumps.

engines from 1994 seem to be more prone to bearing and seal failure, so regular inspection is worthwhile.

In more recent times electric water pumps have started to be fitted to Rover V8 engines, particularly for competition use, where every last horsepower matters. The main advantage of these is that it reduces the drag on the engine, although the increased electrical load on the alternator can counteract this overall parasitic drag reduction slightly. If you are considering using an electric water pump it is important that the system is designed and

The Rover V8 water pumps usually have a small hole located under the shaft, behind the pulley. This is a 'tell-tale' hole that leaks when the pump seals start to fail, the idea being that the owner spots the coolant leak before the water pump fails altogether. One cause of water pump failure is cavitation, where bubbles or pockets of air within the water pump implode, causing impellor, housing or seal failure. This mode of pump failure is usually indicative of a poor coolant system design or a faulty water pump. The water pumps fitted to the later 'Serpentine'

Water-pump tell-tale hole.

Electric water pump.

Aluminium radiator.

installed properly, otherwise it is likely that you will encounter reliability issues. It is absolutely essential to ensure that you purchase the correct specification water pump (in terms of flow rate, size, and so on) and install a robust electrical supply system.

RADIATOR

The purpose of the radiator is to transfer the heat from the cooling system into the surrounding air. A large surface area and a large radiator core area are both conducive to an effective cooling system, maximizing the ability of the cooling system to dissipate heat. Standard Rover V8 radiators are available in both cross-flow and vertical-flow formats, depending on the original application. With a cross-flow radiator there is a header tank on either side of the radiator, and coolant flows horizontally between them via tubes. These tubes are referred to as the 'core' of the radiator, and there are metal fins between these tubes that help dissipate the heat. A vertical-flow radiator is, as the name suggests, the opposite of the cross-flow radiator, with the header tanks located at the top and bottom of the radiator and the coolant flowing vertically between them via the core tubes.

A cross-flow radiator is usually more efficient than a vertical-flow radiator. Double-pass cross-flow radiators are also available; these use a divider within one of the header tanks to force the coolant through the radiator core twice. This means that this type of radiator will keep the coolant temperature noticeably lower than the conventional single-pass types.

All radiators should have a fill or bleed point located at the top; this prevents the radiator from getting an air-lock when filling the coolant system.

Radiators are usually made from either brass or aluminium. Aluminium radiators are more efficient and generally more durable than brass radiators. Some of the aluminium radiators at the cheaper end of the spectrum have plastic header tanks, but these are not very durable and cannot be easily repaired.

SWIRL POTS, EXPANSION TANKS AND HEATERS

In applications with low-mounted radiators (for example TVRs), the hot coolant does not want to flow down from the engine to the radiator. This is because heat rises, and any air bubbles that are trapped in the radiator will try to rise against the flow of coolant to the highest point. In these cases an additional tall coolant reservoir is used, sometimes called a 'swirl pot': these have a fill point at the highest point of the coolant system, a bleed outlet at the top that goes to an expansion bottle, an inlet at the top from the thermostat housing, and an outlet at the bottom that feeds the radiator top hose. The bleed outlet allows the hot air or steam to escape from the radiator, which in turn allows the coolant to flow down to the radiator.

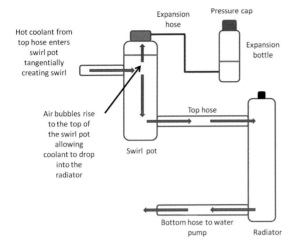

Expansion hose

Pressure cap

Expansion bottle

Hot coolant from top hose enters swirl pot tangentially creating swirl

Air bubbles rise to the top of the swirl pot allowing coolant to drop into the radiator

Swirl pot

Top hose

Bottom hose to water pump

Radiator

Swirl-pot set-up.

Any cooling system needs a way of allowing the coolant to expand as it gets hot. Some older vehicles leave room in the top header of a vertical-flow radiator to allow for this expansion, with a pressure cap fitted to allow the coolant to leave the cooling system via an overflow pipe if the coolant expands too much. However, most Rover V8 applications use an expansion bottle for this purpose, with the radiator being closed off and completely full of coolant. An expansion bottle is typically only meant to be half full of coolant, with the remain-

ing half allowing room for the coolant to expand. Just like the old vertical-flow radiator, the expansion bottle is fitted with a pressure cap that will release coolant out of the cooling system if the coolant system reaches a specified pressure and there is no more room left for further expansion. These pressure caps are rated for a specific pressure – for example 15psi – and the old-style caps can be replaced with higher pressure-rated caps, if required.

If you have an older vehicle that does not have an expansion bottle, your cooling system can be improved by fitting an expansion bottle and converting your radiator so that you can fill it up completely. This effectively increases the volume of coolant in your cooling system, which in turn improves the overall effectiveness of your cooling system.

Another component that improves the effectiveness of the cooling system is the in-car heater. This not only increases the volume of the cooling system, but also acts as an additional radiator, allowing heat to escape from the cooling system. Owners of older vehicles will already be aware of this, particularly if their cooling system is not very effective to begin with, as turning the interior heater on will allow the coolant to flow through the heater matrix and therefore reduce the engine coolant temperature.

Swirl-pot set-up on a TVR Griffith.

Expansion bottle.

Pressure caps.

COOLING FANS

There are two types of cooling fan: mechanical and electric. Many Rover V8 applications were originally fitted with a mechanical fan, usually with a viscous coupling, driven off the nose of the water pump. The viscous coupling is fluid at low coolant temperatures, and locks up once a certain coolant

temperature is reached. These viscous couplings usually fail in the 'locked' position, leading to the fan being driven constantly. This reduces fuel economy and will also reduce performance at lower coolant temperatures. These units can also fail in the unlocked position, resulting in no fan and potential overheating.

A viscous fan can be checked for correct operation by bringing the engine up to full operating temperature and then attempting to stop the fan with a rolled-up newspaper or similar. The fan should easily stall when the engine is cold, but continue to rotate when hot. Extreme care must be taken if doing this, as the rotating assembly, including fan and belts, can easily amputate fingers! A mechanical cooling fan does create additional load on the engine even when working correctly, reducing the fuel economy and performance of the engine. The big advantage of a fixed mechanical cooling fan is reliability.

Electric cooling fans can be used to replace the mechanical cooling fan on a Rover V8 engine. This can improve both performance and fuel economy, although it is important to ensure that the system is designed and installed properly for maximum reliability. In an electric cooling fan set-up a temperature-switched earth is used to power the cooling fan(s) via a relay. The temperature switch can be an otter switch located in the cooling system, an ECU output based on the engine management coolant sensor, or a basic probe. If you are using

Mechanical cooling fan.

Electric cooling fans.

a basic cooling fan probe we recommend locating it between the fins of the radiator, and setting the switch point lower than your target temperature. We do not recommend inserting the probe between the join of a coolant hose and coolant pipe, as this invariably leads to a coolant leak.

There is a lot of choice when purchasing electric fans. The first thing to work out is the physical space available. Fans are ideally mounted on the rear of the radiator so that the cooling fans are pulling rather than pushing air, although they can be front mounted – just check the direction of the fan's

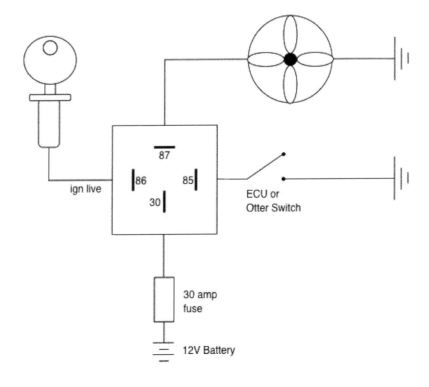

Typical electric cooling fan wiring with four-pin relay.

Bonnet vents on a TVR Chimaera.

COOLING SYSTEM MODIFICATIONS FOR PERFORMANCE ENGINES

An engine that is producing 50 per cent more power will produce approximately 50 per cent more heat. This requires a more effective cooling system to cope with this additional thermal load. In summary, the main methods for improving the cooling system's ability to cope with extra heat are as follows:

More cooling capacity: More coolant means more ability to absorb excess heat, and longer to reach boiling point. There are several methods for doing this: larger radiators, expansion tanks and swirl pots will all increase the physical capacity of the cooling system.

Larger radiator: A larger radiator core will improve the ability of the cooling system to transfer heat from the coolant to the surrounding air, and will usually also increase the cooling capacity by virtue of holding more coolant. If no extra space is available to fit a larger radiator, then the core can often be made thicker. The radiator's efficiency can be further improved by converting from a vertical-flow to a cross-flow or double-pass cross-flow unit.

airflow carefully. Establish what your airflow requirements are, and calculate the total airflow of the various cooling fans that are available. Depending on the dimensions of the cooling fan space you may find that a large single fan will flow more air than two smaller fans. The airflow is usually rated in cubic feet per minute (cfm), and this is dependent on the size of the motor (typically rated in amps), as well as the size and shape of the blades.

Cooling fans usually come with straight blades as standard, but are also available with curved blades. The purpose of curved-blade fans is for quieter operation, but the disadvantage is slightly reduced airflow, although electric fan manufacturers sometimes fit the same size curved-blade fans with more powerful motors to counteract this. Depending on how much space is available, it is always worth considering fitting two cooling fans instead of one. Using two fans obviously improves reliability, particularly when wired in as two parallel systems with separate switches, relays and fused supplies.

To work effectively, the radiator and cooling fan(s) rely on the air in front of the radiator to be of a higher pressure than the air behind the radiator. If the hot air in your engine bay is unable to escape quickly enough, the radiator will be unable to dissipate the heat properly. If this is the problem with your application, you may need to consider bonnet or wing vents to allow the hot, high-pressure air to vent properly.

Increase airflow through the radiator: This includes removing restrictions to airflow through the radiator, and increasing airflow when stationary through the use of improved cooling fans.

Finally, if your cooling system has been properly designed and is definitely working correctly but you are still having problems with overheating, this might be indicative of a problem with the engine or engine management. Problems with camshaft timing, ignition timing or fuelling can cause the engine to run excessively hot. Carry out the necessary checks and refer to the relevant chapters in this book if you think this may be the case.

Remember that the oil system is also part of the engine's cooling system, so fitting an oil cooler can also be beneficial for high performance engines.

CHAPTER 10

FUEL SYSTEM

In this chapter we are going to look at the fuel system in two different stages: fuel supply and fuel delivery. The fuel supply is provided by the fuel tank, fuel lines, pump, filter and, with fuel injection systems, the fuel rail and fuel pressure regulator. Fuel delivery involves either carburettor(s) or fuel injectors.

FUEL SUPPLY

Fuel Tank

When using an original fuel tank it is important to ensure that it is suitable for your requirements. Does it have the required capacity? Does it have adequate surge protection for the intended performance or competition? Are you converting from carburettors to fuel injection, or vice versa?

Fuel tanks are usually made from one of three materials: steel, aluminium or plastic. It is relatively straightforward to modify steel or aluminium fuel tanks – for example with additional baffles, or return line fitting for fuel injection – but more difficult with plastic fuel tanks.

One important feature of any fuel tank is the breather. This is usually plumbed into the filler neck on most applications, and allows the fuel tank to vent to atmosphere, or to the intake manifold via a purge canister (for emissions purposes). This makes filling the fuel tank straightforward, and allows for expansion in warmer weather. In most cases a roll-over valve is fitted in line to ensure that fuel cannot escape from the fuel tank in the event of a vehicle rolling over. A roll-over valve is a basic one-way type valve that will allow fumes

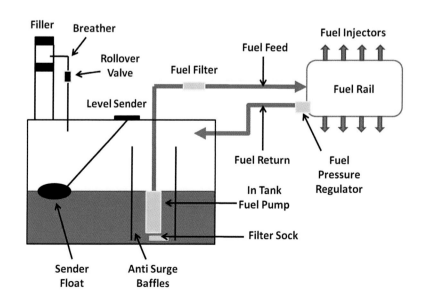

Standard EFI fuel-tank set-up.

Roll-over valve.

to vent but will shut off completely if fuel tries to pass the valve.

A swirl pot can be added to the fuel system to provide protection against fuel surge under hard cornering or acceleration. This is basically a reservoir of fuel which acts as a back-up in the instance of the fuel pick-up pipe becoming momentarily starved of fuel. Standard applications generally do not have, nor do they require an external swirl pot, but some competition applications will benefit from one, to prevent fuel starvation under hard cornering or acceleration. An additional fuel pump is often used with a custom swirl pot installation. Unless the swirl pot is particularly large, we usually recommend that this additional fuel pump has a flow rate of similar volume to the main fuel pump, to ensure that the

swirl pot does not run out of fuel at higher engine loads and speeds.

We also recommend that the fuel return line still goes back to the fuel tank, rather than back to the swirl pot, otherwise there is a risk of the fuel getting too hot whilst circulating in a closed loop at lower engine speeds, and this can cause the engine to run lean as a result. Swirl-pot capacity depends on a number of variables, but a 2ltr swirl pot is usually ample for a 300bhp naturally aspirated Rover V8 used in competition (such as for hill climbs, sprints and so on).

FUEL LINES

A fuel feed line is required for both carburettor and fuel injection systems. A fuel return line is usually only required for fuel injection systems, although it is sometimes used with carburettor systems to help prevent excessive fuel pressure or vapour lock. Rigid fuel line should be used as much as possible, with rubber fuel hoses only to be used for connection purposes and where the fuel hoses connect to the carburettor or fuel injection rail. The rubber fuel hose also allows for engine movement, so it is always worth allowing a little slack in the fuel hoses that connect to the fuel rail on the engine.

Rigid fuel line is usually made from one of four materials: steel, copper, kunifer or plastic. Steel is hard and resistant to puncture, but is prone to

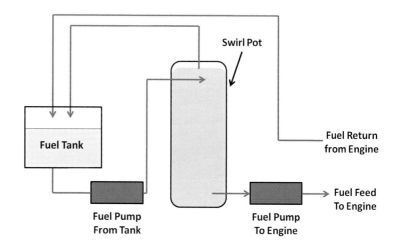

Typical swirl-pot installation.

long-term corrosion and is more difficult to form to shape. Copper is easy to form to the desired shape and less prone to corrosion, but is also less resistant to puncture than steel. Kunifer is a copper-nickel alloy – this means that it is easier to form than steel, not prone to corrosion, and is more resistant to puncture than copper, arguably making it the best all-round material for solid fuel lines. Many modern applications now use plastic fuel lines, which are completely resistant to corrosion but are more difficult to make for custom applications.

Rubber fuel line can vary in quality, and it is important to ensure that it is of the correct grade: 'SAE J30 R6' is the minimum current requirement for fuel-injection applications, and is also the current recommended minimum for carburettor applications. Unfortunately, at the time of writing, there is rubber

fuel line available on the market that is not suitable for modern unleaded petrol. This rubber fuel line quickly degrades and is prone to rupture! The only way to be certain is only to purchase rubber fuel line with the 'SAE J30 R6' grade or higher – R7, R9 or R14 – clearly shown.

It is worth noting that this minimum grade requirement will soon change as the ethanol content of unleaded petrol increases. For longevity, it is worth considering upgrading to R9 specification fuel hose from the outset. R9-spec fuel hose is equivalent to DIN 73379-3E and is suitable for fuel containing a high percentage of bio-ethanol.

For most applications, 8mm ($\frac{5}{16}$in) fuel line is used – this refers to the outside diameter of the solid fuel line, or the inside of the rubber fuel hose. The required fuel diameter depends on the horsepower requirements of the engine – on a fuel injected, naturally aspirated Rover V8 an 8mm fuel line typically supports up to 500bhp, so more than enough for most applications!

The horsepower rating of a fuel feed line not only depends on the inner diameter of the fuel line, but also on the length of the fuel lines and the size or shape of any fittings within the fuel line. As an example, a 4.5m length of 8mm fuel line typically has the same flow rate as one 90-degree fitting. This example clearly shows how the fittings or rigid fuel line bends have a much more significant impact on the flow rate of the fuel system than the overall length of the fuel line.

ABOVE LEFT: Different fuel-line materials.

Rubber fuel hose showing grade.

The key to working out whether or not your fuel system is capable of supporting the engine's power output is to ensure that the pressure drop across the fuel supply system is not significant enough to affect adversely the fuel pump's output.

It is worth noting here that the fuel line requirements for a carburettor equipped engine are different to those for a fuel injected engine. This is largely due to the behaviour of a low-pressure carburettor fuel pump versus the behaviour of a high-pressure EFI fuel pump. In a nutshell, a carburettor fuel pump is much more susceptible to changes in fuel pressure than an injection fuel pump, therefore it will require larger diameter fuel lines than an EFI system would.

FUEL PUMP

There are two main types of fuel pump: in-tank fuel pumps, as fitted to many standard applications, and external in-line fuel pumps. These fuel pumps are then split into two further categories: low-pressure carburettor fuel pumps, and high-pressure fuel-injection fuel pumps.

The in-tank fuel pumps are usually application specific (for example, a Range Rover Classic EFI fuel pump) and are designed to fit the fuel tank for that application, although it is possible to use these pumps with custom fuel tanks if the tanks are designed around that specific fuel pump fitment.

The external fuel pumps are easier to use with custom applications and are simply plumbed in-line with the fuel feed line. A huge range of external fuel pumps is available, including the ubiquitous Bosch

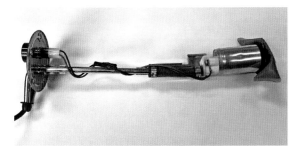

In-tank fuel pump.

044 in various guises. These external fuel injection pumps usually have a larger inlet (for example, 12mm) than the outlet, which is usually 8mm.

It is worth noting that increasing the fuel pressure will reduce the flow rate of the fuel pump, as pump flow is inversely proportional to fuel pressure. The graph overleaf shows how the fuel pump flow is reduced with an increase of fuel pressure for a commonly available fuel injection pump – the Bosch 044 fuel pump.

Bosch 044 fuel pump.

This behaviour is even more pronounced with a carburettor fuel pump; a small change in fuel pressure will give a much more significant change in fuel flow rate with a carburettor fuel pump than with an EFI fuel pump.

Another important factor with an electronic fuel pump is the fuel pump supply voltage. Reduced voltage, caused by a poor earth or failing charging system, will naturally reduce the flow rate of the fuel pump. The graph overleaf shows how a small change in voltage affects the flow rate of the same Bosch 044 fuel pump.

FUEL FILTERS

A fuel filter should be regarded as essential if you plan on keeping your fuel pump and carburettor

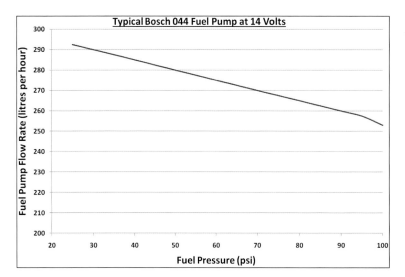

Effect of fuel pressure on the flow rate of the Bosch 044 fuel pump.

Effect of fuel pressure on the flow rate of a carburettor fuel pump.

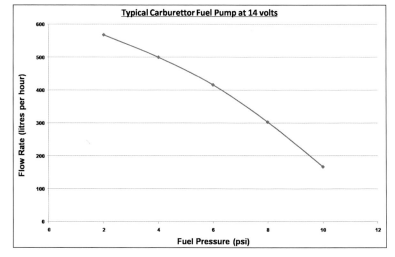

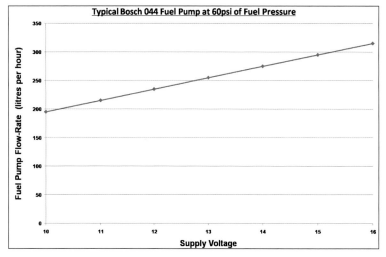

Effect of supply voltage on the flow rate of the Bosch 044 fuel pump.

FRAM G3829 fuel filter.

or fuel injectors running reliably. To be really safe, a basic pre-pump filter should be used, as well as the main fuel filter in the fuel feed line after the fuel pump. The pre-pump filter can be either a basic sock filter on the end of the fuel pick-up pipe, or a gauze filter on the inlet of the fuel pump. The main fuel filter should have a reasonable capacity; the FRAM G3829 is an example of a good main fuel filter, and is standard fitment on a Range Rover Classic, TVR Chimaera and TVR Griffith.

If either fuel filter is not replaced or cleaned at regular intervals, fuel supply issues can arise, leading to running problems and loss of fuel supply. In the worst case a partially blocked fuel filter will cause the engine to run lean at full throttle, potentially causing premature engine failure.

FUEL INJECTION RAIL

The Rover V8 has come with a range of different fuel injection rails, depending on which fuel injection system is fitted. The Lucas 4CU, Lucas 14CUX, GEMS and Thor engine management systems all come with their own design of fuel injection rail. The first three are very similar, comprising a feed loop with an outlet for each fuel injector, and ending with a fuel pressure regulator and the fuel return pipe. The Thor fuel injection rail is a little different, as it is a 'dead-head' type fuel system. This means that there is just a feed pipe to the fuel rail and no return.

The feed to the fuel injection rail is regulated at the fuel pump instead.

It is possible to use this type of fuel rail with a more conventional fuel system, by teeing the fuel return into the feed line just before the fuel injection rail, and locating the fuel pressure regulator into the return line shortly after the tee.

Some Rover V8 fuel injection rails are fitted with a Schrader valve fitment; this allows you to use a basic pressure gauge to check the fuel pressure in the rail. This can be very useful when setting up an adjustable fuel pressure regulator, or for diagnosing fuel system faults. If this is not fitted, fuel pressure can be checked by plumbing a pressure gauge and t-piece into the fuel feed pipe.

Another common feature of many standard Rover V8 fuel injection rails (including Lucas 14CUX &

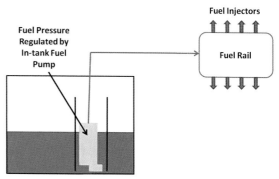

Thor dead-head fuel system.

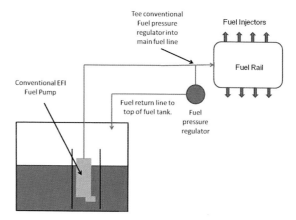

Using a Thor fuel rail with a conventional fuel pump and pressure regulator.

Schrader fuel pressure test valve on fuel rail.

Fuel temperature sensor.

GEMS) is the fuel temperature sensor. This sensor measures the temperature of the fuel rail, and provides this information to the engine control unit (ECU), which uses this information to adjust the fuel quantity provided by the fuel injectors (predominantly for hot-start conditions). This sensor can be removed if fitting an aftermarket engine management system that does not use this sensor.

FUEL-PRESSURE REGULATOR

There are two main types of fuel pressure regulator: fixed and adjustable. Standard fuel pressure regulators are the fixed-pressure type, and these are generally the most reliable.

Standard fuel pressure should be in the range of 34–38psi (+ or –2psi) with the vacuum pipe disconnected. The fuel pressure with the vacuum pipe connected will vary, depending upon the level of

manifold vacuum. Mild camshaft engines will pull more vacuum, and therefore reduce fuel pressure, more than engines with higher overlap camshafts. The maximum pressure you should run with a normally aspirated engine is 60psi, as any more than this can interfere with the injector's ability to open correctly. Forced-induction engines will increase fuel pressure as manifold pressure increases – for example, at 10psi of boost 60psi fuel pressure will increase to 70psi, which would exceed the maximum recommended pressure.

If increased fuel pressure is required, there is a huge range of aftermarket adjustable fuel pressure regulators available. However, the quality of these does vary, and adjustable fuel pressure regulators are inherently less reliable than the fixed-pressure type. It is also possible to increase the pressure of a standard Rover V8 fuel pressure regulator by squeezing it slightly in a vice, but it is easy to overdo this (turning it into scrap), and they have been known to revert back to their original dimensions and cause the engine to run lean! This method is therefore definitely not recommended, and a good quality adjustable fuel pressure regulator is therefore preferable if increased fuel pressure is required.

Standard fuel pressure regulator.

FUEL INJECTORS

Fuel injectors are electrically controlled solenoids that are opened for the required amount of time to

are able to adjust the ECU calibration, you will need to increase the amount of time that the injector is open for. As an example, a TVR Griffith 500 might originally require the injectors to be open for 9.5 milliseconds at wide open throttle (WOT) and 6,000rpm. After some engine modifications the same car will then require 10 milliseconds at the same load/rpm site, and will have the ECU recalibrated to suit.

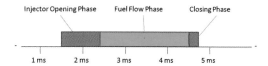

Injector phase diagram.

Adjustable fuel pressure regulator.

deliver a specific quantity of fuel within that time-frame. These solenoids have two electrical connections: a constant twelve volts or more when the engine is running or cranking, and a switched earth. The switched earth is controlled via the engine control unit (ECU), and this dictates how long the injector is open for, which in turn dictates how much fuel is delivered for a given fuel pressure. The length of time the injector is open for is called 'pulse-width', measured in milliseconds, and the percentage of time the injector is open for within a complete engine cycle (two crankshaft revolutions and one camshaft revolution) is called the 'duty cycle'.

Any engine modifications will require the fuelling at least to be adjusted to keep the engine running optimally. Any improvements in performance will require an increase in fuel, and assuming that you

This 0.5 millisecond increase does not mean a lot by itself, but when we look at the duty cycle, or the percentage of time that the injector spends open, you can see where the injector is within its operating range. So the corresponding duty cycle on the TVR Griffith 500 fuel injectors may have increased from 94 per cent to 100 per cent. This is a problem, as the injectors cannot open any more than this, and might even already be beyond their operating range, causing the engine to run lean in a dangerous load/rpm zone. Ideally the fuel injectors will not be operating any higher than 85 per cent duty cycle, so the TVR Griffith 500 in our example ideally required higher flow rate injectors before it was even modified!

Fuel injectors are rated in terms of their static flow rate – this is how much petrol the fuel injectors will flow at 100 per cent duty cycle for a specific amount of time at a specific fuel pressure. Standard Lucas Rover V8 fuel injectors flow approximately 188cu cm per minute (cc/min) at 43.5psi of fuel pressure.

When the fuel injectors are operating at lower pulse-widths, at idle for example, a large proportion of this pulse-width includes the time it takes for the fuel injector to open and to close. If this opening and closing time is the same, or close to the same as the complete pulse-width, the injector will not be able to provide the correct fuel quantity accurately and consistently. In practice this means that the engine will have an unstable

Standard Rover V8 fuel injector.

and inconsistent idle – and it may not even be able to idle without increasing the pulse-width to the point where the engine is running with an excessively rich fuel mixture. Fuel injectors with higher flow rates typically have longer opening and closing times, and are therefore likely to be more difficult to control at lower pulse-widths.

So if you are looking for the correct fuel injectors for your application, you require a fuel injector that operates at no more than 85 per cent duty cycle, and has a minimum operating pulse-width that is comfortably greater than the injector opening and closing times combined.

Remember, a 'bigger' injector is not always better, particularly if you want a smooth idle and a normal idle speed. However, injectors that are 'maxed out' in terms of flow rate – that is, are not 'big' enough – could ultimately damage your engine through lean fuel mixture.

Why can we not simply increase the fuel pressure to provide more fuelling with the original injectors? It is acceptable to increase the fuel pressure to achieve a richer fuel mixture overall, but there is a limit as to how much the fuel pressure can be increased. The fuel injectors have a fuel pressure limit, beyond which they will not be able to function correctly. For

- 3.9- or 4-litre Rover V8 – standard, no modifications, approximately 190–220bhp at the flywheel – 188cc/min
- 3.9- or 4-litre Rover V8 – some engine modifications, approximately 230–260bhp at the flywheel – 215cc/min
- 5-litre Rover V8 – standard, no modifications, approximately 260–280bhp at the flywheel – 215cc/min
- 5-litre Rover V8 – some engine modifications, approximately 300bhp at the flywheel – 240cc/min
- Supercharged Rover V8 – approximately 400bhp at the flywheel – 340cc/min
- Supercharged or turbocharged Rover V8 – approximately 400–500bhp at the flywheel – 440cc/min

this reason, we do not recommend increasing the static fuel pressure to more than 60psi with an EFI system. It is also worth noting that you will need to ensure that your fuel hose is rated to 60psi if you are increasing the fuel pressure to this extent.

There are many on-line calculators to help choose the correct size injectors, but here are a few examples of injectors of a suitable size for Rover V8 engines, based on our experience:

Another consideration when selecting a fuel injector is the spray pattern. The original Lucas injectors are single-hole injectors, whereas more modern fuel injectors (such as the Bosch EV6) are usually multi-hole, giving a finer spray pattern. The finer spray pattern leads to better fuel atomization, which improves combustion at lower engine speeds (better idle quality). This also reduces emissions and fuel consumption. Conversely, if the fuel is too finely atomized it will displace oxygen in the intake charge, which can reduce the power potential of the engine.

Bosch EV6 four-hole injector.

Fuel Injector Location

Fuel injectors tend to be located close to the intake valve to ensure the fuel remains well atomized at low to mid-engine speeds. By spraying the fuel on to the back of a hot intake valve, good mixture atomization is virtually guaranteed. This in turn improves throttle response, whilst lowering hydrocarbon (HC) emissions. However, at higher engine speeds it can be advantageous to locate the injectors further outboard so that the evaporative cooling effect of the fuel can be used to cool the intake and therefore improve mixture density. With particularly high output and high speed engines two injectors per cylinder can be used in a staged injection set-up, and this arguably represents the ultimate configuration. The inboard injectors can be used to achieve a good idle quality and accurate low engine speed fuelling, whilst the outboard-mounted injectors can be staged to activate at higher engine loads and speeds.

GSXR throttle bodies with primary and secondary injectors.

Many aftermarket ECUs can be configured to control staged injection, with most activating the secondary or outboard injectors at a specified engine speed. Some systems also take engine load into account. This is often required when the outboard injectors are located before the throttle plates, otherwise at low throttle openings the outboard injectors will be spraying on to a closed throttle plate. You will need to experiment with the aid of a dynamometer to discover the best point to begin to activate the outboard injectors. We have found that this is usually at, or just below, peak torque with the throttle past 50 per cent.

Low-Impedance and High-Impedance Injectors

It is also worth noting here that early fuel injected engines (such as the Lucas 4CU) were often fitted with low-impedance injectors (typically 3–4 ohms), whereas most fuel injected engines (Lucas 14CUX onwards with the Rover V8) are fitted with high-impedance injectors (13–14 ohms). Lucas 14CUX and GEMS engine management systems both use the same high-impedance fuel injectors (part no. ERR722). These injectors flow approximately 190cc per minute at a working pressure of 2.5-bar. The Thor engine management system uses high impedance injectors (part no. ERR6600). These particular injectors flow approximately 180cc per minute at 3-Bar and are a more modern four-hole type for better atomization.

The early low-impedance injectors (part no. ERC3620, as fitted to the Rover SD1 and Range Rover Classic) are easily identified by the short hose fittings on each fuel injector, and use a ballast resistor box to prevent excess current draw from damaging the ECU.

Early Rover V8 fuel injection systems, such as the Lucas 4CU system, also use a ninth fuel injector mounted on the intake plenum to supply additional fuel for cold starting, as well as when the engine is running below 20°C coolant temperature.

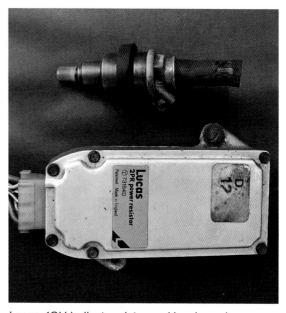

Lucas 4CU ballast resistor and low impedance injector.

Cold-start injector.

FUEL DELIVERY

Carburettors

Throughout the years of production, Rover V8 engines have come with a range of different carburettors, the most common being the SU or Zenith-Stromberg carburettor. Very similar in design, these constant depression-type carburettors are very tolerant of slight tuning errors. These carburettors can be used successfully on both standard and modified engines.

SU HIF6/ HIF44

These SU carburettors are relatively straightforward to set up and tune, offering good mixture control and reasonable airflow for their size. These are excellent carburettors for stock or lightly modified road engines, as they offer better fuel economy and part throttle mixture control than many fixed-choke carburettors due to their excellent fuel atomization characteristics. It is beyond the scope of this book to detail full overhaul procedures, but excellent information can be found on the Burlen Fuel Systems Ltd website.

Set-Up Tips

Regardless of whether your engine is standard or modified, the correct set-up is essential to get the most from an engine equipped with these carburettors. The importance of these checks cannot be over-emphasized. Do not even attempt to tune the carburettors until these checks have been carried out.

Needle heights: Remove the carburettor dashpot securing screws, and carefully remove the dashpots. Remove the piston from the dashpot and carefully check the height of the needle in relation to the piston. The important thing is that both needles sit at the same height in relation to the pistons. Slight differences in height are not uncommon, and cause

SU HIF44 carburettors on a classic MGB engine.

the two carburettors to run slightly different fuel mixtures. If you find that the height changes as soon as you tighten the securing screw, then replace the needle guides with new ones and take care not to over-tighten.

SU carburettor needle.

Jet heights: With the dashpots and pistons still removed, measure the height between the main jet and the bridge. This can be initially set so the jet is around 1mm below the bridge. This should be rechecked after tuning to ensure that both carburettor jets are still at the same height as each other. For example, if you have to turn the jet-adjusting screws a further one turn to achieve the correct idle fuel mixture, then you should remove both dashpots/pistons again after tuning and recheck that both jet heights are equal. Do not assume that a given number of turns on each mixture screw will result in equal jet heights!

Measuring jet height on an SU carburettor.

Float levels: Set the float levels to between 1–1.5mm. It is important that both floats are equal in height, to within 0.25mm of each other.

Balancing airflow: This is also critical to ensure that all cylinders receive the same air–fuel ratio. Use a hand-held airflow meter to ensure that both carburettors are flowing the same amount of air at idle. You can adjust the individual idle screws to achieve equal airflow. It is also important to ensure that both throttle plates are synchronized and reach full opening at the same time. If not, the linkage between the two carburettors will need to be adjusted. Once this is done, ideally you should also check the balance at quarter and half throttle if possible.

Balancing airflow on a pair of SU carburettors.

Dashpot oil level: This is a very important and sometimes overlooked aspect of SU carburettor operation. The oil damps the rising of the piston, and can be thought of as similar to the accelerator pump jet in a fixed-choke carburettor. If the oil level

Dashpot on an SU carburettor.

is low or too thin, then the piston can rise too quickly, resulting in a transient lean spot and engine hesitation. Lack of oil can also cause the piston to oscillate with the pulses in the induction system. The oil slows the rise of the piston so that the engine draws harder on the main jet, creating a temporarily richer mixture, before the piston rises and the airflow increases to match the fuel flow. The oil has a tendency to be consumed over time, so should be checked regularly. Mono grade SAE30 oils are usually recommended, but heavier oils can be experimented with if the mixture still goes lean on transient acceleration.

Fuel pressure: This can be easily checked by installing a fuel pressure gauge in the fuel link pipe between the two carburettors. Fuel pressure should be in the range of 3–4.5psi, and should not drop significantly under heavy engine load. Excessively high fuel pressure will cause the float bowls to flood.

Tuning

First and foremost, the carburettors should be in excellent condition: there is little point trying to tune a set of worn-out carburettors. Air leaks caused by worn throttle spindle bushes are common, along with jet wear, and will make tuning difficult. If in doubt, give the carburettors a full rebuild. There are excellent books available on this subject, and it is well worth familiarizing yourself with their operation before attempting to tune them. In addition to this, the engine should be in good condition, with even cylinder compressions, correct ignition timing and new spark plugs, HT leads, and so on.

Fuel Mixture Tuning

Unlike fixed-choke carburettors, the main jet diameter is fixed in size and is not a variable in tuning. The tuning variables are jet height (adjustable with a screwdriver or spanner) and needle taper profile. There are many different needle profiles available for the SU carburettor. The needle diameter can be measured at various points along its length and is subdivided into sixteen measuring or metering points, with point 1 being the thickest end of the taper and point 16 being the thinnest. It is worth noting that points 13 to 16 usually have very little effect on fuel flow, and therefore fuel mixture. Full load fuelling is mostly influenced by points 10 to 13, depending upon the jet height.

The overall fuel mixture can be altered by raising or lowering the main jet, so that it sits at a thinner or wider point of the needle's taper. Metering points 1 to 3 are very similar across most of the available needles, so it is usually best to use the jet height adjustment to get the idle fuel mixture correct, and alter the mid and full load fuel mixtures by changing the needle profile. The fuel mixture at various points in the engine's load and speed range can be altered by changing or modifying the needle's taper at various points across its length.

If the fuel mixture is too rich or lean across the operating range, from idle to full load, then you can simply raise or lower the jet height by means of the jet-adjusting screw (HIF44) or nut (HS6). If the fuel mixture is found to be too lean at full load but correct elsewhere, then you can substitute the needle for one that has a thinner profile from approximately point 10 to point 13. If the fuel mixture was too lean at part throttle, but correct at full load, then we could substitute a needle that has a thinner profile from approximately point 3 to point 9. Common needle profiles for the HIF44 are listed in Table 17, but this

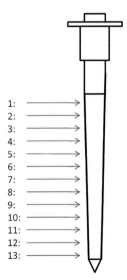

SU carburettor needle with thirteen measuring points.

Table 17: SU needle profile table for HIF44 carburettors

Needle position	BCP	BBG	BBV	BFW	BAK	BAF	BBW	BDR	BAC	BCA	BCV
1	0.099	0.099	0.099	0.099	0.099	0.099	0.099	0.099	0.099	0.099	0.099
2	0.095	0.095	0.095	0.0962	0.095	0.095	0.095	0.095	0.095	0.0955	0.0959
3	0.0929	0.0932	0.0932	0.0939	0.0932	0.093	0.0923	0.092	0.0932	0.093	0.0933
4	0.0905	0.0905	0.0907	0.0914	0.0907	0.0905	0.090	0.0895	0.0907	0.0897	0.0904
5	0.0881	0.0878	0.0875	0.0887	0.0875	0.0875	0.087	0.087	0.0875	0.0854	0.0875
6	0.0858	0.0852	0.0852	0.086	0.0852	0.0832	0.0832	0.0837	0.0852	0.0795	0.0832
7	0.0835	0.0829	0.0829	0.083	0.0823	0.080	0.0792	0.0804	0.0823	0.073	0.0788
8	0.0804	0.0806	0.0805	0.0799	0.0792	0.0768	0.075	0.0758	0.0763	0.0676	0.0746
9	0.0793	0.0783	0.0773	0.0768	0.076	0.0738	0.0717	0.0712	0.0703	0.0639	0.0687
10	0.0781	0.076	0.0742	0.0736	0.0729	0.0709	0.0682	0.0668	0.0642	0.0575	0.0637
11	0.0759	0.0737	0.071	0.0705	0.0697	0.0677	0.0647	0.0623	0.058	0.0519	0.0571
12	0.0737	0.0713	0.0679	0.0674	0.0665	0.0646	0.061	0.0579	0.052	0.0498	0.0497
13	0.0715	0.069	0.0648	0.0643	0.0633	0.0616	0.0577	0.0535	0.046	0.045	0.0445

is far from a complete list of all available profiles. All needle thicknesses shown are in inches.

Zenith Stromberg CD175

These carburettors were used on many Rover V8 engines in the late 1970s and early 1980s, but are not as popular as the more common SU carburettor. Tuning parts are not as commonly available as with the SU type, although rebuild parts and some alternative needles are still available from Burlen Fuel Systems Ltd.

The most common problem experienced on these is split or perished diaphragms, preventing the pistons from operating correctly. This can be easily checked by removing the dashpot assembly and inspecting the diaphragms carefully. Due to the lack of tuning parts, these are best used on standard or near-standard engines, where originality is particularly important.

The overall fuel mixture is adjusted by raising or lowering the needle with a special tool that is located into the top of the dashpot.

Stromberg CD175 carburettors fitted to a Land Rover 101.

Alternative Aftermarket Carburettor Options

There are a number of alternative aftermarket carburettors and carburettor manifolds available for the Rover V8. These are mostly used for EFI to carburettor conversions, or for high performance carburettor applications. Unfortunately it is beyond the scope of this book to detail rebuild and exact calibration procedures for all these different carburettors. There are, however, excellent books available on the subject. The following are the most common options.

Holley 390 carburettor: This used to be a very popular choice for Rover V8-engined vehicles, particularly in replicas of American cars such as Cobra kits, where the appearance is in keeping with the vehicle. These carburettors are of the fixed-choke type, with calibration of the full load fuel mixture being achieved either through changing the removable main jets or via a fixed metering plate. The 4160 carburettor uses a pre-calibrated metering plate, whilst the 4150 uses a metering block with removable main jets. There are both mechanical and vacuum-operated secondary throttles available. The vacuum-operated secondary models are more popular with this engine. There are also automatic and mechanical choke versions available. These are well suited for engine capacities up to 4.6 litres.

Edelbrock four-barrel 500 CFM carburettor: Previously marketed as a Weber 500. This increased capacity four-barrel carburettor is well suited to larger capacity engines (4.6 litres and larger), but can be fitted to any Rover V8 with suitable calibration.

Weber IDA, IDF and DCOE: These carburettors are arguably some of the best fixed-jet carburettors available today; they can be used in single, dual or quad configurations in combination with single-plane, dual-plane or independent runner intakes on the Rover V8. These carburettors are relatively straightforward to calibrate with a very wide range of jets, emulsion tubes and chokes commonly available. Jets can be changed without removing or completely disassembling the carburettors.

Quad SU Boxer set-up: This once relatively popular set-up is uncommon today, although we do still see it from time to time. It offers excellent flow and good bottom-end torque due to the long straight runners and quad SU carburettors. It does, however, have one major flaw, and that is that consecutive firing cylinders 5 and 7 are paired together; this means that one carburettor sees two pulses in quick succession, making it appear to the carburettor as one larger cylinder. To get the most out of these set-ups we need to tune cylinders 5 and 7 so they are richer than the other cylinders to compensate for this. Failure to allow for this will result in cylinders 5 and 7 running lean.

Holley carburettor on an MGB, fitted with a K&N X-Stream air filter.

CHAPTER 11

IGNITION SYSTEM

The Rover V8 ignition system has seen considerable development in its long production life. The earliest engines used a Lucas single contact breaker distributor. This was followed by an electronic breakerless distributor system, with the introduction of the Rover SD1 in 1976. Development continued in the mid-1990s with the introduction of the distributorless ignition systems; it eliminated the mechanical distribution of the HT ignition voltage by using a crankshaft-mounted ignition trigger, an ECU, and four individual double-ended ignition coils.

The main point of this chapter is to illustrate that the ignition timing or ignition advance curve is absolutely critical to achieving optimum engine performance and efficiency. There is no other external adjustment that can gain or lose as much torque or fuel economy as the timing of the ignition. This is even more critical than achieving the ideal fuel mixture or air-fuel ratio. This is a commonly misunderstood area, and many people with modified engines simply leave the ignition timing set as per the factory settings, either because they don't understand how to alter the ignition advance curve, or they simply don't realize how much power and efficiency they are losing. It is the purpose of this chapter to inform the reader what is required in terms of ignition hardware and ignition timing for their particular engine.

IGNITION TIMING

The ideal way to establish the optimum ignition timing values for your engine is with the use of an engine or chassis dynamometer. Certainly we can often improve things with a keen ear, a stop-watch and a clear section of road, but there is no substitute for being able to see the immediate effect of timing changes at more than one point in an engine's speed and load range. Furthermore, we will often observe a drop in torque output on the dyno through excess ignition advance well before we hear the damaging effects of pre-ignition. By the time you hear an engine knock, damage is often already being done.

It is worth pointing out here that the sound of pre-ignition is not always obvious, sometimes a knocking or a tapping, or like marbles rolling around. At other times it can sound like a high-pitched screeching or squealing, depending on the engine specification, the severity of the pre-ignition, and where in the engine's speed range it occurs. The table overleaf should get you close to ideal for most engine specifications and sizes, based on extensive dynamometer testing and the set-up of hundreds of different Rover V8 engines.

Timing Marks

It is vital that we have an accurate reference for ignition timing before we begin any tuning. The factory timing marks should always be checked for accuracy, particularly if the engine is non-standard or the history of a modified engine is not known. We have seen timing marks on front pulley dampers that have been as much as 20 degrees out! It is also useful to add some extra markings, as the original damper marks only extend as far as 10 or 12 degrees before top dead centre (BTDC), so are only any use for checking the idle timing and not for checking the total timing. For example, your extra marks might include 14, 16 and 18 as well as 30, 32 and 34 degrees if your engine is a 3.9- or 4.0-litre. You can

Table 18: Recommended ignition timing values

Engine capacity	Camshaft duration (degrees)	Idle ignition timing (degrees BTDC)	Total ignition timing (degrees)
3.5-litre	260–270	6–8	36–38 @ 4,000rpm
	270–280	8–12	34–36 @ 3,500rpm
	280–290	10–14	32–34 @ 3,000rpm
	300–310	16–20	30–32 @ 2,700–3,000rpm
3.9/ 4.0-litre	260–270	6–8	32–34 @ 4,000rpm
	270–280	8–12	30–32 @ 3,500rpm
	280–290	10–14	30–32 @ 3,000rpm
	300–310	16–20	28–30 @ 2,700rpm
4.2-litre	260–270	6–8	30–32 @ 4,000rpm
	270–280	8–12	28–30 @ 3,500rpm
	280–290	10–14	28–30 @ 3,000rpm
	300–310	16–20	26–28 @ 2,700rpm
4.6-litre	260–270	6–8	26–28 @ 4,000rpm
	270–280	8–12	26–28 @ 3,500rpm
	280–290	10–14	26–28 @ 3,000rpm
	300–310	16–20	26–27 @ 2,700rpm
4.8-litre	260–270	6–8	26–28 @ 4,000rpm
	270–280	8–12	26–28 @ 3,500rpm
	280–290	10–14	26–27 @ 3,000rpm
	300–310	16–20	26 @ 2,700rpm
5.0-litre	260–270	6–8	26–28 @ 4,000rpm
	270–280	8–12	26–27 @ 3,500rpm
	280–290	10–14	26 @ 3,000rpm
	300–310	16–20	26 @ 2,700rpm

* These timing figures assume that the rest of the engine specification matches the camshaft specification – for example, big valve heads with 300-degree duration cam, and so on.

easily add extra timing marks to your damper once you know top dead centre (TDC) by simply measuring another 2.7mm per 2 degrees (with a 154mm crank pulley) and scribing in the extra marks.

It is also possible to buy 'pulley tape' based on your pulley size and stick this on, centred round your TDC mark to give you all the relevant timing figures. Another method is to use a dial-back timing light to establish full load timing values, although care should be taken when working on a wasted spark DIS system such as that fitted to the GEMS or THOR engines, as this can cause errors with such timing lights.

Whatever anyone says, you cannot accurately check timing marks using a screwdriver or simi-lar down the cylinder plug hole. The piston dwells (stops) at TDC for a few degrees of crank rotation, making it very difficult to determine the exact TDC centre point. However, it is very straightforward and quick to find true TDC accurately without resorting to stripping anything apart by using what we refer to as the 'physical stop method'.

Physical stop method of finding true TDC in five easy steps:

1. Create a physical stop from an old spark plug, a nut and a bolt as outlined.
2. Insert this into cylinder 1 spark-plug hole.

Timing tape on crank pulley assembly.

3. Gently rotate the engine in a clockwise direction until it locks against the stop. Mark the pulley where it aligns with the pointer using a fine tip marker or scribe.
4. Rotate in an anti-clockwise direction until it locks, and mark the pulley.

5. True TDC is exactly half way between these points as measured with a small flexible rule or tape. If the points are too far apart to be easily measured, then simply shorten your physical stop so that the marks fall closer together.

CREATING A PHYSICAL STOP TOOL

To create a physical stop tool you need the following:

- Old spark plug from your engine
- M8 threaded bolt and two nuts
- Hacksaw or angle grinder with 1mm cutting disk
- Punch and hammer
- Metal-working file

Take the spark plug and cut through the clinch ring around the base of the ceramic. You only need to cut through the metal clinch, not into the ceramic! Next, cut off the side electrode. Place the plug in a vice, then use the punch to drive out the centre electrode and ceramic, leaving just the threaded metal body of the plug. You can then put the bolt through the hole, and secure it with nuts on either side. The length of the stop can be adjusted by using the nuts, so that more or less bolt protrudes into the cylinder. It is sensible to round the end of the bolt with a file so there are no sharp edges to mark the piston crown. Those with TIG welding equipment may wish to weld the nut to the plug body for quick and easy adjustment.

Physical stop tool.

Checking and Adjusting the Ignition Timing with a Distributor

You must use a stroboscope to check both the idle ignition timing and the total timing. This is very easy once you have marked your front pulley with the relevant timing marks. Alternatively you can use a dial-back timing light to establish total timing:

1. Start the engine and let it idle until it is at full operating temperature. Disconnect the vacuum advance pipe if fitted.
2. Set the idle speed to a speed that suits the engine specification.
3. Connect a stroboscopic timing light to the ignition lead on cylinder 1. If using a dial-back timing light, then set this to zero.
4. Point the timing light at the front damper and timing pointer. The marks should appear stationary with the engine running. Turn the distributor clockwise to retard the ignition, and anti-clockwise to advance as necessary to achieve your desired ignition timing at idle (for example, 10 degrees BTDC). Once the timing has been changed it may be necessary to readjust the idle speed and then re-check the idle timing again. If the idle speed is too high we may find that the bob-weights in the centrifugal advance mechanism have already begun advancing the ignition.
5. Once you are happy with the ignition timing at idle, then you can check the total timing by raising the engine speed and observing the timing advancing until it advances no more – this will usually be between 4,000 and 4,500rpm. This is the total ignition timing figure.

DISTRIBUTORS

Any distributor that is used should be in perfect condition, with no perceptible play in the distributor shaft. This set-up is best described as adequate, and anything in less than perfect condition is unacceptable. Likewise the rotor arm and distributor cap should ideally be genuine OEM components, or at least components of a known good quality. The ignition output of these systems is marginal under high load and engine speed, so any issues here will potentially cost a lot of lost power.

The original Lucas distributors fitted to these engines usually have 11 degrees of centrifugal advance built in. This gives us 22 degrees of timing advance (at the crankshaft) in the fully advanced position, by 2,250rpm at the camshaft or 4,500rpm at the crankshaft. With this in mind we can see that if we set the idle or base advance at 8 degrees – then we will have a total timing of 30 degrees at 4,500rpm.

Many factory settings offer far from optimum performance or efficiency. For example, the stock Rover 3.5 V8 used in various Land Rovers had a specified base ignition advance figure of 4–6 degrees, resulting in a total advance of 26–28 degrees at 4,500rpm. These engines will usually make best power at 12 degrees base timing, or 34 degrees total (12 + 22 = 34 degrees). In some applications, such as heavy towing, this might be a little excessive and it may only tolerate 10 degrees at idle, or 32 degrees total. Either way, there is a lot of free performance and efficiency to be gained for something as simple as loosening a bolt and rotating the distributor. When an engine is standard, or near standard, we can often get away with simply adjusting the distributor.

An engine that has been modified with an aftermarket camshaft or better breathing cylinder heads

Rover V8 distributor.

will almost always require a different advance curve to suit the new characteristics of the engine. As an example, we may have a 3.9-litre engine that was standard and made best power with an idle timing figure of 12 degrees (34 degrees total). Imagine this same engine is now fitted with an aftermarket camshaft and cylinder heads that improve high-speed performance at the cost of reduced cylinder filling at lower engine speeds. This engine will now require more ignition advance at idle and lower engine speeds to compensate for the reduced cylinder filling and slower flame speed. This may want as much as 18–20 degrees at idle compared to the 12 degrees for the standard engine. However, at higher engine speeds the cylinder filling (volumetric efficiency, or VE) will increase over the standard engine and the flame speed will be much higher than standard, therefore requiring less ignition advance – perhaps as little as 30 degrees total.

With the standard advance curve we will have to compromise the idle and low speed timing and set it at 8 degrees to ensure the timing is not over-advanced and detonating at higher engine speeds. This will result in a poor idle quality, poor low speed running, and an unnecessary increase in fuel consumption. What this engine really requires is a timing curve that begins at 18 degrees and ends at 30 degrees. In addition to requiring different beginning and end points to the timing curve, it also requires a different rate of advance, with the total timing figure being achieved at 3,000rpm rather than the 4,500rpm of the standard engine. We will discuss the practical elements of modifying the distributor's advance curve below.

Centrifugal Advance Mechanism

The centrifugal advance mechanism contains two bob-weights and two springs that are flung open centrifugally as the engine speed increases. These bob-weights are attached to the central shaft and cause the rotor arm to rotate clockwise as they move outwards, thus advancing the ignition timing. A single stage or linear advance curve will have two springs of the same strength.

Centrifugal advance mechanism.

A two-stage advance curve will utilize two springs of different strengths. One spring will usually be lighter and will enable the timing to advance relatively quickly on initial acceleration, before the second stronger spring is tensioned and limits the subsequent rate of advance. You can check this advance mechanism is not seized by gently taking hold of the rotor arm and turning it in a clockwise direction: it should move approximately 11 degrees on a standard distributor, and return with a positive action when released.

Establishing the ideal ignition advance curve at full load (full throttle):

1. Firstly, determine the optimum ignition timing at idle by rotating the distributor to achieve the most stable idle. Make a note of this setting (for instance 14 degrees).
2. To determine the best total timing value you can start with the recommendations made earlier: for example, 32 degrees @ 3,500rpm for a mildly tuned 3.9-litre engine. If we know that the distributor is standard, then we must reset the static timing to 10 degrees (10 static + 22 centrifugal = 32 total @ 4,000rpm). We would then carry out two or three power runs on the engine or chassis dynamometer to establish baseline power

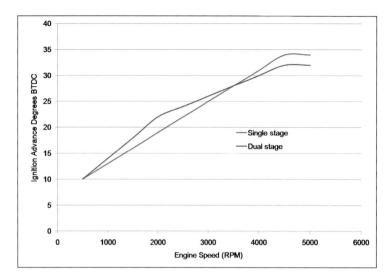

Single- and two-stage advance curves.

figures, whilst keeping a keen ear for detonation or pinking. Once we have established a stable and consistent power curve we would then *retard* the timing by 2 degrees and carry out another series of power runs.

3. Now overlay your two power curves and see which produces the best torque peak. If you lost power everywhere on the retarded run, then try advancing the timing 2 degrees and test again. You will probably find that one timing setting will produce best power in the lower engine speed range, and another will produce best power in the higher engine speed range. The area we are most interested in is around peak torque. For example, if the engine peaks its torque at 4,000rpm during testing, we will look for the ignition timing that gives the best power at this point. Once we have established the best ignition timing setting for peak torque and for smoothest idle, we can begin to modify the centrifugal advance mechanism to achieve this.

As an example we may have found the following:

- Smoothest idle with most vacuum = 14 degrees BTDC @ 1,000rpm
- Peak torque output = 32 degrees BTDC @ 3,500rpm

Clearly, if we set the idle timing at 14 degrees BTDC, then we will end up with 36 degrees total timing. The engine will then under-perform and possibly pink or detonate at peak torque. Equally, we could compromise the idle timing and set it at 8 degrees to achieve our ideal timing of 32 degrees, but we will be losing fuel efficiency and power below the torque peak. The ideal solution is to modify the centrifugal advance curve.

Modifying the Centrifugal Advance Curve

It is possible to modify the advance curve in a distributor by physically limiting the movement of the bob-weights, or rotation of the distributor base-plate, to limit the total amount of ignition advance. There are a number of ways of practically achieving this: from a small screw in the distributor base-plate to limit its rotation, to an adjustable stop bolt. It should be noted that distributor advance is half the crankshaft advance. For example, the standard distributor has 11 degrees of movement or 22 degrees of crankshaft advance. If we determined that we needed 14 degrees initial advance and 32 degrees total advance, then we would need only 18 degrees of ignition advance at the crankshaft, or 9 degrees of distributor advance. To do this we would put a physical stop to limit the rotation of the distributor base-plate from the standard 11 degrees to just 9 degrees.

With the initial and total ignition values set, we can turn our attention to the rate of ignition advance. The rate at which the ignition timing advances is set by the strength of the two springs underneath the distributor base-plate that connect to the two centrifugal bob-weights. If the timing advances too quickly, then we can use stronger springs to limit the rate of advance. If the timing advances too slowly, then we can use weaker springs or even remove one of the bob-weight springs completely.

If we use the example above, then we may find that the initial advance is 14 degrees at 1,000rpm and 32 degrees at 4,000rpm. Dynamometer testing may have shown that best power is made with 32 degrees at 3,500rpm. Clearly, the timing needs to advance at a faster rate. We could achieve this by replacing the bob-weight springs with weaker ones and re-testing until this is achieved.

A lot of experimentation will be required on the dynamometer to establish and then create the ideal distributor advance curve. Optimizing a distributor-based ignition system is a lot more time-consuming than optimizing an aftermarket programmable ignition system.

Aftermarket Distributors with Adjustable Centrifugal Advance Curves

There are now a number of distributors and electronic ignition systems that allow the user to effectively adjust the centrifugal ignition advance curve to the engine. These simplify the process of modifying the full load ignition advance curve. One of the most popular of these is the Mallory distributor from the USA. The total amount of centrifugal advance is adjustable within the range of 16–28 degrees via a slotted hole and an Allen screw on the base plate. The ignition advance is 'all in' or fully advanced by 3,400rpm, as compared to the 4,500rpm of the stock 35DLM8 distributor, making it much more suitable for many modified engines when used straight out of the box. Furthermore there are many spares available to enable you to tailor the ignition timing even more closely to your application, such as different strength bob-weight springs. The ease of adjustment and availability

of parts for modification make these an attractive proposition for those who wish to stick with a basic distributor-based ignition system.

Vacuum Advance Unit

The vacuum advance unit caters for the differing ignition advance requirements of an engine operating at different loads. An engine operating under part throttle will be running at a reduced dynamic compression with less efficient cylinder filling (lower VE). This engine will have a slower burning flame front and therefore we need to ignite the flame earlier.

The vacuum advance unit does this by using the vacuum in the intake manifold under part throttle conditions to pull the distributor base-plate in the anti-clockwise direction, thus advancing the ignition timing.

An engine operating under heavy load (large throttle opening) will create very little vacuum in the manifold, and the ignition timing will be controlled by the centrifugal advance mechanism alone. Under idle conditions, we do not want the vacuum advance unit to be operative as it will tend to advance the timing beyond our ideal idle setting, due to the significant vacuum that can exist in the manifold with the throttle completely shut. OEM set-ups get around this by using a ported vacuum source next to the throttle plate, which is shut off when the throttle plate is fully closed, thus ensuring that no vacuum

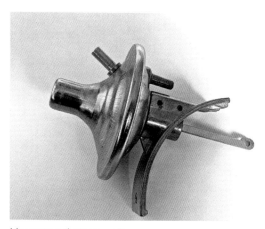

Vacuum advance unit.

is present at idle. It is always worth checking that your vacuum source shuts off completely when the throttle is closed.

A non-functioning vacuum advance unit will result in a significant increase in fuel consumption to the tune of 10–15 per cent, and a loss of part-throttle performance. If you notice a marked increase in fuel consumption you should first check that your vacuum advance unit and associated pipework is intact and functioning correctly.

Many people advocate removing the vacuum advance unit on performance engines, the reasoning being that if it were to stick in the fully advanced position with the engine at full load, then the engine could potentially be damaged through pre-ignition. We have personally never seen a vacuum advance unit fail in this manner. Usually they will fail in a safe manner by not advancing the ignition at part throttle (that is, no vacuum advance).

Engines that use camshafts with large duration and high overlap will produce less vacuum for the same load than engines with standard or low overlap camshafts. For example, two engines may be running at 20 per cent throttle, but the engine with the high overlap camshaft will have significantly less vacuum to drive the vacuum advance unit. The fact is that the engine with the high overlap camshaft

actually requires *more* ignition advance under these cruise conditions than the engine with the standard camshaft, due to reduced cylinder filling (VE) at lower engine speeds and loads. Unfortunately, the engine with the high overlap cam will actually have *less* vacuum advance due to the lower vacuum levels available in the intake manifold.

Fortunately there are measures we can take to rectify this situation. What is needed with these high overlap camshafts is a vacuum advance unit that begins advancing the ignition timing at a lower vacuum level than the original unit.

Modifying the Level of Vacuum Advance

Whilst you cannot modify the vacuum advance unit yourself, you can check the characteristics of a particular vacuum advance unit or capsule by noting the vacuum code numbers stamped on the unit, usually next to the manufacturer part number. The first number in the three-digit code indicates the vacuum level, in inches of mercury, where the unit starts to advance. The second number indicates vacuum level to reach total advance, while the last number is the total ignition advance. For example, a stock 3.5-litre EFI vacuum advance unit reads 5, 17, 8. This indicates that the unit begins advancing the timing at 5in Hg of vacuum, reaches

Ported Vacuum take-off for vacuum advance unit on distributor. The throttle plate blocks this when shut ensuring no vacuum advance at idle. At part throttle openings this port is uncovered by the throttle plate and vacuum is present to advance the ignition timing.

Ported vacuum take-off on standard EFI plenum.

its maximum advance at 17in Hg of vacuum, and achieves a total advance of 8 degrees above the centrifugal advance.

Note that the last number in degrees should be multiplied by two to establish the ignition advance at the crankshaft, because the distributor turns at half the speed of the crankshaft, so the 8 degrees is actually 16 degrees of crankshaft advance. An engine with a high-overlap camshaft would ideally begin advancing the timing at a slightly lower vacuum level, and advance the timing slightly more than the standard unit. Something like a 4, 12, 9 as used on a Rolls-Royce (part #54421585) would be closer to ideal, although the availability of different types is limited and your choice may be more directed by what you can get, rather than what is ideal.

DISTRIBUTOR-BASED PROGRAMMABLE IGNITION SYSTEMS

There are now a number of electronic systems that work with the distributor to provide a programmable ignition advance curve both at full load and at part throttle, such as the Aldon Amethyst and 123-Ignition. These systems require you to fix both the centrifugal and vacuum advance mechanisms, so the distributor is simply used to distribute the HT voltage via the rotor arm.

These systems control the advance curve electronically by delaying or advancing the switching of the coil. They have the major advantage of allowing very quick and immediate changes to the advance curve during engine testing and set-up. Furthermore they allow us to create a non-linear advance curve that is more closely suited to the engine's requirements. For example, we could set the timing optimally at a number of different engine speeds, rather than simply at idle and peak torque. The part-throttle ignition advance curve can also be very easily tailored to the individual engine.

Another possibility with such systems is the use of two ignition 'maps' or advance curves that can be pre-set and toggled between at the flick of a switch

– for example, one curve optimized for LPG and one for petrol.

These systems are still not ideal in that they rely on the mechanical distribution of the HT (high-tension) voltage. The amount of part-throttle ignition advance is still limited compared to a fully distributor-less ignition system. This is because cross-firing between the rotor posts can start to become a problem when using more than 38 degrees total ignition advance, as the rotor arm is so close to the previous cylinder's rotor post in a Rover V8 distributor cap. This is particularly so in damp conditions. That said, if we are restricted to using a distributor on an engine build, then this represents the best compromise between the distributor-based and modern distributor-less systems.

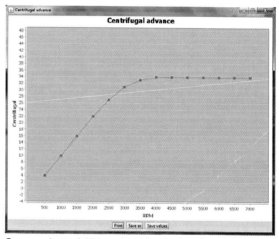

Screenshot of Aldon Amethyst, showing the ignition advance curve.

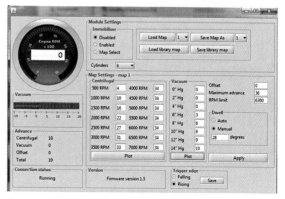

Screenshot of Aldon Amethyst software.

HT IGNITION LEADS

The importance of good quality HT ignition leads cannot be underestimated. The majority of misfires or poor running we see in our workshop can be traced to damaged or old ignition leads. The HT ignition lead arguably has the hardest job of the entire ignition system. It has to carry high-tension voltage in excess of 20,000 volts via a flexible cable, and deliver that voltage to the spark plug whilst resisting engine and exhaust heat. It is not surprising that the insulation invariably breaks down over time under these conditions.

An engine that is not exhibiting any obvious misfiring can still be losing a significant amount of power to micro-misfires. If every one out of sixteen ignition events fails to fire the cylinder, then it stands to reason that we will be losing one-sixteenth of the engine's power – on a 300bhp engine this equates to over 18bhp. This level of misfiring on a V8 would probably not even be noticed by the driver, yet results in a considerable loss of power.

What we require is a good quality, resistive ignition lead. Contrary to popular myth, the HT ignition leads do require some resistance to operate at peak efficiency. An HT lead with very little or no resistance actually causes the spark to extinguish faster than a lead with some resistance in its core. Furthermore, the non-resistive leads will cause a great deal of electromagnetic interference (EMI) that can not only interfere with your radio, but also any ECUs in the vehicle. The amount of EMI given off by a low resistance ignition lead can also easily trigger a crankshaft or camshaft signal, resulting in incorrect ignition timing, incorrect fuelling and an engine misfire.

Many years ago a Range Rover Classic came into our workshop, which had suffered from a breakdown and would not restart. The vehicle had recently been fitted with an ECU-controlled fuel and ignition system, so this was the prime suspect. These systems are normally reliable, so we were doubtful that the ECU itself was the root cause, but when we plugged in our computer to check the system and start our diagnostic work, we found that the ECU was completely blank! There were no fuel and ignition maps, or even any firmware, on the ECU. We would reload the firmware, fuel and ignition maps and the engine would perform flawlessly during

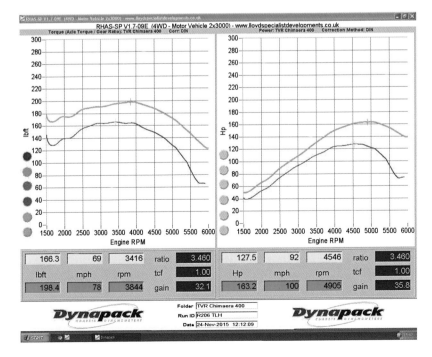

Power and torque directly at the hubs of a TVR Chimaera 400, before and after HT lead replacement.

road-tests, with no faults. Days later the problem would reoccur, leaving us very confused.

Eventually we discovered that a new HT ignition lead set had been made to suit the new ignition coil packs when the system was fitted, and the owner had made the leads out of old-fashioned solid copper core ignition cable! These had no resistance and were emitting such a powerful EMI that they were completely blanking the volatile memory in the ECU. These ignition leads were replaced with resistive ignition leads, and the vehicle has been reliable to date. This is an extreme case, but illustrates the point!

Certainly some resistance is essential, but how much is ideal? In practice anything between 200 and 2,000ohms per 30cm of lead length will work well. Less resistance than suggested is worse than having a little extra resistance. The standard carbon-string type leads are as much as 3,000ohms per 30cm, but will work fine – assuming they are in perfect condition.

A standard specification lead in good condition is better than a fancy aftermarket lead that is not changed regularly, due to the expense. Obviously, some ignition leads are better quality than others. The cheap carbon-string type are adequate, but need to be changed very regularly as they are very easily damaged and degrade fairly quickly. The standard Lucas/Bosch type are the best in this category and are usually good for at least one year. There are a number of aftermarket spiral-wound

steel-alloy cored leads available now, which are more durable than the standard OEM type. This type of lead is available from the likes of MSD, Accel and Taylor, and are recommended if you can afford them. These leads often have better insulation with a greater resistance to heat.

SPARK PLUG EXTENDERS AND IN-LINE SUPPRESSOR CAPS

Some vehicles have a very close proximity between the HT ignition leads and the exhaust manifolds. TVR Chimaeras and Griffiths are an obvious example with their 'up and forward' exhaust routing. These vehicles are fitted with metal-cased spark plug extenders to locate the HT leads further away from the exhaust manifolds. Despite being a little more durable than the HT lead, they still suffer from the effects of heat, and the insulation begins to break down over time.

Spark plug extenders should still be considered a service item and changed with every two or three sets of HT ignition leads. Over 30 per cent of misfires we diagnose on these TVR models are due to ageing or poor quality plug extenders. The supply of these original extenders has all but dried up, and many of the aftermarket replacements are of an inferior quality and are failing to last even the life of a normal HT ignition lead set. Our take on these items is that they are a necessary evil.

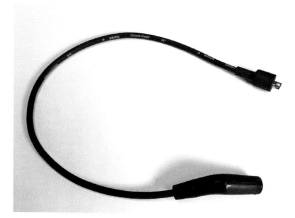

HT ignition lead.

TVR spark plug extender.

We have experimented with all kinds of alternatives to replace these, such as heat-resistant 'socks' to protect the ignition lead. These 'socks', whilst not burning themselves, eventually conduct the heat through to the HT lead underneath, resulting in a breakdown of the insulation and eventual misfire. One effective solution we have found to this problem are the Accel 9002C ceramic-ended HT leads. The HT boot end is made from solid ceramic that can withstand over 1,000°C, whilst the lead is designed to withstand over 300°C. These leads enable us to dispense with the troublesome plug extenders entirely, eliminating yet another cause of power-robbing misfires.

It is also worth a quick mention here of in-line suppressor caps, as we occasionally see these fitted to distributors. These are also best avoided if possible, as they, too, suffer over time and are another common cause of misfires. If these are needed, then make sure to replace them regularly, along with the ignition leads.

SPARK PLUGS

There are two differences in spark plug length used on the Rover V8. The early heads (1967–1976) used a short reach plug of only 12.7mm length, whilst all the heads after 1976 used a long reach plug with a length of 19mm. We recommend the use of projected-tip plugs where possible, as this has a favourable effect on combustion characteristics. Note that your optimum ignition timing settings may change slightly if you move from retracted to projected-tip plugs, or vice versa. The projected-tip plugs often require less timing advance to the tune of 1–2 degrees. Please refer to the table below for suggestions on plug type and heat grade to use for your application.

It is recommended that you check your spark plugs for signs of burning or blistering, and be prepared to move to a colder plug if necessary. If you find that your spark plugs are becoming sooted up quickly, despite having the correct fuel mixtures throughout, then it is worth considering changing to a hotter grade of spark plug.

Iridium Spark Plugs

Iridium spark plugs such as the BPR6EIX have a much finer electrode, which lowers the amount of electrical energy needed to jump a given plug gap. The use of a finer electrode is made possible by the use of a stronger, more heat-resistant material – namely iridium. We have found these plugs to be very effective with LPG-fuelled engines, as these require considerably more ignition energy to create a spark. More powerful ignition coils or increased dwell often results in the HT voltage simply taking the easiest route to ground via the HT leads insulation, or down the ceramic insulator of the plug. These plugs are also useful in non-LPG engines too, as they reduce the likelihood of misfires and cross-firing within the distributor cap by lowering the amount of energy required to create a spark at the plug tip.

Table 19: Recommended spark plugs

Application	Recommended NGK spark plug (12.7mm reach – pre-1976 heads)	Recommended NGK spark plug (19mm – post 1976 heads)
Standard or fast road engines (approx. 150–300bhp)	BPR6HS	BPR6ES
Competition and performance (approx. 300bhp plus)	BPR7HS	BPR7ES
Turbocharged or supercharged engines up to 14psi of boost	BPR8HS	BPR8ES
Turbocharged or supercharged engines over 14psi of boost	BPR9HS	BPR9ES

Non-projected, projected and iridium spark-plug tips.

IGNITION COILS

The function of the ignition coil is to step up the 12 volts supplied from the vehicle's battery to the 15–30 thousand volts required to create a high-power spark across the spark-plug tip. The amount of energy a coil can provide is directly related to the primary voltage supplied, the ratio of turns in the coil, and the dwell time. A single ignition coil has to charge and discharge much more rapidly than a multi-coil set-up, resulting in an increasingly weaker spark as engine speed increases. Multi-coil set-ups have considerably more charging or dwell time, resulting in greater output, particularly at higher engine speeds.

IGNITION AMPLIFIERS AND MODULES

The standard 35DLM8 electronic distributor uses a simple ignition module to step up the low-powered switching from the distributor's VR pick-up, to the higher level required to trigger the ignition coil. Essentially it contains a few switching transistors. There are a few different types – some mount externally whilst others mount to the distributor itself. The remote-mounted units usually last a little longer as they are further away from the engine's heat. It is possible to remote-mount any of these ignition modules, but we recommend the use of shielded cable between the distributor pick-up and module, as these are very sensitive to electrical interference.

ABOVE: *Single ignition coil and GEMS ignition coil pack.*

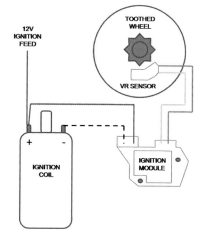

RIGHT: *Ignition amplifier and distributor circuit.*

CHAPTER 12

ENGINE MANAGEMENT

An engine management system performs two essential functions:

- To meter fuel in the correct quantity relative to the engine speed and load
- To provide the ignition spark at the correct time relative to the engine speed and load – this is known as ignition timing

In its most basic form, Rover V8 engine management consists of a carburettor to meter the fuel, and a distributor to control the ignition timing. Although still technically engine management, these mechanical forms of engine management are already covered in Chapter 10, Fuel System, and Chapter 11, Ignition System. This chapter will cover the various systems that use an engine control unit (ECU) for fuel and/ or ignition control. There are several original engine management systems that have been used with the Rover V8, starting with the Lucas 4CU system, first used for the North American market in 1974.

LUCAS 4CU L-JETRONIC FUEL INJECTION SYSTEM

There are a number of different variations of the Lucas 4CU system. The first systems of this type were fitted to Rover SD1s and Triumph TR8s sold to North America and Australia, to comply with their strict emissions regulations. These early systems were relatively crude and unsuccessful, and although they complied with emissions regulations, they also significantly reduced the performance of the engine. This is because they ran a stoichiometric fuel mixture (14.7 parts air to 1 part fuel) at all

times, including under full throttle! This meant that the ignition timing had to be set at a maximum of 20 degrees to prevent engine damage from detonation due to the excessively lean fuel mixture.

The early North American and Australian systems are slightly different to each other, with the American system (ECU part no. 83617) utilizing narrowband lambda sensors, and the Australian system not using any lambda sensors. These early systems used various different intake manifolds (such as the Federal Specification plenum) but the Australian system still ran the engine at 14.7:1 AFR throughout the entire load/rpm range, so also suffered from poor engine performance as a consequence.

In 1983 the Lucas 4CU was introduced with the Rover SD1 for the UK market. This later version of the Lucas 4CU had a number of differences from the earlier American and Australian systems, including full load fuel enrichment, which noticeably improved the engine performance. This version (ECU part no. 83986) did not use lambda sensors for fuel mixture control, and was fitted to the fuel injected versions of the Rover SD1 and Range Rover, including the Rover SD1 Vitesse Twin-Plenum.

The Lucas 4CU system is relatively basic by modern standards, but an overview of the set-up is useful if carrying out diagnostic or tuning work. The main engine load sensor on this set-up is the airflow meter, and the engine speed is picked up from the distributor via the negative side of the coil. This particular airflow meter is basically a spring-loaded flap that is connected to a variable resistor. These 4CU systems use low impedance (approximately 3ohm) injectors that are connected to the ECU (electronic control unit) via a resistor box to limit the current draw.

Lucas 4CU 2AM airflow meter.

With this early engine management system the ignition timing is still controlled via a distributor.

LUCAS 13CU AND 14CU FUEL INJECTION SYSTEMS

These versions of the Lucas Jetronic fuel injection systems were used on 3.5-litre Rover V8 engines for the North American market in the late 1980s. They were designed with EPROM microprocessor chips to comply with OBD1 specification, requiring on-board diagnostics. Although very similar, the later 14CU ECU is more compact than the 4CU ECU. Again, with this early engine management system the ignition timing is still controlled via a distributor.

All systems from this point use high impedance (approximately 14ohm) injectors and are directly connected to the ECU.

LUCAS 14CUX FUEL INJECTION SYSTEM

This system is an evolution of the 14CU system, and probably the most common fuel injection system fitted to the Rover V8. It was released in 1990 for the Range Rover, Land Rover Discovery and Defender,

and then subsequently fitted to various TVRs, Morgans and Marcos. This system uses a 'hotwire'-type airflow meter as the main engine load sensor, and in Rover V8 circles is commonly referred to as the 'hotwire' engine management system. There are two standard airflow meters available for this system – the 3AM and the more common 5AM airflow meter. Other airflow meters can be retrofitted with some modifications to the ECU programming and wiring.

Two narrow-band lambda sensors are utilized for closed-loop fuel control, giving improved emissions and fuel economy, but the system switches to open loop under large throttle openings for maximum performance and engine longevity.

Diagnostic access to the Lucas 14CUX used to be quite limited, but there are now a number of tools available, such as the Rover-Gauge, which make diagnostics very accessible and straightforward for the knowledgeable enthusiast.

The fuel table on a Lucas 14CUX system consists of sixteen engine speed sites and eight engine load sites, making a 16 × 8 fuel table with 128 individual sites. There is linear interpolation between these individual sites.

The use of an EPROM chip allows the same ECU to have a different fuel map calibration by changing the chip. On ECUs with a chip socket, this is simply a matter of opening the ECU case and swapping the

Lucas 14CUX 5AM airflow meter.

Using Rover-Gauge diagnostic software.

ignition system, the GEMS system was a major step forwards for Rover V8 engine management. Introduced in 1994, this set-up uses a 36-1 trigger wheel on the flywheel or flex-plate to measure engine speed and position directly at the crankshaft, along with a camshaft sensor. This system also uses a pair of knock sensors, so if engine knock is detected this system will retard the ignition timing as a consequence. Fuelling is fully sequential and is largely MAF (mass airflow) based. The fuelling and ignition maps are contained within two EPROM chips, and tuning of these systems is largely the domain of experts such as Mark Adams of Tornado Systems Limited.

EPROM chip, whilst other 14CUX ECUs have the EPROM chip directly soldered to the board. Non-socketed ECUs can be modified too, but soldering on an EPROM chip socket makes future EPROM chip changes easier. It is now much easier to tune these systems thanks to the proliferation of tuning suites, such as Tuner-Pro, cheap EPROM burners, and the development efforts of knowledgeable individuals.

GEMS ENGINE MANAGEMENT SYSTEM

The first of the production engine management systems fitted to the Rover V8 with a distributor-less

BOSCH MOTRONIC 5.2.1 ENGINE MANAGEMENT SYSTEM

Introduced in 1999 for the Thor-specification Rover V8 engine, this set-up uses a 60-2 trigger wheel on the flywheel or flex-plate to measure engine speed and position directly at the crankshaft, along with a camshaft position sensor. Knock sensors are also utilized. Fuelling is fully sequential and MAF based. These systems operate the engine under strict closed-loop fuelling control at all times, and offer the lowest emissions of any of the OEM systems. This system offers advanced diagnostic abilities.

Tuning options are extremely limited, with the only current reprogramming options currently available from Mark Adams at Tornado Systems Limited.

GEMS ECU.

GEMS 20AM airflow meter.

PIGGY-BACK ENGINE MANAGEMENT SYSTEMS

These are 'interceptor' ECUs that work in conjunction with the existing engine management system, but can be programmed to modify one or more of the signals going in or out of the original ECU to alter the fuelling or ignition parameters. The best of these piggyback systems can also be used to add features or hardware to the existing engine management, such as additional fuel injectors, or even distributor-less ignition.

These piggy-back ECUs are usually relatively inexpensive, but a thorough understanding of the existing engine management system is required for successful implementation. These piggy-back systems also rely on the original engine management being in perfect working order, as they utilize the sensor and ECU information from the original system. Many of these piggyback controllers use a voltage step convertor to alter MAP (manifold absolute pressure) or MAF signals, and thereby alter the fuelling. For example, if the engine is running larger injectors than stock and now runs excessively rich at part throttle, a piggyback controller can be programmed via a look-up table in its software to reduce the MAF voltage at various points. MAF voltage at 20 per cent throttle and 2,000rpm might be, for example, 2.2 volts, and the piggyback controller

can output a new voltage of 1.7 volts, and thereby fool the existing ECU into outputting a lower injection pulse-width.

Diagnosing faults when using a piggy-back system is usually more challenging than with a single engine management system, as you have to take both systems into account, as well as the interaction between the two.

Most LPG ECUs fall into the category of piggy-back ECUs, as they intercept the petrol injector signals from the original engine management system, and apply a correction to provide the correct signal for the LPG injectors.

STANDALONE ENGINE MANAGEMENT SYSTEMS

There is a huge range of aftermarket engine management systems available that are capable of successfully running the Rover V8 engine. The choice is bewildering, with many options and features. If you are planning on installing and tuning it yourself then you should choose a system that is relatively straightforward to install and tune, with good technical support. A simple system calibrated to a high standard is preferable to a complex system that is not correctly or fully calibrated.

If you are going to purchase an engine management system and get a professional tuner to install and/or calibrate the system for you, then your choice should be dictated firstly by the installer/tuner, and secondly by the individual system and its features. Ideally you want to find a professional tuner who not only knows what it takes to get the best out of your particular engine, but also knows the chosen engine management system inside out. All too often the owner buys a sophisticated engine management system based on its features and glossy software from one source, employs another individual to make the wiring loom, installs this themselves, and then has another rolling-road tuner tune the main fuel and ignition maps in a day or less.

This approach might work out, but is fraught with potential problems. If any issues are encountered with the system, then it is very difficult to get all the

Standalone fully programmable ECUs.

parties involved to work together to find out what is going wrong. The issue could lie with the hardware, the wiring loom, or the ECU calibration.

The most straightforward aspect of the calibration is the main fuel and ignition maps, which can realistically be optimized within a day on a good rolling road. However, all the other important aspects of calibration, such as cold starting, warm-up enrichment, idle control and emissions control can take much longer, requiring many cold starts

at different ambient temperatures. Despite having a large library of maps and settings for the Rover V8 engine, and a great deal of experience, we usually spend at least one week calibrating and testing the starting/warm-up enrichment settings from stone cold to full operating temperature, and every temperature in between. The complexity of getting the whole calibration optimized can be appreciated when you consider that a vehicle manufacturer can spend over a year to get this right on a new vehicle model.

To summarize, it is important that the standard of installation and mapping is excellent to ensure a long-term successful outcome when fitting one of these systems to your vehicle. Engine management calibration is not just a simple case of taking the vehicle to a rolling-road tuner and getting the fuel and ignition maps tuned correctly for optimum full-throttle running. There are many other areas that need to be tuned, particularly on a road vehicle or a competition vehicle that is to be used on the road. These areas include cranking enrichment, part-throttle fuel mixture and ignition calibrations, warm-up enrichment, idle speeds, acceleration enrichment, and so on. We will

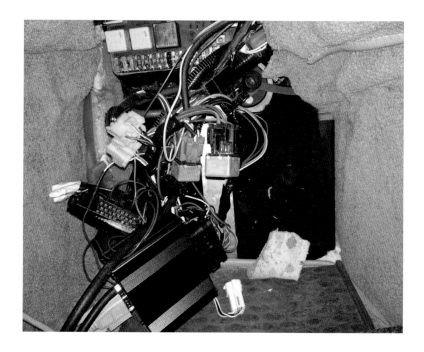

Example of a poor engine management installation.

Engine management wiring loom for a Canems engine management system fitted to a pre-Serpentine Rover V8.

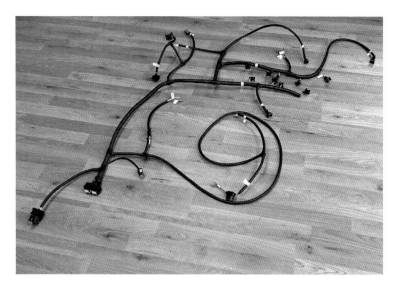

discuss the practicalities of tuning these areas in further detail below.

The beauty of these standalone systems is flexibility and control, in that virtually all the standalone programmable systems available on the market today are capable of running a Rover V8 of practically any specification. This includes engines fitted with individual throttle bodies, superchargers, turbochargers, nitrous, LPG and different injectors.

Engine Speed Sensing: VR versus Hall Effect

Variable reluctance (VR) sensors are the simplest and cheapest form of engine speed and position sensor. They are also one of the most commonly used. These sensors require only two connections: signal positive and signal negative. Their voltage output varies with speed, with low rotational speeds producing low outputs, and high speeds producing higher outputs. These sensors are fussy about sensor-to-trigger wheel gaps: too large a gap and the sensor will fail to generate an output, too close and the output voltage can get too high, causing issues with ECU speed sensing. If when you rev the engine hard you lose the crank signal, this may be caused by the sensor gap being too small. If you lose crank signal at low rotational speeds (for example during cranking) this can be caused by the sensor gap being too large.

VR sensors are susceptible to electromagnetic interference so require careful shielding of the signal wires. One major advantage is their ability to tolerate harsh environments and extremes of temperature.

Hall-effect sensors offer a much cleaner wave form, and the ability to detect very slow rotational speeds, and this makes them particularly suitable for camshaft position sensors. They are typically more expensive than VR sensors. Their voltage output is fixed and does not vary with speed, which makes them far less sensitive to sensor-to-trigger wheel gaps. They are less susceptible to electromagnetic interference in the signal wires. Their output is a clean on/off switch. Hall effect sensors

Crankshaft VR sensor.

require three connections: signal positive, signal ground, and voltage reference. Hall-effect sensors are able to tolerate relatively harsh environments, but are generally not considered to be quite as durable as VR sensors.

Engine Load Sensing: Mass Airflow, Speed Density and Alpha-N

There are a number of different methods used to calculate engine load in a standalone engine management system. Each method has its advantages and disadvantages. The method we would choose to use depends on the engine specification and the components used. Most of us using an aftermarket standalone ECU will be using a speed-density/MAP sensor-based system. We would only choose to use TPS where a speed-density/MAP or MAF-based system has been proven to be unsuitable. Further discussion of each method is given below.

Mass Airflow (MAF)

This is almost universally used on OEM systems due to its low cost and ability to recognize, and compensate for, slight changes in an engine's breathing ability or volumetric efficiency (VE). Most of these use a hotwire or hot-film airflow meter to measure the mass of air flowing into the engine. Some older systems, such as the Lucas 4CU system, utilize a velocity-type airflow meter that uses the air entering the engine to move a spring-loaded flap. This flap is connected to a variable resistor that gives more or less voltage depending upon the position of the flap. This is combined with an air temperature sensor to calculate the volume of air.

Both the hotwire and velocity-type airflow meters give a 0–5v output signal to the ECU, which is proportional to airflow. Their main advantage is the ability to compensate for slight changes in an engine's VE. Their main disadvantage is that they cause a slight restriction to airflow into the engine, particularly the velocity type. This can be reduced to a minimum by using a slightly larger MAF. However, too large a unit will not measure the air correctly, while one that is too small will severely restrict airflow and its voltage

Inside a hotwire airflow meter.

output will max out before peak airflow is achieved. They are not as suitable for engines with aggressive profile camshafts, as the reversions and pulsed flow in the intake can cause metering difficulties.

MAF systems are always used in conjunction with TPS or MAP sensors, to allow the engine management system to respond to rapid changes in airflow.

Speed Density (MAP)

Many standalone and non-Rover V8 OEM engine management systems use a MAP (manifold absolute pressure) sensor to measure the air pressure (vacuum or boost) inside the intake manifold. When the engine is under very little load with the throttle barely open the air pressure in the manifold is low, but when the engine is under heavy load with the throttle wide open, the air pressure will rise. This sensor operates just like a vacuum gauge: high vacuum at part throttle and low vacuum at larger throttle openings. MAP sensor data can be converted to air-mass data using the speed-density fuelling algorithm. Air temperature and engine speed are also required to complete the speed-density calculation.

Most standalone EMS are look-up speed-density systems, as they directly use this MAP sensor data as the load input on the main fuel and ignition look-up tables, without first converting this into air-mass data. Most MAP sensors also operate on a 0–5 volt signal, with 0 volts being the lowest pressure (for example 0 kPa) and 5 volts being the highest pressure (for example 101 kPa with a 1-bar MAP sensor).

MAP sensors have the advantage of not causing any intake airflow restrictions, compensating for barometric pressure changes and responding quickly to changes in load. They are ideally suited to turbocharged and supercharged engines as they can measure above atmospheric pressure (boost). Their main disadvantage is that they cannot compensate for changes in an engine's breathing or VE: the ECU must be remapped after any modifications, as the MAP sensor can only see the manifold pressure, not the actual airflow.

MAP sensors are not suited to engines with very poor or uneven manifold vacuum, such as those fitted with camshafts of particularly aggressive profile that have a lot of overlap. If an engine cannot produce any more than 50–60 kPa vacuum at idle, or has wildly fluctuating vacuum levels, then it is better suited to a throttle-position load input (Alpha-N).

MAP sensor fitted to a TVR Griffith.

Alpha-N (TPS)

Alpha-N or throttle-position systems (TPS) use throttle-position angle and engine speed to estimate engine load. These systems are relatively crude compared to MAF or speed density, and are commonly used in competition engines where rapid throttle response, simplicity of calibration and outright performance are more important than economy or part-load fuelling accuracy. These

systems often use an air temperature sensor to help compensate for air-density changes resulting from changes in air temperature. These TPS-based engine management systems use a direct look-up table where throttle position is cross-referenced against engine speed for fuelling and ignition timing. This makes mapping very simple.

Alpha-N based systems are completely unsuitable for turbocharged or supercharged engines as they cannot measure changes in manifold pressure or airflow, as the turbo or supercharger starts generating boost. The main advantage of this load-measuring method is the stability of the load signal on engines with rough-running camshafts with a lot of valve overlap. TPS-based systems are immune to the effects of reversion or fluctuating manifold pressures caused by such camshafts. Furthermore, TPS gives very good transient engine response. Its main disadvantages are its lack of accuracy and resolution at low throttle openings, and its inability to respond to changes in manifold pressure.

Hybrid Alpha-N and Speed Density

Some standalone systems are able to use a blend of both of these load-sensing strategies. This is not usually necessary, but can be very useful on competition engines that have low or fluctuating manifold pressure at idle and part throttle, but are fitted with a supercharger or turbocharger set-up. Some standalone engine management systems (for example DTA) provide a TPS versus RPM map for main running, and a 2D table of manifold pressure versus additional fuelling for boost.

Throttle-position sensors.

We have found that the simplest way to calibrate such set-ups is to disconnect the supercharger or turbocharger and calibrate the system for naturally aspirated running on the TPS versus RPM fuelling table first. Then reconnect the supercharger or turbocharger boost pipes, and calibrate for additional manifold pressure.

Remember simplicity often yields the best results, so do not resort to such additional complication unless really necessary.

Oxygen Sensing: Narrow-Band versus Wide-Band Lambda Sensors

It is important to remember when tuning that a lambda sensor is really just an oxygen sensor. It does not know how much fuel is going into the engine, or how well it is combusted. All it is telling you is how much residual oxygen is left after combustion. If the engine misfires, then the lambda sensor will read a lean fuel mixture as there will be a lot of oxygen present in the resulting uncombusted exhaust gases. The fuel mixture may actually be rich, causing the misfire! We are inferring how much fuel was combusted based on the residual oxygen.

Narrow-Band Oxygen Sensors

Many OEM oxygen sensors are so-called narrow band, in that they can only accurately measure oxygen content in a very narrow range around lambda 1 or an AFR of 14.7:1. These sensors typi-

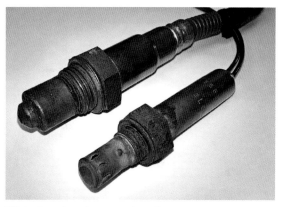

Wide-band and narrow-band oxygen sensors.

cally give a 0–1 volt output, with 0.5 volts indicating lambda 1, or an AFR of 14.7:1. Any voltages higher than this indicate a rich mixture, while voltages below this indicate a lean mixture. These sensors are not linear in their output, and cannot quantify how rich or lean the fuel mixture is. This type of sensor is useful for targeting an AFR of 14.7:1 for emissions purposes, but useless for engine tuning or mapping as they give no usable information beyond lambda 1.

Wide-Band Oxygen Sensors

Wide-band oxygen sensors can measure a much wider range of fuel mixtures, and many can give a linear 0–5-volt output corresponding with a wide range of fuel mixtures such as 10:1–20:1 AFR. These sensors are considerably more expensive than the narrow-band type, but are also far more useful. These are the only type of lambda sensor you should use for engine tuning.

Idle Control

Most EFI systems utilize some form of idle control to allow for the extra airflow required when the engine is cold, or if additional loads are placed on the engine. For example, increased electrical loads on the alternator from cooling fans can create an unstable idle speed, as can mechanical loads from power steering, air conditioning, placing the vehicle into drive, and so on. Most forms of idle control operate by allowing additional air to bypass the throttle plate, thereby increasing the engine speed. These are known as IAC valves, or 'idle air control' valves.

Ignition timing changes can also be used for idle control. This is known as spark-scatter idle control. Modern ECU systems usually incorporate a closed-loop idle control strategy, where the ECU monitors its own idle speed and adjusts the idle air bypass or ignition timing to match its pre-set target. For example, if the idle speed is set at 850rpm but drops to 700rpm when the cooling fans kick in or the air conditioning is activated, then the ECU recognizes this and adds additional air or ignition advance to maintain the pre-set 850rpm.

Fiddle Valve

This is a very simple valve that is either open or closed, and allows a fixed amount of extra air to bypass the throttle plate when the engine is cold. These valves provide a step in idle speed at the switch point. For example, the engine may run at approximately 1,200rpm with the valve activated at coolant temperatures below 60°C, and will drop back to 850rpm when it is closed. This provides the extra air required to match the extra fuel that is injected in the warm-up phase. They are crude, but simple, effective and reliable.

Two-Wire PWM Idle Valve

This is a variable opening valve that is controlled via a pulse-width modulated output from the ECU. These valves can provide a smooth transition in engine speed from cold to warm. They are also suitable for closed-loop idle control where the ECU monitors its own idle speed and regulates the PWM output to maintain a pre-set idle speed. One example of such a PWM idle valve is the Bosch two-wire IAC valve, typically used on VAG (Volkswagen Audi Group) products. They operate over a 30 per cent duty cycle (closed) to a 90 per cent duty cycle (fully open). They are usually very reliable.

Four-Wire Stepper-Motor Idle Valve

This is a stepper-motor controlled valve that is commonly used on the 14CUX and GEMS engine management systems as standard. Many, but not all, standalone systems have the option to control these. These valves also offer variable opening and are therefore suitable for closed-loop idle control. These valves can gum up with carbon deposits over time and require periodic cleaning.

Spark-Scatter Idle Control

This method does not require any additional components or plumbing, and simply uses the ECU's control over the ignition timing to influence idle speed. Its effects are more limited than an idle valve, as it cannot influence airflow. This method is mostly used where simplicity and low weight are the priority, such as on competition vehicles. This is most effective when the air-bypass screw or throttle-stop screws are adjusted to give a slightly fast idle, and then the ignition timing at idle is retarded slightly to slow the engine to the required idle speed. When additional loads are placed on the engine, the ECU recognizes the drop in idle speed and advances the ignition timing to increase the engine speed back to normal. If the idle speed is too high, then the ECU retards the ignition timing to slow the engine.

A simple anti-stall feature can be implemented by creating an engine speed site below the normal idle speed on your ignition advance map, and adding additional ignition advance. For example, if the idle speed is set at 950rpm, you can have a speed site at 950rpm with 10 degrees of ignition advance, and another at,

Bosch two-wire PWM idle valve.

Stepper-motor idle valve.

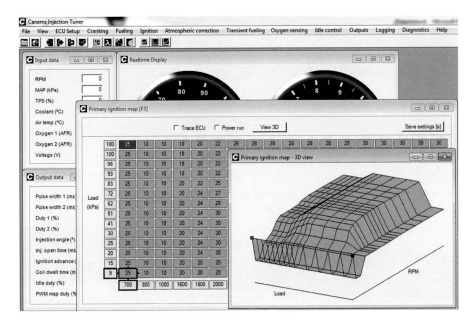

Screenshot of ignition map example with anti-stall – the base map for a competition 4 × 4.

say, 650rpm with 20 degrees of ignition advance. If the engine speed drops below 950rpm then the ECU will immediately begin adding additional advance up to a maximum of 20 degrees at 650rpm. Many OEM ECUs use this method, in addition to an IAC valve to help prevent engine stalling. This feature is useful to help prevent stalling during hill-starts, for example.

Installation

Rather than looking at the inner workings of an electronic control unit (ECU), we will look at the various inputs and outputs on a typical standalone ECU, and see how these would be wired to run a typical Rover V8 engine. In this particular example we show how a standard Canems ECU is wired up to run a Rover V8 engine, previously running with a Lucas 14CUX EFI system. We will use the Canems system as an example, but the same principles apply to many of the standalone systems available today.

All aftermarket standalone engine management ECUs come with a 'pin-out' diagram or table, which tells you the function of each ECU pin and the corresponding wire colour. Table 20 gives the pin-out of the standard Canems ECU.

When building an engine management wiring loom for a vehicle, we always start with the main

relay. This allows the ECU to switch the 12-volt power supply from the main vehicle battery to the various engine management components that require a 12-volt supply – for example fuel injectors, fuel pump, ignition coils and idle valve (*see* Table 20).

Fan Relay Colour Code
Pin A/30 = Battery 12V+ (30A fused) – Red 2mm²
Pin B/85 = Main Relay Output –ECU Pin 2J - Pink
Pin C/86 = Ignition Live (10A fused) & 12V+ ECU Feed to ECU Pin 3B – White 1mm²
Pin D/87 = Fuel Pump 12V+ & 12V+ Supply to Engine Management Components (e.g.: Injectors, Coil-Packs, Idle Valve, etc) – White 2mm²

Main ECU relay wiring.

As you can see, with the standard Canems ECU, pin 3B is the ignition live feed that powers the standalone ECU, as well as being present on one pin of the main relay whenever the vehicle ignition is switched on. Pin 2J is used by the ECU to switch on the main relay via a switched earth within the ECU. This switches on the main relay at the same time as the ECU, but times out after a pre-defined

Table 20: Canems ECU pin-out example

ECU pin	Function	Wire colour
1A	injector earth	black
1B	injector output 1	black/blue
1C	injector output 2	black/grey
1D	injector output 3	black/green
1E	injector output 4	black/red
1F	ignition output 4	grey/red
1G	ignition output 3	grey/orange
1H	ignition output 2	grey/green
1J	ignition output 1	grey/black
1K	ignition earth	black
2A	map switching input	yellow
2B	air temperature signal	blue/red
2C	coolant temperature signal	blue/yellow
2D	throttle position signal	blue/pink
2E	map sensor signal	blue/white
2F	oxygen sensor 1 signal	yellow/brown
2G	oxygen sensor 2 signal	yellow/black
2H	5V reference voltage	orange
2J	main relay output	pink
2K	output 2	purple/green
3A	ECU earth	black
3B	12V supply	white
3C	crank sensor earth	blue
3D	crank sensor signal	red
3E	additional input/output	depends on use
3F	serial ground	green/yellow
3G	serial receive	blue
3H	serial transmit	brown
3J	output 1	purple/yellow
3K	tachometer	purple

amount of time (for example 2 seconds), allowing the fuel system to prime. This output will also be constantly earthed when the ECU receives an engine speed signal, but as soon as the engine speed signal is cut, this output will switch off. This acts as a safety device, cutting the 12-volt power supply to the various engine management compo-

nents, until the next time the ignition is switched back on.

Pins 1A, 1K and 3A are all earth connections required for the Canems ECU to function correctly. We star-earth pins 1A and 1K to the battery earth supply.

Pin 3A is the ECU earth, and we usually earth this on to the stud on the back of the left-hand cylinder head on a Rover V8, and star-earth this to the various engine management components that require an earth (such as air temperature sensor, coolant temperature sensor, and so on). In the case of the Canems ECU, we do this because the ECU earth incorporates the crank sensor shielding, and connecting Pin 3A to a separate earth point from the ignition and injection earths makes the crank signal less susceptible to electrical interference.

Required Inputs

Crank Sensor Signal and Earth

Pins 3C and 3D provide an engine speed and crank angle input to the ECU via a VR sensor. This VR sensor will take a reading from a toothed trigger wheel that is located on the crankshaft. This trigger wheel will have at least one missing tooth to provide a reference point in relation to the top dead centre (TDC) position of cylinder number 1.

With the Rover V8, this trigger wheel can be located on the front crank damper/pulley assembly or on the flywheel or flex-plate assembly. On P38A Rover V8 engines originally fitted with a GEMS or Thor engine management system, there is a 36-1 or 60-2 pattern trigger wheel located on the flywheel or flex-plate, as standard. With this set-up, the crank sensor is located on the opposite side of the engine to the starter motor.

A Hall-effect sensor can be used instead of a VR sensor; these are more expensive, but are less susceptible to electrical interference. If your Hall sensor requires a 5-volt supply, use a connection to pin 2H.

Load Sensor

This is usually either a MAP sensor (MAP) or a throttle-position sensor (TPS). With most naturally

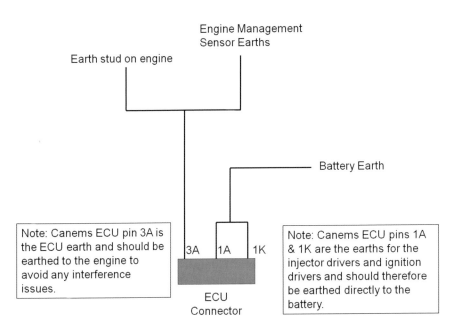

Earth stud on engine

Engine Management
Sensor Earths

*Engine management
earth connections.*

Battery Earth

Note: Canems ECU pin 3A is
the ECU earth and should be
earthed to the engine to
avoid any interference
issues.

3A   1A   1K

Note: Canems ECU pins 1A
& 1K are the earths for the
injector drivers and ignition
drivers and should therefore
be earthed directly to the
battery.

ECU
Connector

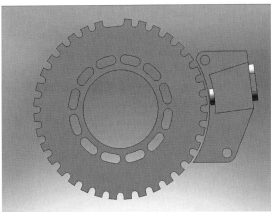

Trigger wheel and crank sensor.

GEMS 36-1 trigger wheel mounted on the flex-plate.

aspirated or boosted Rover V8s we use a MAP sensor as the main engine load measuring device. This is basically like an electronic vacuum/pressure gauge. The MAP sensors that we use are 0–5-volt analogue sensors and require the following connections:

- MAP sensor signal: ECU pin 2E
- 5V reference voltage: ECU pin 2H
- Earth: star-earthed with engine earth and ECU pin 3A

Even when using a MAP sensor as the main load-measuring device, we will still install and wire in a throttle-position sensor. We use this for transient enrichments (additional fuel for rapid throttle openings) and to activate flood-clear mode during cranking. We will also occasionally use the throttle-position sensor as the main engine-load measuring device – when installing one of these standalone engine management systems on an engine fitted with eight individual throttle bodies, for example. The throttle-position sensors are

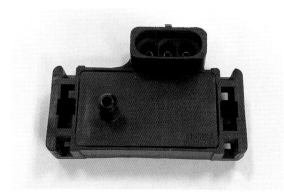

MAP sensor.

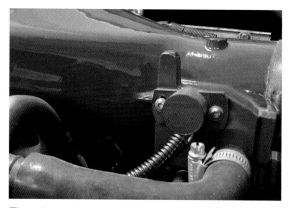

Throttle-position sensor.

0–5-volt analogue sensors, and require the following connections:

- Throttle-position signal: ECU pin 2D
- 5v reference voltage: ECU pin 2H
- Earth: star-earthed with engine earth and ECU pin 3A

If you are using an existing Rover V8 throttle-position sensor, you may find the table below useful.

Coolant Temperature Sensor

This is a thermistor where the resistance varies according to the temperature of the vehicle's cooling system. It will require the following connections:

- Coolant temperature signal: ECU pin 2C
- Earth: star-earthed with engine earth and ECU pin 3A

Most aftermarket standalone engine management systems are compatible with the standard Rover V8 coolant temperature sensors, but some systems will require calibrating to suit. The ECU will require this signal so that it can provide additional fuel when the engine is cold – that is, during the warm-up phase of its operating cycle.

Air Temperature Sensor

This is a thermistor where the resistance varies according to the temperature of the vehicle's air intake. It will require the following connections:

- Air temperature signal: ECU pin 2B
- Earth: star-earthed with engine earth and ECU pin 3A

We usually install a universal air temperature sensor when converting a Rover V8 engine to standalone engine management, although the GEMS system does already have an air temperature sensor that can be used.

Optional Inputs

Map Switch

Pin 2A: connecting this wire to earth switches from the primary fuel and ignition maps to the secondary fuel and ignition maps within the ECU. This is

Table 21: Rover V8 throttle position sensor wiring – common OEM colour schemes

Function	Canems colours	Colour scheme A	Colour scheme B	Colour scheme C
Signal	blue/pink	red	red	green
5v Ref.	orange	yellow	yellow	brown
Earth	black	red/black	green	blue

Coolant temperature sensor.

Air temperature sensor.

Table 22: Typical Rover V8 coolant temperature resistance values, for Lucas 4CU and Lucas 14CUX sensors

Sensor resistance (Ω)	Coolant temperature (°C)
9,200	-10
5,800	0
2,500	20
1,200	40
600	60
350	80
180	100

Oxygen sensor.

particularly useful if you are running your Rover V8 on LPG or high octane fuel.

Oxygen Sensors
Pins 2F and 2G are for oxygen sensor 1 and oxygen sensor 2 signals. These connections allow the ECU to receive a signal from the oxygen or lambda sensors, relating to the air-fuel ratio measured at each sensor. These are used for closed-loop fuelling control, if required.

Required Outputs
Injector Outputs 1, 2, 3 and 4
Pins 1B, 1C, 1D & 1E: these are switched earths that control the fuel injectors. On a Rover V8 with the

standard Canems conversion, we usually wire these in as shown in the illustration.

Note that this example is configured for semi-sequential fuelling: this is where each injector output controls a pair of fuel injectors, corresponding to the firing order of the Rover V8. So with the firing order of a Rover V8 being 1-8-4-3-6-5-7-2, the injector outputs should be wired as follows:

- Injector output 1: fuel injectors on cylinders 1 and 6
- Injector output 2: fuel injectors on cylinders 8 and 5
- Injector output 3: fuel injectors on cylinders 4 and 7
- Injector output 4: fuel injectors on cylinders 2 and 3

Ignition Outputs 1, 2, 3 and 4
Pins 1J, 1H, 1G & 1F: these are switched earths that control the ignition coils. On most Rover V8 applications we will use four double-ended ignition coils and

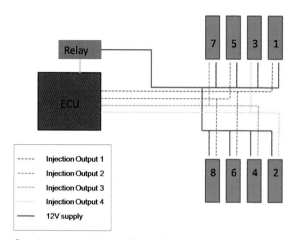

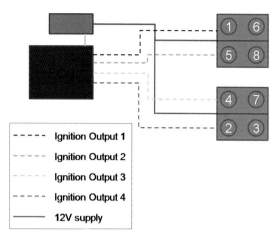

Semi-sequential injection wiring.

Ignition wiring on a standalone EMS installation.

Injector wiring on a standalone EMS installation.

configure them in a 'wasted spark' set-up. This set-up also corresponds to the firing order of the Rover V8, and the ignition outputs should be wired as follows:

- Ignition output 1: cylinders 1 and 6
- Ignition output 2: cylinders 8 and 5
- Ignition output 3: cylinders 4 and 7
- Ignition output 4: cylinders 2 and 3

Optional Outputs
Output 2
Pin 2K, PWM capable: we tend to use this output to control a pulse-width modulated idle valve, but it can also be used as a temperature-based switch, for electronic boost control, or to provide a fixed

frequency output. When being used for a PWM idle valve, then we will wire in the device as shown in the illustration [below].

Output 1
Pin 3J: this output can be used as a temperature-based switch (for example, a cooling fan control), an RPM-based switch (for example, a shift light), to provide a tachometer signal, or for crank sensor

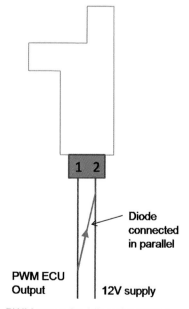

PWM two-wire idle valve wiring.

Cooling fan relay wiring.

Fan Relay Colour Code

Pin A = Battery 12V+ (fused) - Red
Pin B = ECU Signal (Output 1) -
Purple/Yellow
Pin C = Ignition Live - White
Pin D = Electric Fan 12V+ - White

1 – Connect Purple/Yellow 'ECU Switched Earth' wire on electric fan wiring loom to Purple/Yellow wire on main engine management wiring loom;

2 – Connect White 'Electric Fan 12V+' wire to the 12V+ side of your electric fans. Ensure that your electric fans are also correctly earthed;

3 – Connect White 'Ignition Live' wire to a suitable ignition live;

4 – Connect Red 'Battery 12V+' wire to the positive terminal of your battery.

diagnostics. If being used to control cooling fans we would connect this wire to the earth switch on a cooling fan relay, so that the ECU provides a switched earth to the relay via this output once the coolant reaches a specified temperature.

Tachometer
Pin 3K: this provides an engine speed signal to the vehicle's tachometer (also known as a rev-counter).

Obviously, this is just one relatively straightforward example of engine management wiring, based on the standard Canems ECU pin-out, but most aftermarket standalone ECUs would be set up in a very similar way. A higher specification of ECU – for example Motec, Canems Fully Sequential, Pectel – would come with more additional features, such as fully sequential fuelling (using a camshaft sensor), drive-by-wire throttle, coil-on plugs, traction control, knock control, etc. It is worth noting here, however, that it is better to have a less sophisticated system working well than an ECU with lots of additional features working badly!

STANDALONE ENGINE MANAGEMENT SYSTEMS: SET-UP AND MAPPING

Once an engine management system has been installed, there is still some basic set-up work that must be carried out before we can try and start the engine:

1. Establish a connection to the ECU with a laptop PC
2. Load a suitable base calibration or base-map
3. Set and check the static ignition timing
4. Calibrate the engine sensors

Establish a Connection to the ECU with a Laptop or PC

Most standalone ECUs will use an RS232 or USB cable to communicate with the ECU. Many laptops nowadays do not have an RS232 connection, and ECUs equipped with this connection will therefore have to use an RS232 to USB adaptor. It is worth checking with the ECU supplier before using a generic adaptor, as many engine management systems (for example Canems and Emerald) will use a specific adaptor cable. Other cables will not work with some of these systems, as the internal wiring connections are different. These RS232-USB adaptors often require specific drivers to operate correctly, and these should be supplied with the adaptor.

Check that you can establish connection by plugging the interface cable into the ECU connection

EMS software on a laptop.

port and the laptop computer. Turn the ignition on and then open the tuning software. Most tuning software will have an indicator that the ECU connection has been established. You can view the various gauges such as coolant and air temperature to ensure that the ECU is live and that realistic values are displayed.

If no connection can be established, then first ensure that the ECU is definitely powered up, then check the cable connection between the laptop and ECU. Try closing and reopening the tuning software. If this fails, then you may need to select the communication tab or options on the tuning software, and select the COM port you are using (for example, COM3). You can usually find this information by selecting 'Control Panel' or 'My Computer', and right clicking > Manage > Device manager > Universal Serial Bus Controllers. The connection should appear and disappear as you plug and unplug the cable with this window open. The exact details for this are obviously operating-system specific. Once a connection is established we can move on to the next step.

Load a Suitable Base Calibration or Base-Map

The easiest thing to do is to acquire a suitable base-map from the ECU supplier, or a fellow owner with

a similar set-up. It is possible to create your own base-map from scratch, although this will require experience and detailed knowledge of the engine management software and the engine's requirements. Once you have a suitable base-map, it is often a simple matter of opening the tuning software and loading the base-map on to your ECU. You can then view the fuel and ignition maps to check that the maps have been loaded on to the ECU, and can be edited.

Set and Check the Static Ignition Timing

This is absolutely critical on any installations that incorporate ignition-timing control, and should always be checked before attempting to crank the engine. Failure to do this can result in catastrophic engine damage. Do not assume anything. Engine management specific details can be found in the instructions that were supplied with your chosen ECU, but the general idea is to ensure that the ECU knows precisely where the engine is in its cycle. Most systems will use a trigger wheel and crank sensor. The ECU needs to know where this reference is in relation to cylinder number 1 at top dead centre (TDC). From this reference, the ECU can work out the firing sequence and timing for all the other cylinders.

Standard crankshaft trigger patterns for the Rover V8 are 36-1 and 60-2 for the GEMS and THOR systems respectively. Most standalone engine management systems will use a 36-1 trigger mounted to the crank pulley or flywheel, although other patterns are occasionally used. With a 36-1 trigger pattern, each tooth corresponds to 10 degrees of crankshaft rotation. The 36-1 trigger will have thirty-five teeth, plus one missing tooth for reference. With a standard GEMS engine, the missing tooth is positioned so that the ECU sees this missing tooth when cylinder 1 is 340 degrees BTDC. As soon as the ECU 'sees' the missing tooth, it knows where it is in the engine's cycle and can time the ignition for every other cylinder. Some systems require the trigger to be set at a specific point – for example, GEMS needs the missing tooth positioned at exactly 340 BTDC, and Ford's EDIS 8 system requires it set at 50 BTDC. Many standalone systems can be set with the trigger wheel in any position, and this information is then set in the software.

Setting the Static Trigger Position

We would usually begin by rotating the engine so that cylinder 1 is at TDC, and then count the number of teeth between the crank sensor and the missing tooth in the clockwise direction, as viewed from the front of the engine. For example, if there are approximately six and a half teeth between the crank sensor and the missing tooth on a 36-1 trigger wheel, then we would enter a static trigger position of 65 degrees BTDC (6.5 teeth × 10 degrees = 65 degrees). This only needs to be close at this stage. Once the engine is running, we would set the base ignition timing to 10 degrees BTDC and recheck this trigger position with a stroboscopic timing light connected to number 1 cylinder. If the light were flashing at 13 degrees rather than 10, then we would trim the static trigger position in the software until the timing light was flashing at exactly 10 degrees.

If your ECU is retaining the distributor and single coil, then you would need to rotate the engine until it is at TDC on the firing stroke for number 1 cylinder, and rotate the distributor so that the rotor arm is pointing exactly at number one HT lead post in the

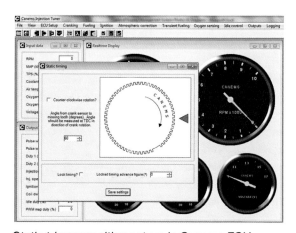

Static trigger position set-up in Canems ECU software.

Trigger wheel and timing mark.

Eight-lobed rotor in Rover V8 distributor.

distributor cap. The ECU then uses the eight-lobed rotor in the distributor as its timing reference.

Calibrate the Engine Sensors

Throttle-Position Sensor Calibration

All standalone engine management systems will require calibration of the throttle-position sensor so that the ECU knows the position of the throttle plate. This is set in the tuning software for the ECU. Most systems allow the user to click a button to capture the TPS voltage with the throttle shut, and another to capture the voltage at wide-open throttle (WOT). The ECU uses this range of voltages to create a linear voltage curve between these minimum and maximum voltages. Once this is set, you should check that you get a clean sweep by turning on the ignition with the software connected and ensuring that the throttle position smoothly and linearly changes from 0 per cent to 100 per cent and back to 0 per cent as you operate the throttle pedal. Once this is set, then save the calibration.

Spiky or inconsistent readings point to a bad throttle potentiometer. As the throttle potentiometer track wears it can have 'gaps' in its sweep. For example, as you smoothly apply the throttle it might read 10 per cent, then 0 per cent, then 20 per cent, as this wear in the potentiometer's voltage track creates gaps in the voltage output. If this is the case, then it is advisable to replace the throttle-position sensor.

Temperature Sensor Calibration

Some ECU systems will come pre-set for the standard Rover V8 coolant and air temperature sensors. Other systems may require this data to be entered into the tuning software's sensor calibration tables. These calibration tables allow the ECU to be able to convert a resistance reading into a temperature reading. The calibration data for the standardized Bosch Rover V8 temperature sensors can be seen in Table 23 overleaf. This data can be directly entered into your ECU software's sensor calibration tables.

Once all this has been set, then you can check that all the sensors are reading realistic values in the tuning software. The throttle position should be smooth and accurate, and the static trigger position should be double-checked. Only then can we move on to the exciting step of starting the engine.

First Start-Up

The initial start-up is one of the most exciting times during the installation, but it is important not to rush this stage as it is also fraught with the potential for engine damage. Our aim here is to get the engine

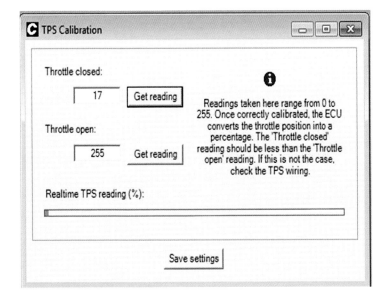

Throttle-position sensor calibration in Canems ECU software.

Table 23: Sensor resistance versus temperature for standard Rover V8 sensors

Sensor resistance (Ω)	Coolant, air or fuel temperature (°C)
9,200	−10
5,800	0
2,500	20
1,200	40
600	60
350	80
180	100

running smoothly, to set the idle fuel mixture and speed, check the timing with the engine running, and ensure that all sensors are operating correctly. The vehicle should not be driven until this first stage is complete, no matter how well the engine appears to be running on the base-map. It is essential to have an assistant to monitor the engine as you tune, particularly if the engine is a fresh build. You will be concen-

Double-check the following before attempting to start the engine:

- Establish a connection to the ECU with a laptop or PC
- Load a suitable base ECU calibration (also known as a base-map)
- Set and check the static ignition timing
- Calibrate the engine sensors
- Double check the HT lead order and coil-pack wiring to ensure correct firing order
- Check coolant and oil levels
- Ensure that the battery is fully charged
- Connect a wide-band lambda gauge and sensor to monitor the air-fuel ratio (AFR)
- Ensure adequate ventilation – do not run the engine in an enclosed environment without adequate exhaust extraction!
- Have a fire extinguisher handy and a suitable spanner to disconnect the battery quickly if required

trating on tuning the ECU and may fail to notice any external issues, such as coolant and oil leaks.

Sit in the vehicle with the ignition on, with the laptop connected and the engine management software showing live data. Locate the wide-band gauge somewhere where you can see it easily (if not displayed on the tuning software). Crank the engine and observe the engine speed in the tuning software – this should show a cranking speed of at least 100rpm. If no speed is shown, but the engine sounds as if it is turning over at a normal speed, then you have a problem with your ignition pick-up or crank sensor arrangement. If the engine is turning very slowly, then test/charge the battery and investigate battery cables, earth connections and so on. Most engine management systems are sensitive to low voltages, so a full battery charge is essential.

Crank the engine in 5 seconds bursts until it starts or coughs. If the engine backfires loudly through the intake or exhaust, then carefully check the ignition firing order, HT leads and static ignition trigger position. Do not continue to crank or run the engine if it is banging, popping or knocking heavily, as this indicates that the engine is firing at the wrong time and can cause catastrophic engine damage very quickly.

Once the engine starts, then attempt to keep it running until it warms up a little. It may be necessary to hold your foot on the throttle pedal slightly to keep it running. With the engine running, take a quick glance at your wide-band lambda gauge. Is it showing rich or lean fuel mixtures? Is it fluctuating wildly, indicating a misfire? Look at the live data in the tuning software. The sensor values should be stable and realistic. If the engine is using a MAP sensor, then this should be reading a value below 80 kPa, even when running poorly. Any less, and the MAP sensor vacuum connection is not connected, is obstructed, or the MAP sensor is not working correctly. Throttle-position values should read 0 per cent with your foot off the throttle. Coolant and air temperature should be realistic and not fluctuating wildly.

If the wide-band AFR (air-fuel ratio) reading is stable but showing a rich or lean mixture, we can open the fuel table or map and simply add or subtract fuel as is necessary to get the AFR in the range 11.8:1–14.5:1.

Do not be concerned with getting this absolutely exact at this stage, just ensure the engine is rich enough to continue to run, but not so rich that it quickly carbon-fouls the spark plugs or lambda sensor. Once the fuel mixture is roughly set around the idle point, attempt to let the engine idle with your foot removed from the throttle pedal. If the engine speed is too low, then either open up the idle bypass screw or increase the throttle-stop setting until it will idle satisfactorily.

Idle bypass screw on EFI plenum.

With the engine idling at a sensible speed we can double-check our ignition trigger position. This is essential to ensure that the timing values we set in the software are the same as the actual timing fired at the spark plug. This was set only statically before start-up, and now needs to be dynamically checked using a stroboscopic timing light (strobe). To do this, connect the pick-up to the HT ignition lead for cylinder number 1, power up the strobe and point at the timing mark pointer. Some tuning software has the option of locking the timing at a fixed figure (for example 10 degrees BTDC), regardless of the settings in the ignition table or map. If so, lock the timing at something sensible that corresponds with your timing marks on the front pulley (for example TDC or 10 degrees BTDC).

If your ECU tuning software does not have this option, then set all the cells in the ignition table to 10 degrees BTDC (save a copy of the original base-map settings to reinstate later). Check your live data to ensure the ECU is indeed set at this timing figure.

Timing pointer and pulley marks.

Using the strobe, check that the timing mark aligns correctly with the timing pointer at your chosen timing figure. If the marks do not align, make a note of the error. For example, if we set the timing in the software at 10 BTDC, but our timing marks align at 7 BTDC, then we need to alter the static trigger position by 3 degrees, then re-check with our timing light. Many ECU tuning softwares offer the ability to trim or adjust the static trigger position in the software. In this case all we need to do is trim this until the marks align correctly. If this option is not available, then you will need to adjust the ignition pick-up or trigger wheel physically until the timing set in the software exactly matches the actual ignition timing.

Fuel and Ignition Calibration

Once the engine starts, idles satisfactorily, and we have verified that the timing displayed in our tuning software matches the actual ignition timing, then we can move on to calibrating the fuel and ignition maps. You should begin by ensuring that you have a safe, conservative ignition map. The ignition timing and fuelling are essentially inter-related. The fuelling should be calibrated first, then the ignition timing, and then back to check the fuelling again.

Large changes in fuel mixture (AFR) will affect the flame speed inside the engine, and therefore the optimum ignition timing point. Excessively rich fuel mixtures will burn more slowly and will there-fore respond to increases in ignition advance. Fuel mixtures that are lean will often burn faster and will therefore respond to less ignition timing. If we optimized the ignition timing first on an engine that was running excessively rich, it would be over advanced and would potentially pre-ignite once we reduced the fuelling, as making the mixture leaner would increase the flame speed. Conversely, engines that are running excessively retarded will often respond positively to lean mixtures, as the lean air-fuel mix will increase the flame speed so the engine requires less ignition advance.

Tuning the Fuel Map

Connect up your wide-band lambda sensor and gauge. With the tuning software open and connected, select the primary fuel map. Tick the 'Trace Map' box to highlight the area on the map that the engine is operating, if this option is available.

Start the engine and let it settle to an idle if possible: if it stalls when the throttle is released, then use the minimum amount of throttle to keep it running. Take a look at the wide-band readout. Is it stable or jumping around all over the place? The readout should remain reasonably stable. Large fluctuations indicate a misfire on one or more cylinders; this can

be caused by an excessively rich or lean air-fuel mixture, amongst other things.

How does the engine sound? Is it running smoothly or is it lumpy? The engine should run reasonably well on any mixture between 11.8:1 and 15:1 AFR. Do not immediately assume any rough running is caused by a fuel mapping issue. Re-check the basics, including plug-lead order against coil outputs, static timing and so on, before trying to continue calibration.

Click in the particular fuel site in which the engine is currently operating – this is usually highlighted in most programmable ECU software. What does the wide-band gauge display?

Ideally the fuel mixture should be in the range given in Table 24 on page 177. With most software you can simply adjust the highlighted site up or down to increase or decrease the fuel quantity by clicking in that site and entering the new fuel value. With some software you can simply press shift and the up/down keys to increase/decrease fuelling. It is best to make small adjustments at a time. Be aware that most engine management systems use interpolation between fuel sites. This means that the fuel sites immediately closest to the highlighted one will

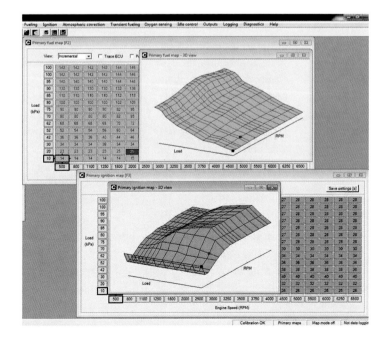

Fuel and ignition maps in Canems ECU software.

also be having an effect on the fuel quantity, so you may need to adjust these slightly too. Click 'Save Settings', 'Burn Calibration' or 'Write Map' to activate any changes.

It is worth noting that the smoothest idle mixture can be easily set by adjusting the fuel mixture until the highest vacuum or lowest MAP value is achieved. Adjust the relevant fuel site again if necessary until the desired air-fuel ratio or highest vacuum is achieved, remembering to click 'Save Settings' or 'Burn Calibration' and so on, to activate each change. Once the idle mixture is set, you may need to adjust the idle valve duty within the software (or physical air bypass) to achieve the desired idle speed.

With the engine idling smoothly we can proceed with checking and adjusting the main fuel map as necessary. Raise the engine speed gently and watch the wide-band gauge closely, making a note of any excessively rich or lean areas on the fuel map; adjust as necessary and save the changes. Repeat this process until the engine will rev up cleanly, with no excessive rich or lean spots indicated by the wide-band gauge.

The engine is now ready to be carefully driven on the dyno or road. For this you will need a dynamometer or volunteer driver. The engine should be operated under light load (up to 30 per cent throttle, or 75 kPa load) and at lower engine speeds (less than 4,000rpm). The tuner should keep a very close eye on the wide-band gauge at all times, and make a note of any excessively rich or lean areas on the main fuel map. Suggested air-fuel ratios are given in Table 24, although exact fuel mixtures are not critical at these low load areas, so simply ensure that the engine is not running excessively rich, or lean surging. If your vehicle is fitted with catalytic converters, we would aim for an air-fuel mixture of between 14.35:1 and 14.7:1 AFR to prolong the life of these components.

Repeat this checking and adjusting procedure as necessary until the engine is running smoothly, with no excessively rich or lean spots as indicated by the wide-band gauge. With the light load and low engine speed fuel mixtures calibrated, take a break and have a close look at both the fuel map and the 3D view by clicking on the 'View 3D' tab. The fuel map should be reasonably smooth with no sharp peaks or troughs, and all fuel values should be progressively and smoothly increasing or decreasing. Any numbers that do not follow the visible trend should be adjusted slightly to smooth the map.

Look at the load/rpm values just above those you have already checked and adjusted: are the numbers increasing progressively as expected,

Example of an AFR target table.

or decreasing? Is there a large step? The engine will always require more fuel at higher loads and less fuel at lower loads, so ensure this is the case before continuing, and correct any fuel numbers that do not follow this trend. Fuel numbers will always increase with extra load, but not necessarily with engine speed. At high engine loads (over 50 per cent throttle, 80 kPa MAP) we would expect to see the fuel numbers progressively increasing until peak torque, and then steadily decreasing thereafter.

Now we can continue with checking and adjusting the fuel mixtures at progressively higher engine loads (over 30 per cent throttle, 75 kPa MAP), whilst still keeping the engine speed below peak torque (approximately 3,000 to 4,000rpm, depending on the engine specification). It is very important that you keep a constant eye on the wide-band gauge from this point, as the fuel mixtures over 30 per cent throttle

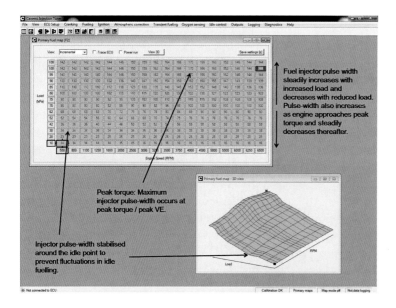

Example of a Rover V8 fuel map on Canems ECU software.

Fuel injector pulse width steadily increases with increased load and decreases with reduced load. Pulse-width also increases as engine approaches peak torque and steadily decreases thereafter.

Peak torque: Maximum injector pulse-width occurs at peak torque / peak VE.

Injector pulse-width stabilised around the idle point to prevent fluctuations in idle fuelling.

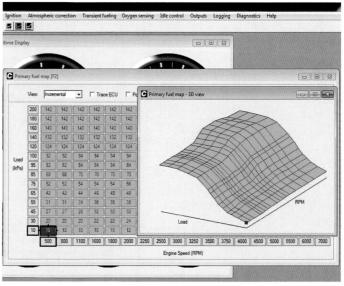

Example of a supercharged Rover V8 fuel map.

Table 24: Recommended fuel mixtures at different engine loads

Approximate load in kPa	Approximate load in TPS	Air-fuel ratio	%CO	Lambda
20 kPa	1%	13.5–14.7:1	2.6–0.5%	0.92–1
30 kPa	5%	13.5–14.7:1	2.6–0.5%	0.92–1
40 kPa	7%	13.5–14.7:1	2.6–0.5%	0.92–1
50 kPa	10%	13.5–14.7:1	2.6–0.5%	0.92–1
60 kPa	15%	13.5–14.7:1	2.6–0.5%	0.92–1
70 kPa	20%	13.2–14:1	3.3–1.6%	0.90–0.95
80 kPa	40%	12.7–13.2:1	4.7–3.3%	0.86–0.90
90 kPa	70%	12:1–12.7:1	6.5–4.7%	0.82–0.86
100 kPa	90% +	12:1–12.7:1	6.5–4.7%	0.82–0.86

are much more critical. An excessively lean mixture under these greater loads could be damaging to the engine and cause pre-ignition or detonation. Brief forays into higher loads (at a maximum of 5 seconds at a time) should be all that is necessary to determine in what direction the fuel mixture is heading. Ensure that the driver fully releases the throttle before activating changes. Activating ECU calibration changes whilst applying the throttle can be tough on the engine, particularly at higher loads and engine speeds.

Once these higher load and lower engine speed sites have been both checked and corrected, we should stop and take another close look at the fuel map, including the 3D view. All the fuel values in the fuel map should follow the logical trend of progressively increasing with load and engine speed. Correct any visible anomalies in the 3D view. The greatest amount of fuel is required at peak torque and peak load, *not* at peak engine speed. If you know where your engine produces maximum peak torque, then ensure that the fuel values at full load are increasing progressively right up to peak torque and slightly beyond. Fuelling values can level off or remain the same from peak torque up to maximum engine speed. If you don't know where peak torque occurs, then simply ensure that the fuel values increase progressively to maximum engine speed, until we have carried out a full load acceleration run.

We are now ready to attempt a full load acceleration run – this is easiest on a chassis dynamometer, although it can be carried out on a quiet open road with a co-operative driver. The tuner should not take

their eyes off the wide-band gauge for a moment, as peak torque is where the engine is most likely to detonate or overheat. Drive gently up through the gears until in fourth or fifth at approximately 1,500–2,000rpm. Bury the throttle and let the engine labour up through the engine speed range – 2,000, 2,500, 3,000, 3,500, 4,000 and so on. Abort the run immediately if the mixture is found to be lean (any leaner than 13:1 for naturally aspirated engines), whilst making a mental note of any areas that are excessively rich (richer than 12:1 for naturally aspirated engines).

Make any changes as necessary to the full load areas of the fuel map, adding a generous amount of extra fuel where the wide-band gauge indicated a lean mixture (for example +4 to +6), and decreasing the fuelling numbers slightly where it indicated excessive richness (for example, –2). Save any changes and do another full load acceleration run, and repeat this procedure until the wide-band gauge indicates no rich or lean spots across the engine speed range. Aim to have a consistent fuel mixture across the engine speed range at full load (for example 12.5:1 AFR) from minimum to maximum engine speed. Peak power is produced between rich best torque (11.8:1) and lean best torque (13.2:1). We would usually aim for somewhere in the middle (for example 12.5:1) on a normally aspirated engine, and rich best torque on a forced induction set-up (that is, 11.8:1).

Optimum fuel mixtures will vary from engine to engine. The throttle position and manifold pressure at a given engine load will vary depending on engine breathing and throttle area. Engines with high overlap camshafts often require richer fuel mixtures around idle and at low engine speeds. The comparison between AFR, per cent CO and lambda is approximate and not exact.

Tuning the Ignition Map

Determining the optimum ignition timing is absolutely critical to achieving peak engine efficiency. A fully programmable ignition system gives us the ability to optimize this critical parameter at every load and rpm point in a way that was never possible with a mechanical distributor set-up. The ignition timing is more critical, with a narrower window of error than the fuel settings. Whilst an engine may run peak power safely with a relatively wide range of fuel settings, a difference of as little as 2–3 degrees of ignition timing can be the difference between peak efficiency and pre-ignition. Optimum ignition timing for a given engine varies depending upon engine loading and engine speed. The aim is to achieve peak cylinder pressure with the piston around 15 degrees after top dead centre on the power stroke.

The relationship between ignition timing and volumetric efficiency (VE) is inverse, because the denser air-fuel mixtures burn much faster than the less dense mixtures. There is also a time element, because when the engine is rotating at higher speeds a combustion event of fixed duration must be started or ignited earlier so that peak pressure is still achieved at the same degrees of crankshaft rotation. It can be seen that combustion speed and engine speed in degrees of crank rotation per millisecond are independent variables. An engine turning at high speed and with low load will require a large amount of ignition advance. This is due to the fact that flame speed will be low because cylinder filling (VE) is poor, with low throttle openings, and the time frame to get the combustion event concluded is very small.

To achieve peak pressure by 15 degrees after top dead centre, we might initiate the combustion process as early as 42 degrees before top dead centre (BTDC). If we now suddenly opened the throttle wide open we would find that the VE or cylinder

filling would be high and the denser air-fuel mixture would burn much more rapidly through the cylinder. If we initiated combustion at 46 degrees BTDC, we would find that peak cylinder pressure would be achieved much sooner in the engine's cycle, perhaps as early as 10 degrees before top dead centre. With the piston still travelling up the cylinder bore and the flame front pushing down against the piston, engine knock and the resultant destructive damage would occur. Clearly, at wider throttle openings with the increase in VE we require less ignition advance – perhaps as little as 20 degrees before top dead centre at peak torque.

Ignition Timing at Idle with 'Mild' Camshafts

With the engine idling, we should begin by setting the idle ignition timing. This should be in the range of 8–20 degrees BTDC, depending upon the camshaft specification. Engines with relatively mild camshafts should use 8–12 degrees and no more; certainly the engine may sound smoother and respond a little faster with more timing, but it will also idle faster, requiring less throttle opening or idle bypass to achieve your target idle speed. This means there is a massive change in airflow from idle (throttle plates shut) to just above idle. This makes it very difficult to get the fuel mixture correct here, resulting in flat spots and poor engine response just above idle. Furthermore, with less air flowing through the engine for a given idle speed the exhaust emissions will be higher.

Ignition Timing and Idle Emissions

Interestingly, if you are struggling to get acceptable emissions at idle then you can retard the ignition timing at idle from, say, 12 degrees to 4 degrees, and increase the throttle stop or air bypass to compensate for the drop in engine speed as a result of the retarded ignition timing. With more air flowing through the engine at idle, it is much easier to achieve acceptable emissions. We can also use this technique when the injectors are too large to achieve a reasonable fuel mixture at idle (for example with a heavily boosted engine with very large injectors).

Ignition map and 3D view on Canems ECU software.

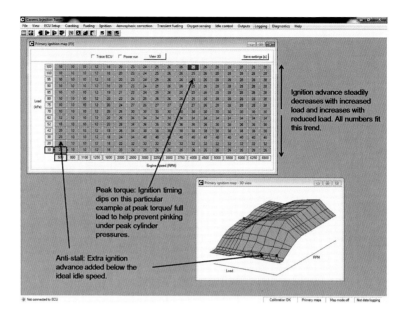

Ignition advance steadily decreases with increased load and increases with reduced load. All numbers fit this trend.

Peak torque: Ignition timing dips on this particular example at peak torque/ full load to help prevent pinking under peak cylinder pressures.

Anti-stall: Extra ignition advance added below the ideal idle speed.

Ignition Timing at Idle with 'Aggressive' Camshafts

Engines with more aggressive camshafts, with a lot of overlap, valve lift and duration, will require considerably more ignition timing at idle to counteract the slower burning fuel mixture that results from exhaust dilution and poor cylinder filling at lower engine speeds. Please refer to the table below for suggested idle ignition timing values. Only the more extreme camshafts will require ignition advance settings of 16–20 degrees at idle.

Ignition Timing Calibration

The place to optimize the ignition timing is on a chassis dynamometer or rolling road. Whilst we can calibrate the fuel mixtures on the road adequately, we cannot set the ignition timing correctly. Simply advancing the timing until we audibly hear the engine pinking or pre-igniting, then retarding the timing by a few degrees, will get you close but is fraught with danger and will not be the optimum. If you are calibrating the ECU yourself and do not have access to a rolling road, then we recommend you keep to known safe settings until you can hire some dynamometer time. Big gains or losses in efficiency can be made here, so it is worth getting this aspect right.

With the fuel mixtures and idle ignition advance set correctly we can calibrate the rest of the ignition map. Unlike with the fuel map, here we will often begin at full load and work backwards into the lower load areas. We would start by ensuring that the engine is running well with no audible pinking or pre-ignition noted under load.

There are two methods of optimizing full load ignition timing on a dynamometer: under steady state engine-speed holding, or on a transient test/power run. The most commonly used method, and easier on the engine, is during a transient test or power run.

Optimizing Full Load Ignition Timing during a Transient Test/Power Run

To do this we will begin with a safe ignition map and perform two or three back-to-back power runs

Table 25: Ignition timing at idle versus camshaft overlap

Overlap	Idle ignition timing	Idle speed
15–40°	6–8° BTDC	600–750rpm
40–55°	8–12° BTDC	750–900rpm
55–75°	12–16° BTDC	900–1,050rpm
75–100°	16–20° BTDC	1,050–1,300rpm

Optimizing ignition timing with the aid of a chassis dynamometer.

until the power and torque has stabilized. Set the ramp rate on the dynamometer to at least 400rpm per second, or a rate that reflects the vehicle's likely engine acceleration in fourth (or 1:1) gear on the road. Once we have a consistent and stable torque graph, we would retard the ignition timing by 2 degrees and repeat the power runs. Overlay the two torque graphs on top of one another. If you lost torque on the retarded run at every engine speed, then simply add 4 degrees to this retarded setting, or 2 degrees above the baseline ignition settings.

Repeat the runs again, taking great care to listen for the sounds of audible pre-ignition. If the torque increases notably everywhere, then try increasing the ignition timing a further 2 degrees and overlay the torque curves again. If you lost torque at one engine speed but gained at another, then return the timing values to the previous setting at the engine speed site where you lost torque, and leave it advanced where torque was gained. Repeat this process until adding more ignition advance results in the same or no extra torque. The aim here is to achieve the least ignition advance for best torque, at every engine speed. If the engine makes the same torque at 4,000rpm with 32 degrees as it does with 30 degrees, then set it at 30 degrees.

Once you have this close to optimum, you can try subtracting 1 degree from the entire ignition map and see if torque is lost or gained anywhere. Repeat this process until you have the best torque curve with the least ignition timing. This method is quick and effective for optimizing the full load values, but you should note that if you set the ramp rate on the dynamometer too fast, then the ignition timing will inevitably end up over-advanced in real world use.

Optimizing Ignition Timing under Steady State Engine-Speed Holding

The other way to set the full load ignition values is under a steady state load or engine speed holding. This is far harder on the engine, so be sure to allow the engine to cool down at regular intervals. Here

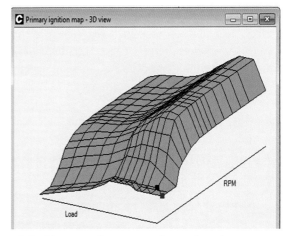

3D ignition map for a supercharged engine.

Ignition map for a supercharged engine.

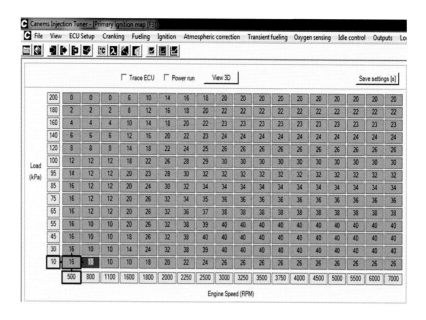

Load (kPa)	500	800	1100	1600	1800	2000	2250	2500	3000	3250	3500	3750	4000	4500	5000	5500	6000	7000
200	0	0	0	6	10	14	16	18	20	20	20	20	20	20	20	20	20	20
180	2	2	2	8	12	16	18	20	22	22	22	22	22	22	22	22	22	22
160	4	4	4	10	14	18	20	22	23	23	23	23	23	23	23	23	23	23
140	6	6	6	12	16	20	22	23	24	24	24	24	24	24	24	24	24	24
120	8	8	8	14	18	22	24	25	26	26	26	26	26	26	26	26	26	26
100	12	12	12	18	22	26	28	29	30	30	30	30	30	30	30	30	30	30
95	14	12	12	20	23	28	30	32	32	32	32	32	32	32	32	32	32	32
85	16	12	12	20	24	30	32	34	34	34	34	34	34	34	34	34	34	34
75	16	12	12	20	26	32	34	35	36	36	36	36	36	36	36	36	36	36
65	16	12	12	20	26	32	36	37	38	38	38	38	38	38	38	38	38	38
55	16	10	10	20	26	32	38	39	40	40	40	40	40	40	40	40	40	40
45	16	10	10	18	26	32	38	40	40	40	40	40	40	40	40	40	40	40
30	16	10	10	14	24	32	38	39	40	40	40	40	40	40	40	40	40	40
10	16	10	10	10	18	20	22	24	26	26	26	26	26	26	26	26	26	26

Engine Speed (RPM)

you set the dynamometer to lock at an engine speed that corresponds with the engine speed site in your ignition map that you wish to optimize (for example 1,500rpm). Bring the engine up to that engine speed and increase the load (via the throttle) until the engine is running at full load. Hold for approximately 3 seconds whilst noting the torque readout. Release the throttle and retard the ignition timing at that particular engine speed by 2 degrees. Bring the engine up to full load again and make a note of the torque readout. Has it increased or decreased? Simply add or subtract ignition timing until you achieve the most torque for the least amount of ignition advance.

Once you have optimized the ignition timing at that particular engine speed and engine load, then move on to the next engine speed, and keep repeating this process until you reach the maximum engine speed you wish to tune using this method. This method is also used to optimize part-throttle ignition timing by methodically working through every engine load and speed combination, finding the highest torque for the minimum amount of ignition advance.

Optimizing Part-Load Ignition Timing

Generally we will begin by optimizing the full load ignition timing using a transient test or power run.

Once we have the full load values optimized we would take a break and have a look at the ignition map and 3D view. Generally we would use the same full load ignition timing values all the way down to approximately 80 kPa or 50 per cent throttle. Below this amount of load the ignition timing can steadily increase all the way down to a maximum timing value at approximately 40 kPa or 5 per cent throttle. The ignition advance at around 40 kPa or 5 per cent throttle will be as much as 10–12 degrees more than the ignition advance at full load. In overrun conditions (less than approximately 30 kPa or 5 per cent throttle) it can be advantageous to retard the ignition timing a little to aid engine braking.

Too much ignition retard when lifting off the throttle can result in excessive engine braking and popping or crackles from the exhaust, while too much ignition advance can cause the engine to 'hang on' or decelerate very slowly.

A steady state or engine speed holding test can be used to further fine-tune the part-throttle ignition advance by simply locking the dynamometer at a given engine speed, using the throttle to hold the load site, and increasing or reducing ignition timing until peak torque is obtained. Once the calibration

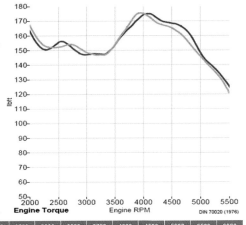

First power runs with the ignition advance curve set as standard. This is the red curve.

We would then begin by retarding the ignition timing to see where we lose power. The orange curve is with the timing retarded 2 degrees.

Although we lost power in some areas we also gained power in others.

We would then keep the original ignition advance values everywhere we lost power and retard the timing everywhere it stayed the same or we gained power.

This is only possible with a fully programmable ignition system. With a distributor we would have to strike a compromise between these values.

Comparing torque curves to optimize ignition timing.

Engine Torque Engine RPM DIN 70020 (1976)

	1000	1500	2000	2250	2500	3000	3500	3750	4000	4500	5000	5500	6000
Original	12	16	20	22	24	26	28	28	28	28	28	28	28
-2 degrees	10	14	18	20	22	24	26	26	26	26	26	26	26
Final Setting	10	14	18	20	24	24	26	26	26	28	28	28	28

is concluded, we should take a good look at our 3D ignition map view and ensure the entire map is as smooth as possible. Look for any areas that do not fit the visual trend. Ignition timing should always decrease with extra engine load and increase with engine speed, at least until peak torque is achieved. For example, if you notice that you have 30 degrees at 90 kPa and 28 degrees at 85 kPa, then set both load sites to 29 degrees (the average of two values). The aim is to make the map as smooth as it can be within the requirements of the engine, with no unnecessary dips or peaks. A smooth map creates a smooth engine response.

Warm-Up Enrichment

Warm-up enrichment is the electronic equivalent of a carburettor's choke. In a cold engine, much of the fuel fails to vaporize correctly or condenses on the cold metal in the engine and ends up as large, incombustible droplets of fuel. To counter this it is necessary to inject considerably more fuel when the engine is cold to keep it running smoothly. The colder the temperature, the more enrichment is needed, tapering to no enrichment at full operating temperature. Almost all engine management systems specify warm-up enrichment as a percent-

age of the main fuel map. For example, if the pulse-width on the main fuel map is 4 milliseconds (ms), and the enrichment is at 10 per cent, then the final pulse-width will be 4.4ms at that temperature point.

To set the warm-up enrichment, we must first make sure that the main fuel map is set correctly, and then start the engine from cold. Observe the wide-band AFR gauge, and increase or decrease the warm-up enrichment percentage as necessary to achieve smooth running at all temperatures. Fuel mixtures as rich as 11:1 may be necessary when the engine is very cold (around freezing), progressively decreasing as the engine warms up. Refer to the warm-up enrichment AFR table opposite for a rough guide. Experiment here and use the least warm-up enrichment conducive with smooth running. If you have too little warm-up enrichment, then the engine will have poor throttle response and will suffer from flat spots. Too much warm-up enrichment will increase fuel consumption, increases engine wear, and will lead to ignition misfires due to carbon fouling of the spark plugs.

Starting and Idle Tuning

We should only begin the final tuning of the starting and idle settings once the main fuel and ignition

Table 26: Examples of warm-up fuel mixtures

Coolant temp. (°C)	−20	−10	0	10	20	30	40	50	60	70	80	90	100
AFR	11	11.5	11.8	12	12.7	13	13	13.2	13.5	13.8	14.35	14.7	14.7
Lambda	0.75	0.78	0.80	0.82	0.86	0.88	0.88	0.90	0.92	0.94	0.98	1	1

maps have been set correctly. The start-up settings usually include the following:

- Cranking Pulse-width
- Idle Air Control – fixed and adjustable versus coolant temperature
- After-start Enrichment
- Cranking Pulse-width Enrichment – cranking pulse-width versus coolant temperature
- Priming Pulse-width

We would begin by setting the fixed idle air control and cranking pulse-width with the engine fully up to temperature. After we have finished the full temperature calibration is an ideal time, as the engine will be fully heat-soaked. Once we have set the cranking pulse-width with the engine hot, we would then set the after-start enrichment, followed by allowing the engine at least twelve hours to cool fully. Only once fully cool will we set the cranking pulse-width enrichment and priming pulse-width at the lower engine temperatures.

Cranking Pulse-Width

With the engine at full operating temperature, we can set the cranking pulse-width by starting with a relatively low setting, such as 3ms. Crank the engine and count the number of seconds or revolutions until the engine fires. Increase the cranking pulse-width in small increments, such as 0.5ms at a time, until the fastest starting is achieved. Remember to let the engine run at approximately 2,500rpm for a suitable period of time between starts to allow the battery voltage to recover, or you will find the starting will get progressively worse due to low voltage. Try and achieve the fastest hot starting with the best average pulse-width, as this will make starting easier. For example, if the engine starts equally fast with 6ms pulse-width as it does with 7ms, then set it at 6.5ms.

Idle Air Control – Fixed and Adjustable versus Coolant Temperature

The fixed air bypass includes the throttle-stop screw and air-bypass screw (if fitted). This should be set with the engine fully warm and idling. We would start by setting the idle valve to its minimum effective opening – for example, 32 per cent for the Bosch two-wire PWM idle valve. The air-bypass screw or throttle stop can then be set to your desired hot idle speed – for example, 900rpm. Any additional air that is required for cold running or additional engine loads is then provided by the idle valve.

Most engine management systems offer an idle valve duty cycle or stepper motor position versus coolant temperature. This idle bypass versus coolant temperature should be set with the engine fully cold. Start the engine and set the idle valve duty or stepper position at each temperature, as required to achieve the desired engine speed. We would usually run the engine a little faster when cold to ensure there is plenty of air speed to support complete combustion in the cold engine. The slightly faster idle also decreases warm-up times and helps reduce engine wear by ensuring strong oil pressure. For example, if the idle speed were 900rpm when hot, we would set the idle speed when cold to approximately 1,250rpm, gradually tapering back to 900rpm as the engine warms up.

Many engine management systems also offer a closed-loop idle speed option that will target a certain idle speed under specific conditions – for example, at engine speeds below 1,500rpm and throttle positions below 2 per cent. This should only be activated once your open-loop or ECU-controlled idle bypass has been correctly set. The aim here is for the closed-loop idle control to be applying the minimum amount of corrections to your base settings.

After-Start Enrichment

After-start enrichment is provided to smooth the transition from the engine firing on the priming and cranking pulse-widths, to running on the main fuel map. At very low engine speeds, between initially firing and idling, a great deal of the fuel injected will drop out of suspension due to the low intake airspeed, and fail to combust properly. As a result, almost all engines require a little extra fuel after initially firing to keep them running until the engine settles and is operating from the main fuel map.

Most engine management systems will specify after-start enrichment quantity and duration. Some systems will have a fixed after-start setting for all temperatures, whilst others will specify in terms of coolant temperature. This setting is not usually so fussy: too little after-start enrichment and the engine will fire, then stall, too much and the engine will fire, then stall, or idle very slowly with a rich mixture until the after-start enrichment shuts off. We should aim to use the minimum amount of after-start enrichment to ensure a smooth transition from firing to running.

Cranking Pulse-Width Enrichment: Cranking Pulse-Width versus Coolant Temperature

Once the cranking pulse-width is set at full operating temperature, we can set the cranking pulse-width at the lower coolant temperatures. Some ECU types will set the hot and cold cranking pulse-widths on one table or graph, others will set the hot cranking pulse-width separately and have an enrichment table for the lower coolant temperatures with an enrichment value that is a percentage of the hot cranking value. However it is implemented, the aim is the same: to get the engine to start as fast as possible at all coolant temperatures.

Start at the coldest temperature you can see on that day (for example 10°C), and attempt to start the engine. Count the number of seconds or revolutions until it fires, and increase or decrease the cranking pulse-width or percentage correction at that temperature as necessary to achieve the fastest starting possible. We do not want the engine to warm up too fast during this process, so turn it off as soon as it fires.

If you notice the battery voltage falling, or the engine begins to crank more slowly, then you may need to connect a battery starter charger to ensure that the starting is not being affected by low battery voltage. This process can take some time, and you will need to leave the engine to cool for a minimum of twelve hours before repeating this.

We spend at least one week setting cold starts on every engine management system we install, and even then we sometimes need to revisit this when the weather turns colder.

Priming Pulse

The priming pulse is used to aid starting from stone cold by injecting a small amount of fuel from the injectors when you turn on the ignition. When the ECU first powers up, it commands a small pulse-width to the fuel injectors to wet the manifold slightly with fuel. Most engines do not require a priming pulse beyond 30°C coolant temperature. Some ECU systems give the option of a different priming pulse, depending upon coolant temperature; other systems will just use one priming-pulse figure. If you give the engine too large a priming pulse, then it will flood easily, while too small a priming pulse and it may take a little longer to start.

When setting from scratch it is easiest to set this to something small, such as 2ms, and come back to this once the cranking pulse-width and after-start enrichment has been set correctly for all temperatures. It is easy to compensate for too small a cranking pulse-width by increasing the priming pulse, but this is not ideal, as too large a priming pulse makes the engine particularly prone to flooding or even hydro-locking. The priming feature can be used to guide your cranking pulse-width settings from stone cold.

If you are not sure if the engine requires a larger or smaller cranking pulse-width, simply set the priming pulse to at least 2ms and turn the ignition on and off several times: if the engine is quicker to start, then the engine requires a larger cranking pulse-width, but if it is now harder to start or becomes flooded, then it requires a smaller cranking pulse-width.

CHAPTER 13

LIQUID PETROLEUM GAS

The use of LPG with the Rover V8 is a fairly common practice, but still widely misunderstood. Many LPG systems have acquired a bad reputation due to poor quality components and less than optimum installation or set-up. As a result, many people are convinced that a large power reduction is inevitable when converting to LPG. This need not be the case – for example, our own Range Rover 4.6-litre engine only loses 1.6 per cent power over petrol when fully optimized.

LPG systems and kits fall into a very budget-conscious market, and many suppliers are competing to produce cheaper kits. Unfortunately, the old adage that you get what you pay for is often true with vehicle components. Nevertheless, this situation has improved considerably in recent years, with the demand for better quality systems and components driving product development. It is now possible to purchase and assemble a system that is both highly functional and cost-effective. However, the situation is confusing when it comes to component selection, so we will discuss both complete kits and individual components to try and make things clearer.

LPG has a slightly lower calorific content than petrol, resulting in reduced fuel efficiency when compared to petrol: there is simply less energy contained in each litre of fuel. There is approximately 27 per cent less energy in a litre of LPG than a litre of petrol though, interestingly, an optimally tuned LPG-powered engine does not need to suffer the full 27 per cent reduction in fuel efficiency that might be expected. This is for a number of reasons. LPG has a higher octane rating than standard unleaded petrol, with much greater knock resistance. The octane rating of LPG is approximately 110 RON compared to 95–97 RON for pump petrol. This higher octane allows us to run higher compression ratios and a

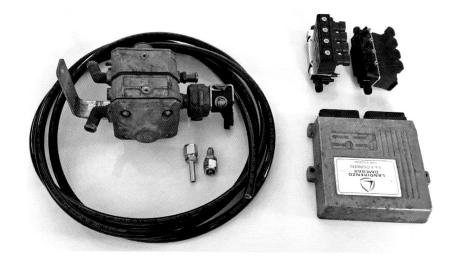

LPG components.

more aggressive ignition advance curve, with less risk of pre-ignition.

Another factor is the combustion characteristics of this fuel. LPG is usually introduced to the engine as a vapour rather than a liquid. Air and LPG in vapour form makes a much more homogenous mix than air and petrol. With petrol we can get cool pockets in the cylinder where the liquid fuel does not fully vaporize, or it separates from the air, resulting in unburned pockets of fuel. With LPG, the gas tends to mix much more thoroughly with the air, resulting in far fewer unburned hydrocarbons out of the exhaust than with petrol. This is evident when we look at the exhaust emissions of a vehicle running on LPG, as it has far lower HC emissions (it has far lower emissions of most other pollutants, too). The downside of injecting a vapour fuel is that we do not get the desirable evaporative cooling effect of injecting a liquid fuel such as petrol. This evaporative cooling effect

increases the charge density and therefore the power output.

Interestingly, the auto-ignition point of LPG is nearly twice that of petrol.

These different factors mean that the ignition advance requirements of LPG are completely different to the ignition advance requirements of petrol. For this reason, it is essential to be able to modify the ignition advance throughout the engine speed and load range in order to optimize the performance and fuel economy on LPG. This is difficult to achieve with a distributor set-up but straightforward with a fully programmable ignition system.

TYPES OF LPG SYSTEM

Most LPG systems are very similar in layout and operation, with a few slight variations. Almost all commercially available systems introduce the gas to the engine as a vapour, although there are also a

Table 27: Energy content, auto-ignition temperature and octane of various fuels

Fuel	Typical energy content (higher heating value)	Auto-ignition temperature	Typical octane (RON)
Petrol	32,232 BTU/ltr	257°C	95
Methanol	17,226 BTU/ltr	481°C	117
LPG	24,153 BTU/ltr	454–510°C	110

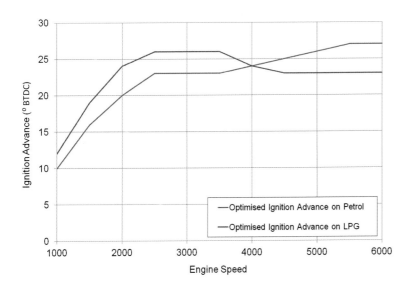

Ignition timing requirements of petrol versus LPG.

few liquid injection systems now commercially available worldwide.

Mixer Ring Systems

The most basic systems comprise an LPG tank, multivalve, 6–8mm liquid feedpipe, vaporizer (known as a reducer), and a mixer ring to introduce the gas into the engine's intake. Almost all carburettor-equipped engines will use this layout, although fuel-injected engines can also be equipped with mixer ring LPG systems.

In addition to these LPG components, there will also be a changeover switch to open and shut the LPG solenoids via a relay. A carburettor-equipped engine will then have a means of switching off the fuel supply to the carburettors, usually with a timed delay between the changeover. Many fuel-injected engines will require 'emulators' to fool the existing engine management system into thinking that the petrol injectors are still being operated.

When the LPG solenoids are activated, liquid propane will flow out of the multivalve on the tank, to the LPG vaporizer. The vaporizer uses coolant heat to convert this liquid propane into gas vapour and regulate the vapour pressure. The vaporizer is connected to the mixer ring via a low-pressure vapour hose. The mixer ring is very similar in construction and appearance to the gas ring on your gas stove. This is placed in the intake between the air filter and carburettor or throttle body, and forms a venturi, much like a carburettor. The pressure drop across the mixer ring draws gas out of the vaporizer. The vaporizer contains a diaphragm that operates much like a sea-diver's demand valve: the greater the engine draws on the intake, the greater the gas delivery.

These systems are crude but effective. They are simple to install and tune for anyone familiar with basic carburettor tuning. There are usually two or three adjustment screws for adjusting the fuel mixture. One adjustable restrictor, much like a tap between the mixer ring and vaporizer, alters the full load fuel mixture by increasing or reducing the gas flow. This can be thought of as equivalent to the main jet in a carburettor. There is a pressure screw on the vaporizer that alters the pressure of the vapour. This adjustment alters the fuel mixture throughout the engine load and speed range from idle to full load.

Some vaporizers also have an idle mixture screw that alters the fuel mixture only when the diaphragm is in the idle position. The mixer ring, by design, creates a pressure drop in the air intake, and this reduces airflow into the engine, causing a performance loss at higher engine speeds. This can be reduced to a minimum by correctly sizing the mixer ring: too small and the engine's airflow is choked, too large and it is virtually impossible to get the air-fuel mixture correct, so the engine will run lean.

These systems tend to like a certain restriction in the intake, therefore free-flow air filters (for example K&N) will require a smaller mixer ring to ensure that there is an adequate pressure drop, thus negating the benefits of the free flowing filter. As a guide, Table 28 shows the correct size mixer rings for your application.

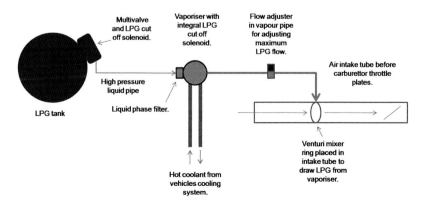

Mixer ring LPG system.

Table 28: Mixer ring diameters

Brake horsepower at flywheel	Single mixer ring	Twin mixer rings
130–190	32–40mm	28–30mm
190–270	40–50mm	30–32mm
270+	Single ring unsuitable. Size for required gas flow would not give a strong enough metering signal to the vaporizer to fuel correctly at low engine speeds and loads	32–40mm

Note: There is no such thing as a completely unrestrictive mixer ring. The ideal size will minimize loss of airflow whilst still maintaining a good metering signal to enable the engine to fuel correctly at lower engine speeds and loads.

Multipoint LPG Injection Systems

The majority of modern LPG conversions will employ a multipoint injection system that operates alongside, or 'piggybacks' off the original petrol-injection system. Multipoint systems comprise an LPG tank, multivalve, 6–8mm liquid LPG feed pipe, an injection vaporizer, a set of LPG injectors, a wiring loom and an ECU unit. Most of these kits employ an automatic changeover function that will switch from petrol to LPG and back automatically, depending upon changeover switch position, coolant temperature and gas pressure or temperature.

Typically when the user selects the LPG position on the changeover switch, the LPG ECU will moni-tor when the correct coolant temperature has been reached, and will activate the LPG solenoids. When the LPG solenoids are activated, liquid propane will flow out of the multivalve on the tank to the LPG vaporizer. The vaporizer will use coolant heat to convert this liquid propane into gas vapour, and will regulate the vapour pressure to approximately 0.8 to 2.5-bar (12–36psi), depending on the set-up. This vapour is supplied from the vaporizer to the LPG injectors. If there is sufficient gas pressure detected in the LPG injector rails, then the LPG ECU will switch on the LPG injectors and simultaneously switch off the petrol injectors.

The original petrol injectors are connected via the LPG ECU and its internal emulators. The emulator's purpose is to fool the original petrol-injection system into believing it is still firing the petrol injectors without activating any fault codes within the original petrol ECU. Most LPG ECUs fall into the category of piggyback ECUs, as they intercept the petrol injector

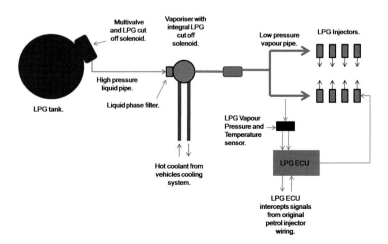

Sequential LPG injection system.

signals from the original engine management system and apply a correction factor to provide the correct signal for the LPG injectors. The petrol EFI system continues operating the ignition and firing the LPG injectors as though it is running on petrol.

The factory lambda sensors and closed-loop fuel correction within the petrol EFI system will increase or decrease the injection duty cycle as normal to correct the fuel mixture within normal limits. If, for some reason, the gas pressure falls below the pre-set minimum, such as running out of LPG or insufficient gas flow under high demand, then the LPG ECU will reinstate normal petrol injection and switch off the LPG solenoids. If the LPG changeover switch remains in the LPG position, then it will automatically repeat this process as soon as it detects that sufficient coolant temperature and/or gas pressure has been restored.

LPG Kits

A complete LPG kit with all the required components is usually the preferred route for most people. There is a bewildering number of kits available, with some kits even having several different options for injectors, vaporizers or tanks. Which kits work well and which do not? It is beyond the scope of this book to discuss every kit that we have ever tested, but there are a few names that are typically well regarded, such as Prins, BRC, LPG-Tech, OMVL, Stag.

It is worth remembering that the quality of the installation and tuning is as important as the brand or make of the hardware. If you are getting the installation work done by somebody else, then it is worth listening to their advice on component selection, as they will know what they are familiar working with, and will have experience with what works for them. Be clear about your criteria and ask questions. If you require an LPG system that can operate at full load without switching back to petrol, then make this clear.

A surprising number of systems under-spec the components, as they assume that you only want to use LPG for gentle economy driving, so use cheaper components that are unable to keep up with the demand of a large V8 engine running at wide-open

throttle. The attitude 'it's LPG, so why do you want performance?' is common amongst installers, and contributes to the generally poor reputation of LPG. With correct component choices there is no need to accept these compromises. We will discuss the individual component choices below and you can use this to help guide your kit selection.

LPG COMPONENTS

With the correct components it is perfectly feasible to assemble your own LPG kit that is both highly effective and cost competitive. Your component choices will be driven by your requirements.

LPG ECU

There is a large choice of highly effective ECU types available, with most being the 'piggyback' or 'slave' type, which operate in tandem with the original engine management system. There are, however, standalone systems available that can control LPG injection on carburettor vehicles. There are also completely standalone engine management systems, such as our own Canems Dual-Fuel ECU kit, which will control all engine management functions on both LPG and petrol, including full ignition control.

Piggyback LPG ECU.

Canems Dual-Fuel ECU.

When choosing an ECU, look for interface software that is easy to use and tune. Your choice will be largely dictated by compatibility with your existing fuel system and associated hardware. Some ECU types have greater flexibility than others, so if you are assembling your own collection of LPG components then you should check to make sure the ECU you choose is capable of controlling your choice of hardware. Any decent system should ideally have an 'open-loop' injection map for tuning the injector duty cycles when the engine is running at full throttle and the petrol-injection system is disregarding the oxygen sensor (lambda) feedback.

Many 'self-tuning' systems are heavily reliant on the lambda trims to bring the fuel mixture within specified limits. This is useful when the engine is running part throttle and the factory engine management system is in 'closed-loop' operation. Under heavy loading, however, most factory systems switch to 'open-loop' fuelling and disregard the oxygen sensors, as the fuel mixture needs to be much richer than stoichiometric to allow greater power production and cool running. We have seen some LPG systems that run very lean (or rich) under these open-loop conditions.

Some installers do not even tune the 'open-loop' fuel mixtures at all and just use the 'closed-loop' lambda trims to correct the mixture under part throttle conditions, and simply ignore the engine's critical full throttle fuel mixture requirements. The

combination of lean fuel mixtures and the naturally elevated combustion temperatures that are experienced on LPG can be very damaging to the engine, particularly to the valves and valve seats.

LPG Injector Filtration

In addition to the liquid-phase LPG filters, it is necessary to install vapour-phase filters between the LPG vaporizer and the LPG injectors. These filters are critical to the longevity and correct operation of any LPG injector. There are essentially two types of vapour-phase filter: paper cartridge and coalescing filters. Paper cartridge filters are old technology and do not adequately remove sticky oily impurities from LPG. These sticky impurities are often referred to as 'heavy ends', and pass easily through the paper element when suspended in the gas. Such impurities wreak havoc with injector operation by gumming up the moving internals of the injectors, causing them to stick, especially when cold.

The recommended type of filter is the coalescing type that spins or centrifuges the vapour, keeping such deposits in the filter housing. These operate in much the same way as an air-water separator on a workshop air compressor. They are highly effective and should be considered an essential fitment on your LPG set-up. There are a few coalescing filters on the market such as the LPGTECH Perfect Blue filter, E.G. Filter and Ultra 360.

Coalescing LPG filter.

LPG Injectors

There are no other individual components in an LPG injection system that have more of an impact on performance, drivability and cold weather performance than the LPG injectors, so it pays to do your research here and get the best you can afford. Many LPG injectors often struggle to meter LPG accurately at low injector pulse-widths and low engine speeds.

Keihin Injectors

These Japanese LPG injectors are without doubt the most highly regarded injector on the market. They are suitable for LPG, CNG and hydrogen. Their cold weather performance is excellent, and their flow is linear right down to low duty cycles. The injectors are of the peak and hold design, drawing 4 amps at peak and 1.5 amps in the hold phase. Their resistance is 1.25 ohms and they are available in various sizes – for example 32cc, 42cc, 52cc, 62cc, 73cc and 100cc. They can operate in a temperature range of −40°C to +120°C. These are the basis for the Dutch Prins LPG kit, and arguably are the main reason for the kit's great reputation and performance.

Pros: Good linearity, accurate, fast response and excellent cold weather performance. Good reliability.

Cons: Expensive compared to other brands, and incompatible with many LPG ECU types due to their low impedance (resistance) and unusually high current draw.

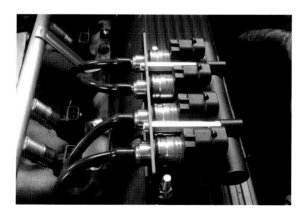

LPG injectors.

Barracuda Injectors

These Polish designed and built injectors are amongst our favourites. They are great value for money, offering a combination of excellent linearity at low duty cycles, good cold weather performance, and a very high flow rate (particularly with the high flow or 'BF' version). These injectors are also of the 'peak and hold' type, drawing 4 amps at peak and 2 amps to hold. Their 1.9 ohms resistance makes them compatible with more ECU types than the Keihin type. These injectors are fast operating with a 1.9ms opening time and 1.2ms closing time. They operate from −20°C to +120°C, and are one of the few LPG injectors we have tested that are happy to start from cold in sub-freezing temperatures.

These units utilize a modern, anti-freeze, frictionless coating that prevents the sticking issues typically experienced with LPG injectors in cold weather. These units are available in normal flow and large flow ('BF') versions that are capable of a maximum of 115 NL/min (nanolitres per minute) and 130 NL/min respectively. These units are calibrated to the individual engine's flow requirements, with removable nozzles that set the maximum flow rate.

Pros: Outstanding value for money, good linearity and fast response. Great cold weather performance. Good reliability.

Cons: Sensitive to impurities in the fuel, and must be used with a coalescing-type vapour phase filter to ensure longevity. They have a higher current draw than some other types of injector.

Hana Injectors

These Korean-built injectors are similar in construction to the Keihins. They have good linearity and relatively high flow rates. The Hana injectors also have fast opening and closing times of approximately 2.1ms and 1.2ms. There are different flow rates of injector available, much like the Keihins, and these different flow injectors are designated with a colour (for example Hana Blue or Hana Gold). The Hana Gold injector can be further calibrated with different size nozzles. These injectors also operate on the 'peak and hold' principle, with 4 amps at peak and 2 amps in the hold phase. Although they are very similar to the Keihins in construction and performance, their cold weather performance is inferior to both the Keihin and the Barracuda types. The Hana injectors offer great value for money and are an excellent budget choice, provided that you do not require the LPG system to operate in freezing conditions.

Pros: Good value. Good linearity and relatively fast response. High flow rates available.

Cons: Sensitive to impurities in the fuel, and must be used with a coalescing-type vapour phase filter to ensure longevity. They have a higher current draw than some other types of injector. They do not work well in very low temperatures.

OMVL Fast Reg Injectors

These LPG injectors are included here as a budget option as they offer outstanding value for money. They have 3-ohm coils, making them highly compatible with most ECU types. Their cold weather performance is excellent, and they can be easily stripped and serviced due to their very simple construction. They offer a combination of reasonably accurate fuelling control, good low temperature performance and longevity for a low price. The main criticism is that the body is made of very weak plastic and it is very easy to snap the vapour hose-tails when fitting the calibration jets or vapour hoses if you do not take great care when installing or removing.

Pros: Very low price, good cold weather performance, simple construction and ease of servicing.

Cons: Cheap plastic construction; easily broken when fitting or removing calibration jets or vapour hoses.

Vaporizer (Reducer)

The vaporizer's job, as the name suggests, is to convert the liquid gas into a vapour. As well as this, it needs to regulate the gas flow and pressure

to match the requirements of the engine. There are a great number of different vaporizers available, with a range of different sizes and flow rates. Mixer ring systems will often use two, or even three stage diaphragms to ensure accurate gas delivery under different loads. These multistage vaporizers are ideal for large V8 engines running a mixer ring set-up. Most vaporizers are rated in terms of horsepower or KW rather than their flow rate. We recommend over-sizing your vaporizer by at least 10 per cent to ensure it can keep the gas pressure at the injectors stable under full load. Gas pressure should ideally not drop by more than a few psi when under full load. A drop of more than approximately 20 per cent in gas pressure under load indicates that the vaporizer or gas supply is insufficient for the engine's demands.

LPG Tank, Fittings and Pipework

The size and shape of your LPG tank will be determined by your particular vehicle and the space available. All LPG tanks must be R6701 approved and meet the LPG COP 2 standard. All LPG tanks include the following functions:

- A filling hose connection with an 80 per cent shut-off to allow for thermal expansion within the tank
- An over-pressure relief valve that opens at approximately 27-bar to prevent explosion in case of fire or excess heat

LPG vaporizer.

- A shut-off valve to close the tank – this is usually an electronic solenoid, but many also incorporate a manual shut-off valve
- A fuel gauge to give an indication of the amount of LPG left in the tank
- Any tank that is mounted inside the vehicle must also have all valves and connections enclosed within a gas-tight cover that is vented to avoid the possibility of leaking LPG entering the car

There are tanks available in just about every configuration and size. LPG tanks can be divided into two types: single-hole and four-hole.

Single-Hole Tanks

Single-hole tanks use a single multivalve to contain all these functions. The filling hose connection is smaller than with a four-hole tank, and this makes filling much slower than with petrol or a four-hole tank. The outlet on the multivalve is often smaller than the four-hole types, and this can cause a flow restriction issue at high engine speeds on higher output engines. Our own Range Rover Classic 4.6-litre engine experienced this problem at approximately 270bhp and 5,200rpm. At the time there was no multivalve available for our tank that could flow sufficient liquid gas, so we fitted a four-hole type. An alternative would have been to fit a second single-hole tank and link the two together. High-flow single-hole multivalves are now available on the market. Single-hole tanks are cheaper to buy and often more compact due to the smaller area required for these vital functions.

Four-Hole Tanks

Four-hole tanks, as their name suggests, have a separate hole for each function rather than combining these into a single unit. The outlet is often larger on four-hole tanks, meaning they can flow more liquid gas. This makes them more suitable for high output engines. Their main advantage is that they can use a much larger filling hose connection, which speeds up refilling times considerably.

LPG Pipework

LPG-resistant vapour hose should be used for all low pressure LPG vapour connections, as normal rubber hose degrades rapidly in the presence of LPG, cracking and eventually leaking.

6/8mm copper: 6mm copper pipe is really only sufficient for low output engines up to approximately 190bhp. 8mm copper pipe can be used on higher output engines. Copper pipe is gradually going out of favour and being replaced by the easier to install, and higher flowing, polyflex pipe.

6/8mm polyflex: Over a length the 6mm polyflex pipe has a similar flow rate to an 8mm copper pipe, due to its reduced flow restriction when bent. We use 8mm polyflex pipe on all our high output engines, as this has the greatest flow rate of all and there is little price difference between the 6mm and 8mm pipework.

LPG tank.

LPG pipework.

LPG IGNITION REQUIREMENTS

The real Achilles heel of many LPG conversions is not the fuel hardware at all, but the existing ignition system. The need for an excellent ignition system cannot be over-emphasized, and the requirements for an effective ignition system for LPG can be broken down into two elements for clarity: ignition energy and ignition timing.

Ignition Energy

An ignition system that is adequate for petrol is often woefully inadequate for LPG. The ignition requirements of LPG and CNG are very different to petrol. The energy required to ignite LPG is much greater. There are a number of reasons for this. Firstly, the ignition temperature of LPG is almost twice that of regular petrol. Secondly, LPG is usually a dry, vaporous fuel that provides much more electrical resistance than the 'wet' air-fuel mix found inside a petrol engine. In addition to this, LPG typically burns hotter than petrol, resulting in higher combustion temperatures; this increased heat also creates more resistance to the spark inside the cylinder.

At first, the obvious move seems to be to provide a more powerful spark by providing a higher secondary voltage. There are many ways of achieving this, including more powerful coils and ignition amplifiers, and distributor-less ignition systems that employ multiple coils. However, the main point here is that we require more ignition energy *at the spark-plug electrode.* It is all very well providing more ignition energy, but we need to ensure that it is actually delivered to the spark-plug electrode inside the cylinder. As we all know, electricity takes the easiest path to ground, and unfortunately the easiest path is not always the plug electrode inside the cylinder.

If the electrical resistance across the plug electrode inside the cylinder is greater than the resistance of the plug lead insulation or the spark plug's ceramic insulator, then the spark will simply track down the plug lead or insulator to ground. Extra ignition energy will simply make this worse, therefore throwing extra ignition energy at the problem will often not help. The resistance at the plug electrode varies as the engine is running. Extra engine load (more throttle opening), for example, will increase the plug-electrode resistance, as will increased heat inside the cylinder. A leaner fuel mixture will also increase resistance. Consequently, the engine will only occasionally misfire. These sporadic or 'micro' misfires, as we refer to them, may not be obvious unless severe, but will serve to reduce engine power, increase fuel consumption, and generally make the engine's running less smooth.

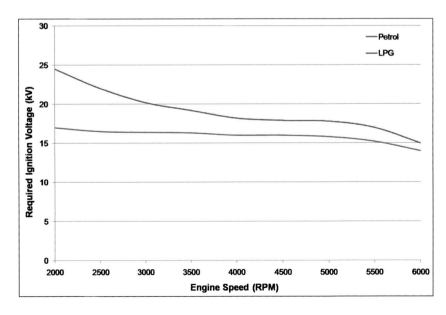

Ignition voltage required to ignite petrol and LPG.

Quite often the user is unaware that there is a problem, or will blame the occasional backfiring and lumpy running on the LPG hardware or installation. Many users simply resign themselves to the fact that LPG running is not as powerful or smooth as it could be because they don't realize there is a problem. To see this for yourself, you can run your LPG-powered engine with the bonnet open on a very dark night and look carefully around the coils, ignition leads and spark plugs, and watch the pretty blue lightshow!

WARNING! Be very careful to keep your body and hands away from any ignition components and rotating parts. The voltage here can be in excess of 40KV and can be fatal!

Every one of these blue flashes or bolts of electricity that you see is a missed ignition event. It only takes ten of these in every hundred ignition events (not at all uncommon) to be losing 10 per cent power and efficiency. So what is the solution? The solution depends upon where the ignition is tracking to ground. The first thing is to have a very good set of ignition leads routed as far from any metal components as is practical. Secondly, we need spark plugs that offer less resistance at the electrode.

Ignition Leads

Standard carbon-string ignition leads offer the essential level of resistance for electronic fuel-injected (EFI) engines, but they are prone to rapid deterioration, resulting in excessive resistances

over time. Copper-core leads are out of the question for any vehicle fitted with an ECU. The best solution that we have found to date are the excellent spiral-wound types made by the likes of Accel, Moroso and Taylor, to name but a few. These use a metal wire that is spiral-wound around a strong core, which offers less resistance and greater durability than the standard carbon-string types. They give sufficient resistance to ensure that our ECUs are kept happy and free from electrical interference. Double or triple silicone insulation helps to prevent electrical tracking.

Spark Plugs

We often find that once we have increased the ignition energy and fitted a set of good quality ignition leads, the ignition can be clearly seen tracking down the plug's ceramic insulator. We need to find a way of reducing the resistance at the spark-plug electrode inside the running engine. One common solution is to reduce the spark-plug gap by 0.2mm to a minimum of 0.6mm. This is a compromise as it reduces the duration of the spark. Another option is to run a non-resistive spark plug. However, this can play havoc with ECU-controlled systems, in the same fashion as very low resistance ignition leads, so it is not recommended on EFI engines.

The best solution we have found is to use an iridium-tipped spark plug such as the NGK BPR6EIX in place of the standard BPR6ES. The iridium tip can be made much thinner than a standard plug electrode, whilst still retaining the necessary durability and strength. This thinner electrode reduces the electrical resistance considerably, without having to resort to smaller plug gaps. We have found that an iridium-tipped plug with a 0.8mm plug gap requires less ignition energy, and suffers from fewer micromisfires, than a non-iridium-tipped plug with a 0.6mm gap.

Many spark-plug manufacturers, such as NGK, are aware of the problems with LPG ignition systems and now offer LPG-specific spark plugs, such as the BPR6EIX LPG. Whilst being undoubtedly effective, these are often very expensive and we have found them to be little better than a standard iridium

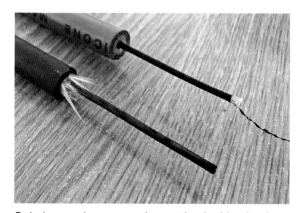

Spiral-wound versus carbon-string ignition lead.

electrode plug. Straight platinum-tipped plugs (as opposed to a platinum/iridium combination) are not recommended as these can actually increase the resistance across the spark plugs electrode, exacerbating the ignition issues that we experience with LPG.

Ignition Timing and LPG

A lot of power and efficiency is lost on conversions that are still using the original petrol ignition advance curve for LPG running. LPG requires more ignition advance at lower engine speeds than petrol, but conversely, it needs the same or less ignition advance at higher engine speeds. This is due to the fact that LPG and air burns more slowly than petrol and air at lower speeds, but faster at higher speeds. This means that most LPG-converted cars are running over-advanced at higher engine speeds and retarded at lower engine speeds, leading to very high combustion temperatures. These high temperatures can potentially lead to bore scuffing and burnt exhaust valves after high mileage. Exact ignition timing requirements naturally depend on engine specification.

Table 29: Example of ignition timing requirements of petrol versus LPG with a modified 4.6-litre Rover V8

Engine speed (rpm)	Optimized ignition advance on petrol (° BTDC)	Optimized ignition advance on LPG (° BTDC)
1,000	10	12
2,000	20	24
3,000	23	26
4,000	24	24
5,000	26	24
6,000	27	24

LPG AND ENGINE WEAR

There is a common misconception that LPG damages valve seats, exhaust valves, cylinder bores and valve guides due to lower lubrication levels in a 'dry' gas. Petrol actually has very little lubrication ability and will break down lubrication in the cylinder bores when run excessively rich, leading to 'bore wash'. Many LPG-converted engines are not set up correctly and are often found to be running retarded at low engine speeds and/ or over-advanced at higher speeds, sometimes with lean fuel mixtures further compounding these problems.

Valve seat erosion can be a real issue on some engines (for example the Jaguar AJV8) due to a combination of soft valve seats, higher exhaust gas temperatures, and the lack of cooling given by a non-liquid fuel. This is not a major problem on a correctly set up Rover V8 engine however, due to its relatively hard valve seat material.

In fact, LPG can actually reduce engine wear as it is a very clean-burning fuel that does not produce the same carbon soot, acids and other corrosive by-products that we get with petrol combustion. All piston engines suffer from a certain amount of blow-by past the piston rings. With a petrol engine we get a certain amount of fuel trapped between the top of the piston crown and the first piston ring. This fuel does not fully combust as it is no longer a homogeneous mixture of air and fuel. It works its way past the piston rings and ends up in the sump, where over time it breaks down and thins out the lubricating properties of the oil. With an LPG system we do not have this issue, and the oil stays clean and at the correct viscosity for much longer.

CHAPTER 14

FORCED INDUCTION

A close ancestor of the Rover V8, the Oldsmobile 215, was in one of the first ever turbocharged production cars – the 1962 Oldsmobile Jetfire. Despite this, it is only in more recent years that turbocharging and supercharging have become more commonplace with the Rover V8 engine. This is largely due to the intro-duction of modern programmable engine manage-ment systems, giving full control over the fuel quantity and ignition timing throughout the entire engine load and speed range, which allows us to convert these engines to forced induction, with fewer compromises and less risk of engine destruction during use.

Oldsmobile Jetfire engine bay. JAMES
PERKINS, OLDSJETFIRE.COM

Oldsmobile Jetfire. JAMES PERKINS,
OLDSJETFIRE.COM

All methods of forced induction involve the process of force feeding the intake system with additional oxygen, either by means of compressing the intake air or by injecting an additional fuel that contains the additional oxygen (that is, nitrous oxide). If the air is being compressed, this is done using either a supercharger or a turbocharger; this compressed air is commonly referred to as 'boost'. This term 'boost' is essentially how much the air has been compressed beyond atmospheric air pressure. So an engine running on 5psi of boost will actually have approximately 19.5psi of intake air pressure inside the intake manifold at peak boost. This is because atmospheric air pressure is approximately 1-bar, or 14.5psi, giving the total of 19.5psi.

MECHANICAL REQUIREMENTS FOR FORCED INDUCTION

It should be obvious that the main mechanical requirement is having an engine that is strong enough to take the expected increase in power. Compression ratios should be suitably matched to the boost and airflow levels. Suitable static compression ratios are suggested in the table below; these assume that the camshaft specification is sensible, and that the dynamic compression is not unusually high, relative to the static compression. This table is a rough guide, and also assumes that you are using fuel with a 95–97 RON octane rating.

When building an engine specifically for forced induction, there are several considerations regarding component selection. The bottom end of the

Table 30: Compression ratio versus maximum boost level

Static compression ratio	Maximum recommended boost level
9.75:1	5psi
9.35:1	10psi
8.8:1	15psi
8:1	20psi
7.5:1	25psi
7:1	30psi

engine, including pistons, connecting rods and crankshaft, needs to be strong enough to handle the additional stresses involved. Fortunately the Rover V8 is relatively strong in these areas, and it is only once the boost and airflow exceeds a certain level that we need to consider forged pistons, stronger connecting rods and so on.

It is commonly believed that the airflow of the cylinder head is not as important, as we are able to overcome any inherent restrictions with boost. Whilst it is true that we can still make good power despite these restrictions, an engine equipped with forced induction will still benefit from increased airflow through the cylinder head. Additional pressure may help overcome airflow restrictions, but will also generate heat, which will serve to reduce air density. Engines with forced induction will almost always benefit from extra exhaust flow, as additional exhaust gases will be produced from the extra air-fuel mixture that is combusted.

It is a commonly held belief that the camshaft fitted should be relatively mild, with low levels of valve overlap. This is true if there is a high level of exhaust back pressure, as is often the case with many forced induction engines. The bottom line here is that the camshaft's specification should be related to the pressure ratio between intake and exhaust. If we can achieve a 1:1 pressure ratio between intake and exhaust, then everything that applies to normally aspirated tuning will apply to our supercharged or turbocharged engine. For example, if you had 10psi of intake pressure, then you would have no more than 10psi of exhaust back pressure between the engine and the turbocharger. For those seeking the highest levels of performance it is worth monitoring the exhaust back pressure by making a small pressure tapping into the exhaust manifold, and running a length of metal pipe to a pressure transducer or pressure gauge.

Many engines will not achieve this 1:1 pressure ratio however, and in these cases valve overlap should be kept to a minimum. Most engines with forced induction can achieve the level of performance required without resorting to high overlap camshafts.

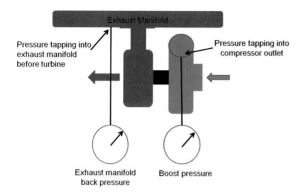

How to use pressure tappings to measure the pressure ratio on a turbocharged engine.

So how much boost or additional airflow can the Rover V8 safely handle? This depends on both the specification and the state of health of the engine: thus a healthy, otherwise standard, non-cross-bolted engine can have a moderate sized supercharger or turbocharger installed, running approximately 5–7psi of boost, provided the fuel and ignition requirements are met. With careful fuel and ignition management we have seen stock engines tolerate more than 10psi of boost. A cross-bolted engine with forged pistons will usually handle in excess of 15psi of boost.

It is important to note at this stage that, although we often talk about boost, it is actually airflow that is the significant factor when it comes to making power with forced induction. Different forced induction systems or set-ups can actually give higher airflow, and therefore more power, for the same amount or even less boost than other systems. There are a number of factors in play here, including compressor design, intake system design, and so on.

FUEL AND IGNITION REQUIREMENTS FOR FORCED INDUCTION

Modern engine management systems can provide distributor-less ignition, programmable fuel injection, and closed-loop knock control. As modern specification turbochargers, superchargers and the associated equipment are now relatively cost effec-

tive, forced induction on the Rover V8 is a much more realistic option. This is reflected in the fact that both supercharger and turbocharger conversions for the Rover V8 are now being offered by specialists such as SC Power, Torque V8, Powers Performance, and ourselves at Lloyd Specialist Developments Ltd. Prior to this, specialists and enthusiasts alike had to control the ignition timing and fuelling via mechanical fuel and ignition systems, leading to significant compromises between longevity, drivability and performance.

Fuel systems need to be able to cater for the wide range of fuel mixture and fuel flow requirements. A boosted engine may need to run as lean as 14.7:1 AFR at idle, with very little fuel flow, to 11:5 AFR under boost with a very large fuel flow. In some cases even modern electronic fuel injectors can struggle to satisfy both the idle and full boost fuel requirements. One solution to this is staged injection, with lower flow rate injectors to cope with the off-boost and idle requirements, and higher flow rate injectors to provide the fuel flow needed at high boost and high engine speeds.

Ignition systems need to be able to cater for both the naturally aspirated and the boosted ignition requirements of the engine. At part throttle and lower engine speeds, the engine may require as much as 44 degrees of ignition advance to provide efficient combustion, particularly if it has a low compression ratio. However, at the same engine speeds it may require as little as 16 degrees advance when placed under wide-open throttle and at maximum boost. This wide range of ignition advance requirements is very difficult, if not impossible, to satisfy accurately with a conventional distributor-based ignition system. With careful modification it is possible to satisfy the requirements of the boosted engine, but then a great deal of efficiency is often lost when driven at part throttle and off boost.

In addition to the ignition timing of these boosted engines, we should also consider the necessary ignition energy requirements. In summary, the higher the cylinder pressure, the greater the ignition energy that is required to initiate combustion. The higher cylinder pressures resulting from forced

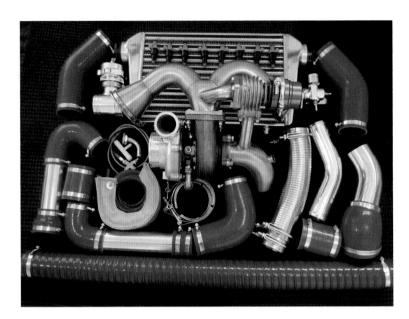

Turbocharger kit for TVR Chimaera or Griffith. EANN WHALLEY, *TORQUE V8*

induction require more ignition energy to generate a strong spark in the cylinder. A lack of ignition energy is experienced as a high-boost misfire. This is commonly, yet erroneously, referred to as the boost 'blowing out the spark'.

Possible solutions include more powerful or multiple ignition coils, increased coil dwell (within safe limits), and smaller spark-plug gaps. Plug gaps as small as 0.5–0.6mm are often used with heavily boosted engines. However, where possible we do not want to resort to such crutches, as smaller gaps can lead to reduced efficiency and difficulty starting. Distributor-less ignition systems with multiple coils are ideal in this regard, as each coil sits idle when charging, or 'dwells' for longer than a single coil. This results in greater ignition output. In addition to this, there are fewer places for the HT voltage to track to ground, such as the rotor arm or distributor cap on a distributor-equipped engine.

SUPERCHARGERS

There are two main types of supercharger used on Rover V8 engines: positive displacement and centrifugal. Positive displacement superchargers – such as Eaton M112, Roots – provide additional airflow at all engine speeds, whereas centrifugal superchargers – Rotrex, Procharger, Powerdyne – provide additional airflow in proportion to increased engine speed. Both types are effectively air pumps that are driven by the engine's crankshaft, usually via a drive belt.

On the face of it, the positive displacement supercharger appears to be superior for any application, as these provide additional airflow at all engine speeds. There are, however, many other factors that should be considered. Firstly, a centrifugal supercharger is more straightforward to install, as it is mounted in the manner of an external engine ancillary (for example alternator, power-steering pump) and often has its own external oil supply.

Secondly, as the centrifugal supercharger delivers the additional airflow at a higher engine speed, it transfers less shock loading on the drivetrain and transmission than a positive displacement supercharger. This is because the transmission and drivetrain are already rotating at a higher speed as the additional forces are applied, which is significantly less harsh than if the additional forces are applied with little or no rotational speed already present in the transmission. Naturally, this means that a centrifugal supercharger set-up can be used with a

Rotrex supercharger installation. SC
POWER

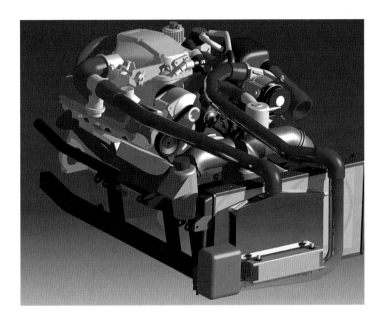

wider range of transmissions without risk of transmission failure, whereas a positive displacement supercharger conversion is more likely to require an upgraded transmission and drivetrain.

This benefit of the centrifugal supercharger over a positive displacement supercharger also applies when it comes to the traction limitations of a vehicle. If the available traction on a vehicle is exceeded, then the additional power and torque supplied at that particular engine speed is not only wasted, it is actually undesirable. In those cases it would be

more beneficial for the supercharger to provide the additional airflow, and therefore performance, at higher engine speeds where the vehicle is more likely to be travelling at some speed and hence less likely to lose traction.

Although the positive displacement supercharger is often harder to install, there are some applications where this set-up is more desirable. The additional airflow that is delivered at low engine speeds is ideal for heavier vehicles, towing and off road, where increased performance at low engine speeds

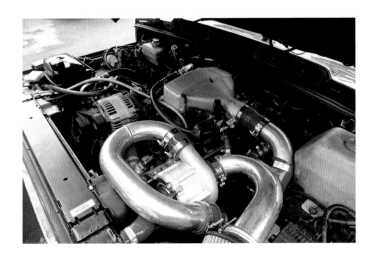

Rotrex supercharger on a Range Rover Classic.

Rotrex supercharger on a TVR Chimaera.

is the main requirement. Naturally, this means that the transmission and drivetrain needs to be strong enough to cope with the increased performance at low rotational speeds. With most standard Rover V8 applications (for example Land Rover) this means that some fairly expensive transmission upgrades may be required, with a positive displacement supercharger set-up.

Selecting the Correct Size Supercharger and Reading Compressor Maps

The first step before attempting to select the supercharger for your engine is to work out the pressure ratio and theoretical mass airflow. With this information you can choose the optimum supercharger, and make sense of the various supercharger compressor maps.

Pressure Ratio

The first step is to decide on your maximum boost pressure. This depends on your engine hardware, fuel octane available and desired power level. We can then calculate the pressure ratio. For example, if we have a maximum boost pressure of 14psi:

$$\text{Pressure Ratio} = \frac{\text{Ambient Pressure} + \text{Boost Pressure}}{\text{Ambient Pressure}}$$

Ambient pressure at sea level is approximately 14.7psi, therefore the pressure ratio with 14psi of boost equals 1.95.

Mass Airflow

In a naturally aspirated engine, volumetric airflow is often measured in cubic feet per minute (cfm). But once you begin compressing the air it has a different oxygen content, or air density, than the same volumetric airflow at ambient pressure. Because of this, it is commonly measured in terms of mass airflow. The formula we use for mass airflow in lb per minute is:

$$\frac{0.5 \times \text{CID} \times \text{Engine Speed}}{1728} \times \text{VE} \times \text{DR} \times .069$$

Where:
CID = cubic inch displacement
VE = volumetric efficiency
DR = density ratio

For example, we have a 4.8-litre Rover V8 rated at 250bhp at 5,000rpm in normally aspirated configuration. We want to boost it to a maximum of 14psi and use an intercooler to keep intake temperatures at a safe level.

Boost and airflow delivery of centrifugal versus positive displacement supercharger.

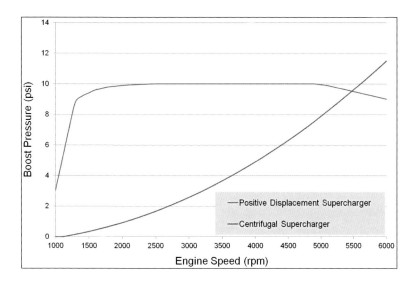

- This 4.8-litre engine has a cubic inch displacement (CID) of 292
- We will assume a volumetric efficiency of 70 per cent
- We will aim for a supercharger compressor efficiency of 70 per cent

We then use a density ratio chart to find our density ratio for an intercooled set-up running with a pressure ratio of 1.95:1. This density ratio chart plots air density as a function of compressor efficiency and pressure ratio.

By looking across the density ratio chart's X-axis to the 1.95:1 pressure ratio and extending up to the 70 per cent compressor efficiency line, we see that we have a density ratio (DR) of approximately 1.7. Applying these example values into the mass airflow equation shown above gives us the following:

$$\frac{0.5 \times 292 \times 5000}{1728} \times 0.7 \times 1.7 \times .069 = 34.7 \text{ lbs per minute}$$

(For reference, 1lb/min = 0.00756kg per sec (kg/s), so 34.7 × 0.00756 = 0.26kg/s.)

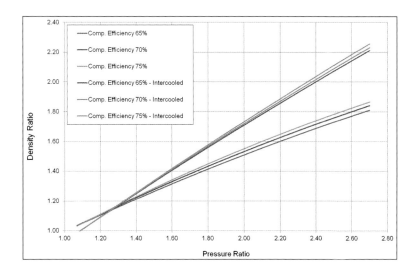

Density ratio chart for intercooled and non-intercooled supercharged engines.

Now we have calculated our pressure ratio and mass airflow we can select a suitable supercharger for our application. In this example we will look at the technical data for a Rotrex C38-61 supercharger. This has a maximum mass airflow of 0.48kg/s, a stated power range of 272 to 557bhp, and a maximum pressure ratio of 2.9:1. So this supercharger easily exceeds our requirements.

Looking at the compressor map, we want to find the point at which the mass airflow of 0.26kg/s meets the pressure ratio of 1.95:1. We can then see that this point falls within the 70 per cent compressor efficiency zone.

We can also see that our supercharger is operating near the centre of its peak efficiency. This means that at lower airflow and pressure ratios, we will still remain in a relatively high efficiency zone.

Surge and Choke
Surge occurs when the airflow 'stalls' at the compressor inlet due to lack of airflow, coupled with a pressure ratio that is too high. This effectively creates a momentary negative volume flow rate,

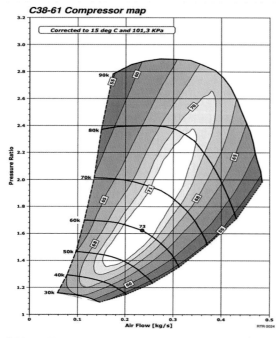

C38-61 Rotrex compressor map. ROTREX AS

which intermittently stops the supercharger from supplying the intake with compressed air. This stop-start behaviour is why it is commonly referred to as surging. If this occurs, the supercharger is probably too large for the airflow and pressure ratio requirements of your particular engine.

Surge can also occur when the throttle is closed and not enough pressure is released, creating a situation where the pressure ratio is too high for the amount of airflow passing through the supercharger. This is where a recirculation or blow-off valve is used, to release the excessive pressure and ensure that the supercharger does not suffer from surge.

The maximum airflow is limited by the 'choke line', which is the physical limitation that the compressor inlet imposes on the airflow. Put simply: the larger the compressor inlet, the greater the maximum airflow. If choke occurs, the supercharger is probably too small for your airflow and pressure ratio requirements.

Impellor Speed and Pulley Diameter
Next we must calculate our impellor speed to ensure that we are not under-driving or over-speeding our supercharger. The impellor speed is calculated by using the following formula:

$$\frac{\text{Max. Engine Speed (rpm)} \times \text{Crank Pulley Dia. (mm)} \times \text{Supercharger Ratio}}{\text{Supercharger Pulley Dia. (mm)}}$$

So if we go back to our example 4.8-litre with forged pistons, running with a maximum engine speed of 6,000rpm, and using a Rotrex C38-61 supercharger:

$$\frac{6000\text{rpm} \times 166\text{mm} \times 7.5}{85 \text{ mm}} = 87882\text{rpm impellor speed}$$

The maximum impellor speed for the C38 range of superchargers is 90,000rpm, so this combination of engine speed and pulley diameters is just about within specification in that respect. To maximize the potential of the Rotrex supercharger, we need to gear it so that maximum supercharger speed is close to maximum engine speed. If you under-drive it you will lower both the boost and airflow over the entire engine speed range.

RECIRCULATION OR BLOW-OFF VALVES

Also known as a 'dump valve', this is often used on both turbocharged and supercharged engines. Its function is to release excess pressure when the throttle is suddenly closed. Imagine that an engine is at full boost, maximum flow and the throttle is suddenly closed: the pressurized air will back up quickly against the closed throttle plate, putting the turbocharger or supercharger into surge. This air needs to go somewhere, and can momentarily flow backwards as the air pressure equalizes; however, the turbocharger or supercharger will still be spinning forwards, so the air will flow forwards, then backwards repeatedly until this energy dissipates. This surge can put damaging loads on the compressor and bearings, as well as heat up the intake air considerably.

The dump valve is a vacuum-activated valve placed between the compressor and throttle plate. When open, it releases or dumps the compressed air to atmosphere or back into the low pressure side of the compressor's intake. This valve is held shut by spring pressure, and is opened by a diaphragm connected to a vacuum pipe between the throttle plate and the engine. When the throttle is closed, vacuum is generated between the engine and the closed throttle plate. This vacuum pulls against the spring pressure to open the valve. The vacuum at which the valve opens is set by using different strength springs.

Dump valves can be the atmospheric type, which simply dump the boost pressure to atmosphere, or the recirculation type, which dump pressure back into the low pressure side or the air intake. Atmospheric dump valves create the characteristic 'whoosh' noise that many associate with high power turbocharged engines. The advantage is that any heated air is simply dumped to atmosphere and not recycled back into the engine's air intake. Atmospheric dump valves are not suitable for engines that use a mass airflow (MAF) sensor, because the valve will act as an air leak between the engine and MAF sensor, resulting in inaccurate fuelling.

Recirculation-type dump valves are also known as 'compressor bypass valves', and are much quieter in operation. It should be remembered that the dump valve will often be open and leaking air into the intake tract under certain off-boost, high-vacuum conditions such as part-throttle cruise or closed-throttle engine braking. Because of this, atmospheric dump valves should ideally be fitted with an air filter to prevent dust and dirt bypassing the main air filter. Our preference for road-going applications is usually a recirculation-type valve.

It is important to choose the correct spring strength in order to set up and tune these valves correctly. Too heavy a spring will prevent the valve from opening fully, causing the compressor to go into surge, while too weak a spring will allow the valve to leak boost pressure when under wide-open throttle.

TURBOCHARGERS

Turbochargers are turbines that are driven by waste exhaust gases. In other respects, the turbocharger is very similar in design to a centrifugal super-

Dump valve.

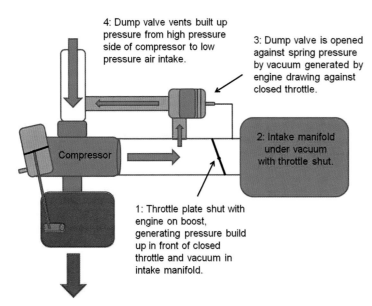

4: Dump valve vents built up pressure from high pressure side of compressor to low pressure air intake.

3: Dump valve is opened against spring pressure by vacuum generated by engine drawing against closed throttle.

Compressor

2: Intake manifold under vacuum with throttle shut.

1: Throttle plate shut with engine on boost, generating pressure build up in front of closed throttle and vacuum in intake manifold.

Dump-valve installation.

BELOW LEFT: Dump-valve springs.

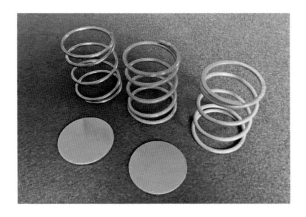

charger, but with the compressor impellor powered by an exhaust gas-driven turbine instead of by the crankshaft via a belt. The main advantage of a turbocharger is that it utilizes waste exhaust energy to power the intake turbine. This makes the turbocharger a particularly efficient device.

The turbocharger's main bearings require a continuous supply of clean oil for lubrication and cooling. This is usually supplied via an oil feed from the engine's own lubrication system; it can be taken from a fitting in line with the oil pressure switch via a braided line to the turbocharger core. A minimum of a 16mm (⅝in) oil drain is required to return the oil back to the sump. This must return oil back to the sump above the oil level. The oil feed is often restricted to prevent excess oil flow to the turbocharger. A 1mm restrictor is common for ball-bearing turbochargers, and 1.5–2mm is typical for journal-bearing turbochargers. This depends on the particular turbocharger and oil pressure generated, and advice should be taken from the turbocharger supplier regarding this. Journal-type bearings in turbochargers often do not require any restrictors, but ball-bearing types commonly do.

Most turbochargers require at least 40psi of oil pressure at the maximum engine speed. Too little pressure or flow and the turbocharger can seize, while too much results in oil entering the intake system, causing blue smoke and potential detonation.

Selecting the Correct Turbocharger(s) for your Application

Choosing the right size turbocharger or turbochargers for your application can be confusing. Your engine specification and intended usage both need to be considered carefully. In addition to a large number of different manufacturers, there are a great number of options regarding compressor wheel, turbine, turbine housing and compressor housing dimensions.

The compromise when specifying a turbocharger is between power or response, as improving one generally negatively impacts the other. A large turbine and housing A/R will give excellent high-speed performance, but poor response or slow 'spool' times. A small turbine and housing A/R will give excellent response and very quick 'spool' times, but will limit or restrict gas flow at higher engine speeds.

To get started, it can be helpful simply to select a range of turbochargers that fall right in the centre of your intended horsepower target. For example, if your horsepower target is 400bhp, then select a turbo that the manufacturer states is suitable for petrol engines in the 350–460bhp range. This 'ball-park' matching is not the most scientific method of sizing a turbo, but it will help you to draw up a short-list of potentially suitable types that should at least flow sufficiently to avoid choke, and not be in danger of surge. If you are using two turbochargers, then obviously specify turbochargers that are individually capable of at least half your horsepower target.

Compressor Sizing

In a naturally aspirated engine, airflow is often measured volumetrically in cubic feet per minute (cfm). But once you begin compressing the air to pressures above ambient conditions it has a different oxygen content, or air density, than the same volumetric flow rate at ambient pressure. Because of this the flow rate is commonly measured in terms of mass. In fact, even under normally aspirated conditions, a given volumetric flow rate will not always have the same oxygen content due to temperature and atmospheric pressure variations. The formula we have used for mass airflow in lb per minute (lb/min) is:

$$\frac{0.5 \times CID \times Engine\ Speed}{1728} \times VE \times DR \times .069$$

CID = cubic inch displacement
VE = volumetric efficiency
DR = density ratio

For example, we have a 4.6-litre Rover V8 rated at 225bhp at 4,800rpm and wish to boost it to no more than 10psi to allow us to use normal octane fuel and a moderate sized intercooler. This 4.6-litre engine has a cubic inch displacement (CID) of 281.

Now we need to calculate the engine's approximate volumetric airflow as a normally aspirated engine. To do this we use the basic formula:

$$\frac{0.5 \times CID \times Engine\ Speed}{1728} = Volumetric\ Flow\ Rate\ (cfm)$$

Turbocharger conversion on a TVR Chimaera. EANN WHALLEY, TORQUE V8

Therefore:

$$\frac{0.5 \times 281 \times 4800}{1728} = 390 \text{ cfm}$$

This formula assumes 100 per cent volumetric efficiency, which this engine definitely does not achieve. If we assume an 80 per cent VE, then this is 390 × 0.8 = 312cfm.

This is the flow potential of our 4.6 V8 in its normally aspirated configuration. We need to adjust this by the increase in actual airflow once turbocharged. This is done using a density ratio chart. This density ratio chart plots air density as a function of compressor efficiency and pressure ratio (PR). The pressure ratio is simply ambient pressure + boost pressure divided by ambient pressure: ambient pressure at sea level = 14.7psi + 10psi = 24.7/ 14.7 = 1.68 PR

Now we have the pressure ratio (PR) of approximately 1.7, we can look up the density ratio on the density ratio charts. Notice that there are two charts, one for non-intercooled and one for intercooled set-ups. This is to be an intercooled set-up due to its boost level. To read this chart we also need an approximation of compressor efficiency: we have used 70–74 per cent as this is realistic and achievable.

By looking across the density ratio chart's X-axis to the 1.7 PR and extending up to the 70–74 per cent compressor efficiency line, we can find a density ratio (DR) of approximately 1.5.

Volumetric Flow Rate × DR = Volumetric Flow Rate when Turbocharged

Therefore:

$$312 \times 1.5 = 468 \text{ cfm}$$

We now need to convert the volumetric flow rate into mass flow rate (lb/min). This is simply done by multiplying the volumetric flow rate by the standard air density of .069lb mass per cubic foot.

$$469 \times .069 = 32.3 \text{ lbs/min}$$

Now we have calculated our mass airflow in lb per minute, we can begin to look at our compressor maps.

Reading Compressor Maps

So in our example we have a 4.6 Rover V8 running 10psi of boost. With an atmospheric pressure of 14.7psi, this equates to a pressure ratio of 1.68. If you draw a horizontal line across from the pressure

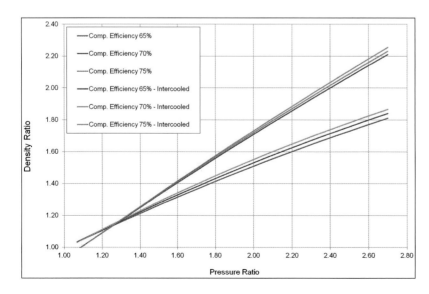

Density ratio chart for intercooled and non-intercooled turbocharged engines.

Example of a compressor map for a turbocharger similar to a Garrett GT3076R.

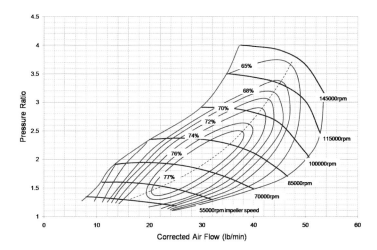

ratio of 1.68, you can see that the lowest available airflow is subject to the 'surge line'.

Surge occurs when the airflow 'stalls' at the compressor inlet, due to the lack of airflow coupled with a pressure ratio that is too high. This effectively creates a momentary negative volume flow rate, which intermittently stops the turbocharger from supplying the intake with compressed air. This stop-start behaviour is why it is commonly referred to as 'surging', and it can be very damaging to the turbocharger's bearings. If this occurs, the turbocharger is probably too large for the airflow and pressure ratio requirements of your particular engine specification.

Turbocharger and exhaust manifold for a TVR Chimaera or TVR Griffith. EANN WHALLEY, TORQUE V8

Surge can also occur when the throttle is closed and not enough pressure is released, creating a situation where the pressure ratio is too high for the amount of airflow passing through the turbocharger. This is where a recirculation or blow-off valve is used, to release the excessive pressure and ensure that the turbocharger does not suffer from surge.

The maximum airflow is limited by the 'choke line', which is the physical limitation that the compressor inlet imposes on the airflow. Put simply, the larger the compressor inlet, the greater the maximum airflow. If choke occurs, the turbocharger is probably too small for your airflow and pressure ratio requirements.

The aim here is to match your mass airflow requirements and pressure ratio to ensure that the turbocharger is operating efficiently throughout the engine's speed range. Modern turbocharger compressors will commonly hit efficiencies as high as 76–80 per cent, but the wide speed range of the engine will operate any given compressor through a wide range of flow efficiencies. Each compressor has areas of varying efficiency called 'efficiency islands', and we need to ensure that the compressor is operating well away from surge point (too large a compressor) and in the opposite direction of choke (too small a compressor).

If we consider that we want the full boost pressure of 10psi to occur from 3,000rpm to 5,000rpm, then we can calculate mass airflow for 3,000rpm and 5,000rpm, using the formula above. This gives us a mass airflow of 20.2lb/min at 3,000rpm, and 33.7lb/min at 5,000rpm.

From this we can see that we want a turbocharger that is operating at high efficiency, between 20lb/min and 34lb/min, and certainly well away from surge or choke. As a rule of thumb, you should not match a compressor to an engine if you expect it to be less than 65 per cent efficient. Below that level of efficiency the compressed air becomes very hot, reducing air density and increasing the chance of detonation.

By looking closely at turbocharger compressor maps for turbochargers in the right horsepower range, we can select one that is suitable. The Garrett GT3076R is stated as being suitable for engines in the 310–525bhp range. If we look horizontally across the mass airflow axis to 20lb/min, and then vertically up the pressure ratio axis to 1.7, we can see that the compressor would be operating at approximately 72–74 per cent efficiency at 3,000rpm. If we do the same for 34lb/min at the same pressure ratio of 1.7, then we can see the compressor would still be in the 72–74 per cent efficiency range at 5,000rpm. At 4,000rpm the compressor would pass right through its peak efficiency zone. This turbocharger represents an excellent match to this example engine.

We have only considered the Garrett range in this example. There are, of course, other brands of turbocharger that will be equally suitable.

Table 31: Suitable turbochargers for various Rover V8 applications

Engine capacity	Single turbocharger @ 10psi	Twin turbocharger @ 10psi
3.5	GT3071R	GT2052
4.0	GT3071R	GT2052
4.6	GT3076R	GT2052
5.0	GT3582R	GT2252

* This table assumes that the engine is operating at approximately 80 per cent VE and producing maximum horsepower at about 5,000rpm. This is using an air-to-air intercooler and a maximum boost pressure of 10psi.

Compressor/Turbine Trim

'Trim' is used to describe the ratio between the inducer and exducer diameters of a compressor or turbine wheel. The inducer of the compressor wheel is the smaller inlet diameter, where the air is induced or sucked into the compressor wheel, while the compressor exducer is at the maximum diameter, where the air exits the wheel. Conversely the turbine inducer is the larger diameter of the turbine wheel, where the exhaust gases first hit the wheel. The exducer of the turbine is the smaller diameter of the turbine wheel, where the gases exit the wheel.

$$\text{Compressor Trim} = \frac{\text{Compressor Inducer Diameter}}{\text{Compressor Exducer Diameter}} \times 100$$

$$\text{Turbine Trim} = \frac{\text{Compressor Exducer Diameter}}{\text{Turbine Inducer Diameter}} \times 100$$

For each particular turbocharger you have a compressor trim and turbine trim. Turbines are usually not as sensitive to flow changes as compressors. Because of this, there are commonly more options of compressor trim within a turbocharger model than there are turbine trims. Generally speaking, compressors with large inducers and smaller exducer diameters will flow more air at lower pressures, while smaller inducers with larger exducer diameters will flow less air at slightly higher pressures.

The trim characteristics of a compressor wheel will heavily influence the compressor map and a turbocharger's airflow potential. If the compressor map matches the engine perfectly, then there should be no need to alter the compressor trim. If you already have a given turbo and find that the airflow is slightly lower than desired, then it may be advantageous to move to a larger compressor trim, provided that the larger trim has a larger inducer diameter. If the larger trim has the same exducer diameter as your old compressor wheel, then you know that the inducer must be larger.

Turbine Housing A/R and Sizing

A/R (area/radius) describes a geometric characteristic of all compressor and turbine housings. The

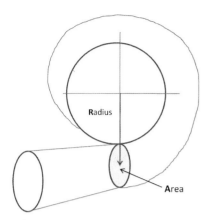

A/R-compressor housing.

A/R of a turbine housing is the inlet cross-sectional area divided by the radius from the turbo centre line to the centroid of that area.

Compressor performance is relatively insensitive to changes in A/R, and because of this there are no A/R options available for compressor housings. However, turbine performance is very sensitive to A/R as this determines the flow capacity of the turbine.

Using a smaller A/R will increase the exhaust velocity into the turbine. This will give increased turbine power at lower engine speeds, resulting in faster spool times. However, a small A/R also causes the flow to enter the wheel more tangentially, which reduces the ultimate flow capacity of the turbine wheel. This will tend to increase exhaust back pressure, and hence reduce the engine's ability to breathe well at higher engine speeds – effectively the engine is choked with excess back pressure.

Using a larger A/R will lower exhaust velocity, and increase spool times. In a larger A/R housing the exhaust gas enters the wheel in a more radial fashion, increasing the wheel's effective flow capacity, resulting in lower back pressure and better power at higher engine speeds.

A/R selection is a compromise between fast spool and peak flow. When selecting a suitable A/R it pays to be honest with yourself about the intended vehicle use, and match the A/R to the desired characteristics. If your current turbocharger creates plenty of top-end power for your needs but has a slow spool time (lots of turbo lag), then it may be worth dropping a size on the A/R. Conversely, if you find there is a lot of back pressure generated between the engine and turbo in relation to the boost pressure, then you may wish to select a larger turbine A/R. Ideally, we would have a 1:1 pressure ratio between intake and exhaust.

WASTE-GATES AND BOOST CONTROL

The waste-gate is simply a valve that opens between the engine and the exhaust turbine to relieve excessive exhaust back pressure and control the boost pressure that is generated. The waste-gate is activated by a boost pressure actuator connected via a small pipe to the turbocharger's compressor housing or the engine's intake manifold. The waste-gate is held shut by a spring inside the actuator. The actuator also contains a diaphragm with a pressure connection. When the boost pressure acting on the diaphragm exceeds the strength of the spring, then the waste-gate opens. When the waste-gate opens, the extra exhaust pressure bypasses the exhaust turbine, limiting turbine speed and therefore boost pressure.

We can understand why a waste-gate is necessary when we consider that a well-sized turbo might be making peak boost by 3,000rpm, but the engine will operate right up to 6,000rpm. Without a waste-gate, boost pressure would continue to rise with increasing engine speed, leading to excessive boost pressures.

Many turbochargers have the waste-gate built in, or integral to the exhaust turbine housing. This creates a compact and neat installation. Beyond a certain flow level the internal waste-gate may not be able to bypass enough exhaust pressure to prevent the turbine speed and boost level from increasing. This is when an external waste-gate is used. As a rough rule of thumb you should consider using an external waste-gate if the power level is likely to exceed 400bhp per turbocharger.

The spring pressure inside the waste-gate actuator controls the boost pressure. Increasing the spring strength means that the boost pressure will

Waste-gate actuator and threaded rod.

rise higher before it overcomes the spring pressure and opens the waste-gate. Internal waste-gate actuators are connected to the waste-gate via a threaded rod. This rod can be shortened to increase the boost pressure, or lengthened to decrease it. Shortening the length of the actuator arm increases the spring pressure by compressing the spring more. If we shorten the actuator rod too much, then the spring inside the actuator will reach coil bind

and prevent the waste-gate from opening properly. Boost pressure can usually be increased by about 5psi by adjusting the threaded rod. A larger boost increase than this requires an actuator with a stronger spring, or some form of boost controller.

A boost controller in its most basic form is a controlled air leak or 'bleed'. By bleeding off boost pressure between the turbo and waste-gate actuator we can fool the actuator into 'seeing' a lower pressure than is actually being generated. For example, let's say we require 15psi of boost and our turbo is generating 10psi of boost before the actuator spring strength is defeated and the waste-gate opens. If we introduce a controlled air leak or 'bleed' into the pressure line to the actuator, then we can bleed away 5psi of pressure so the waste-gate actuator only 'sees' 10psi when the boost pressure is actually 15psi.

Manual boost controllers allow a fixed rate of leakage or bleed that can be set with an adjustable valve. The best manual boost controllers are typically the ball and spring type. Electronic boost controllers are pulse-width modulated (PWM) solenoids that allow precise control over the boost pressure. A typical PWM boost control solenoid usually operates over a 10–90 per cent duty cycle, with higher duty cycles allowing greater air bleed and

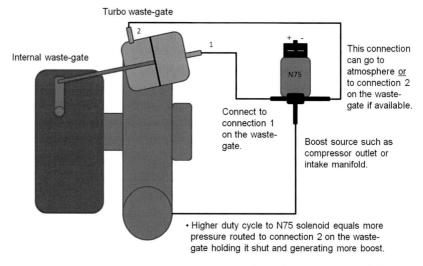

Plumbing of boost controller.

Boost pressure graph of mechanical versus electronic waste-gate control.

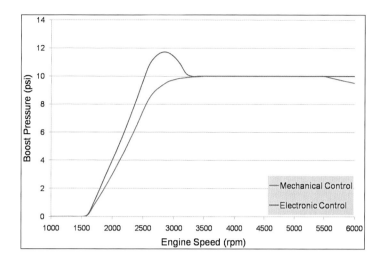

therefore greater boost pressure. The use of electronic boost control enables much more sophisticated boost control strategies, such as two-stage boost controlled by a switch or different boost levels for different gears.

We can also use modulated boost to ensure there is less boost and torque at lower speeds to preserve the transmission or maintain vehicle traction. There are many types of programmable boost controller available in the market today. Many aftermarket

PWM boost control solenoid.

ECUs contain a programmable PWM table or map that can be used to control a boost control solenoid. We have implemented such strategies with switchable boost, fuel and ignition maps to enable low- and high-power set-ups that can be activated at the flick of a switch.

Another advantage of electronic boost control is that it can enable us to make more boost pressure lower in the engine speed range than with a fully mechanical waste-gate control. This is because a mechanical actuator does not hold the waste-gate shut right up to the pre-set boost pressure, when it opens suddenly. Instead it begins to open at a much lower pressure than the peak, and bleeds off valuable exhaust pressure before the peak boost pressure is reached. This creates lag. If we look closely at the waste-gate actuator on an engine running 10psi of boost pressure, then we will see that the actuator begins to open at, say, 5psi and then continues to open progressively until it is fully open by 10psi. With electronic control we can keep the waste-gate shut right up until the peak pressure of 10psi is achieved. This ensures that more exhaust pressure is available to drive the turbine right up until the desired peak boost is achieved. This creates more torque below peak boost.

The disadvantage is that the boost pressure can 'spike' or overshoot briefly. On some vehicles a slightly softer boost rise is desirable, particularly when traction is limited.

Intercooler.

Intercooler pipework on a TVR Chimaera.

INTERCOOLERS AND CHARGECOOLERS

Whilst compressing the intake air does increase the amount of oxygen, it also increases the intake air temperature, which in turn reduces the amount of oxygen in the intake air charge and causes increased combustion temperature. The purpose of an intercooler or chargecooler is to cool the intake air after it has been compressed by the super-charger or turbocharger. This then increases the oxygen density of the intake charge and reduces the combustion temperature. An intercooler is an air-to-air radiator, whereas a chargecooler is a water-to-air radiator.

Do we need an intercooler? This really depends on many factors, but as a general rule we would install an intercooler on any forced-induction set-up that is producing more than 7psi of boost. This does not mean that set-ups with less than this boost pressure will not necessarily benefit from an intercooler, or that higher boost set-ups cannot operate without one. We have seen non-intercooled supercharged Rover V8 engines running in excess of 10psi with intake temperatures approaching 100°C! This is far from ideal, however, and the likeli-hood of detonation and resultant engine damage is greatly increased.

It is common to see some pressure drop across an intercooler and its pipework, particularly if the pipework is long. The reduction in intake tempera-tures is usually worth a slight drop in pressure, but we have found that some centrifugal superchargers – for example, Powerdyne BD1A – will suffer from a significant drop in pressure when used with an inter-

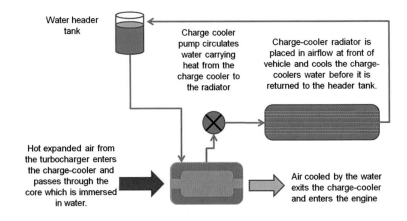

Water header tank

Charge cooler pump circulates water carrying heat from the charge cooler to the radiator

Charge-cooler radiator is placed in airflow at front of vehicle and cools the charge-coolers water before it is returned to the header tank.

Hot expanded air from the turbocharger enters the charge-cooler and passes through the core which is immersed in water.

Air cooled by the water exits the charge-cooler and enters the engine

Typical chargecooler layout.

cooler. Those particular superchargers therefore do not work properly with an intercooler.

Intercooler efficiency is simply the ratio of how many degrees of temperature that were removed from the charge air by the intercooler, to the original temperature that is put into the charge air by the turbocharger or supercharger. For example, if a supercharger heats the intake air up to 100°C, and the intercooler reduces this temperature to 25°C, then it has reduced the temperature of the intake air by 75°. If we divide the temperature reduction by the original temperature at the intercooler inlet (75/100 = 0.75), this gives us an intercooler which is 75 per cent efficient.

There are two main types of intercooler construction commonly used in automotive intercoolers: tube and fin design, and bar and plate design. Tube and fin designs are typically used in standard original fitment intercoolers, as they are quicker and cheaper to mass produce. These comprise individual tubes brazed or welded to the header plates and separated by fins, much like the construction of a radiator. The more robust tube and fin types use extruded aluminium tubes and can withstand higher boost pressures. The cheaper designs use tubes folded from flat plate and welded along the seams. These cheaper types are generally unsuitable for boost pressures above approximately 14psi.

The most robust intercoolers are made of the bar and plate construction, and are capable of withstanding very high boost pressures. The bar and plate design uses a series of bars and plates

stacked up to form the air tubes. Making a wider intercooler is easier with the bar and plate design as you can simply make the plates wider to provide greater heat transfer to the surrounding air. With the tube and fin design this is limited by the tube width.

What size intercooler should we use? Many intercooler manufacturers rate intercoolers in terms of horsepower capability. This is very crude, but will get us in the right way of thinking. It is better to oversize the intercooler slightly than to undersize it.

Chargecooler set-ups typically consist of the chargecooler itself, a water pump, and a water-to-air radiator. The hot compressed air passes through the chargecooler core, which is much like an intercooler immersed in a water jacket. The chargercooler transfers heat from the air to the water. This water is then pumped from the chargecooler to a water-to-air radiator placed in the airflow at the front of the vehicle; the cooled water is then returned to the chargecooler. The heat transfer between aluminium and water is over ten times greater than the heat transfer between aluminium and air, making a chargecooler much more efficient than an intercooler of the same size. Furthermore a small chargecooler can often be packaged into a tight engine bay where there would be little room for an intercooler set-up.

WATER/METHANOL INJECTION

Water and/or methanol injection is another effective way of reducing the intake air temperature and increasing the effective octane of the fuel. Aircraft engines in World War II, as well as the 1962 Oldsmobile Jetfire, used water injection to reduce intake temperatures and reduce the likelihood of pre-ignition.

Water injection is a well-established technology. Not only does water injection reduce the likelihood of pre-ignition by cooling the intake charge and combustion chamber, it also temporarily increases the compression (water is an incompressible liquid) and can reduce harmful nitrogen oxide (NOx) emissions by lowering combustion temperatures. Water injection also keeps the engine internals very clean and free from detonation promoting carbon deposits. Water injection by itself will not increase engine

Bar and plate intercooler.

power but can enable the use of more boost than the engine would otherwise tolerate with its existing fuel octane and intake temperatures.

Any water-injection set-up must work properly in conjunction with the existing fuel and ignition systems, to ensure a successful and reliable outcome. Some systems incorporate a failsafe that can activate a switch if the water flow stops. We have connected these failsafe switches into the switchable map function on aftermarket ECUs to switch fuel, ignition and boost to safe settings when the water injection ceases to operate.

One disadvantage with any water injection set-up is that it can run dry, which is less than ideal if your set-up relies on water injection to keep the engine within safe operating limits. The other potential yet unlikely disadvantage is that a faulty or incorrectly installed system could inject too much water. This could lead to significant engine damage, including bent con-rods and stripped head bolts. There are many aftermarket water injection kits available on the market today, from AEM, Aquamist, Snow Performance and Devils Own, to name just a few.

Water Jet Location

It is worth giving a little thought to the placement of the water injection nozzles and the resultant distribution of water to the individual cylinders. Most modern EFI intake manifolds such as the Gems and Thor units are 'dry' manifolds insofar as they are designed to distribute air evenly to each cylinder, but not liquids. Nice sweeping bends that create excellent airflow may serve to centrifuge heavier

Water-injection nozzle.

liquids out of suspension, resulting in some cylinders receiving more water than others. If a single nozzle is used, then it should be placed after any intercooler, but before the throttle plate(s). The water vapour will hit the throttle plate, helping to mix the air and water.

We do not recommend placing the injection nozzle before the turbocharger or supercharger, as we have seen evidence of water erosion of compressor turbines when set up in this way. Multipoint water-injection systems can ensure even distribution between cylinders, but require very small nozzles, which are more prone to clogging than one larger nozzle. We would always recommend using only distilled or deionized water, as clogging of the fine water jets is a very real problem.

Water Injection Jet Sizing and Flow Rates

Water flow rates should be approximately 10–25 per cent of the total fuel flow, depending on the boost level and the ratio of water to methanol. As a rule of thumb, for a 100 per cent water injection set-up we should target 10–15 per cent of total fuel flow; for a 50:50 water-methanol mix we should target 15–20 per cent of total fuel flow; and for a 100 per cent methanol set-up we should target 20–25 per cent of total fuel flow.

For example, if we had a turbocharged Rover V8 using eight 350cc injectors running at 90 per cent duty cycle, we would have a maximum of approximately 2520cc per minute (cc/min) of fuel flow. 15 per cent of this would work out at 378cc/min of water flow. We could use a single 380–400cc jet, or eight 50cc jets for a multipoint system.

The water injection jets are sized in flow rate at a given water pressure, so the pressure that the pump is running at should be considered when calculating the flow rate. If we run at a higher pump pressure than the jet was rated at, then we will achieve a higher flow rate. Do not forget to subtract boost pressure from the water-pump pressure, as the pump will be injecting against the boost pressure in the intake. For example, if the boost pressure were 10psi and the pump was running at 120psi, then we would calculate the pump pressure as 110psi.

Example of a basic water-injection set-up.

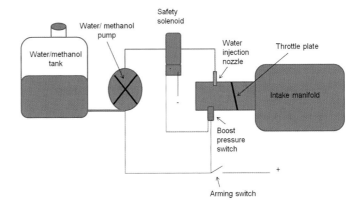

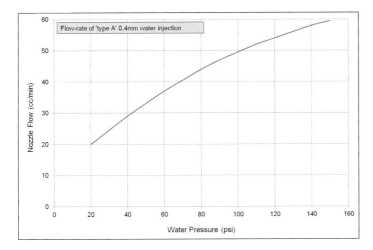

LEFT: *Nozzle flow rate versus pump pressure.*

BOTTOM: *Nitrous oxide installation in a TVR Chimaera.* DEREK BECK

Looking at this chart of nozzle flow against pump pressure, we can see that at 110psi of pump pressure we would require eight of the 0.4mm jets to achieve a total water flow of just over 400cc per minute. This would be an ideal match for our example above.

NITROUS OXIDE

Nitrous oxide is still regarded as a method of forced induction because it contains more oxygen than air – therefore the use of nitrous oxide adds more oxygen into the intake system.

Significant performance gains can be made with the use of nitrous oxide, but there are also significant risks with its use. Single-point injection systems are best avoided, as these often lead to large variations in fuelling between the different cylinders on the Rover V8. Multipoint injection systems can be made to work well, but a properly calibrated engine management system with built-in safeguards should be regarded as essential. Forged pistons are also highly recommended with nitrous oxide installations.

APPENDIX

Engine numbers

Engine code	Applications	Notes
84xxxxx1A	Rover P5B	3.5-litre, 1967–73, 10.5:1 Static CR
425xxxx1A	Rover P6	3.5-litre, 1968–77, 10.5:1 Static CR
427xxxx1A	Rover P6	3.5-litre, 1968–77, 8.5:1 Static CR
430xxxx1A	Rover P6	3.5-litre, 1968–77, 10.5:1 Static CR
432xxxx1A	Rover P6	3.5-litre, 1968–77, 8.5:1 Static CR
451xxxx1A	Rover P6	3.5-litre, 1968–77, 10.5:1 Static CR
453xxxx1A	Rover P6	3.5-litre, 1968–77, 8.5:1 Static CR
455xxxx1A	Rover P6	3.5-litre, 1968–77, 10.5:1 Static CR
466xxxx1A	Rover P6	3.5-litre, 1968–77, USA spec
48xxxxx1A	Rover P6	3.5-litre, 1968–77, 10.5:1 Static CR
10Axxxx1A	Rover SD1	3.5-litre, 197687, 9.35:1 Static CR
11Axxxx1A	Rover SD1	3.5-litre, 1979–80, 9.35:1 Static CR
12Axxxx1A	Rover SD1	3.5-litre, 1979–80, 8.13:1 Static CR, USA spec
13Axxxx1A	Rover SD1	3.5-litre, 1979–80, 8.13:1 Static CR, USA spec
14Axxxx1A	Rover SD1	3.5-litre, 1976–87, 8.13:1 Static CR, Sweden spec
15Axxxx1A	Rover SD1	3.5-litre, 1976–87, 8.13:1 Static CR, Australian spec
16Axxxx1A	Rover SD1	3.5-litre, 1976–87, 8.13:1 Static CR, Japanese spec
17Axxxx1A	Rover SD1	3.5-litre, 1979–87, 9.35:1 Static CR
18Axxxx1A	Rover SD1	3.5-litre, 1979–87, 9.35:1 Static CR
19Axxxx1A	Rover SD1	3.5-litre, 1976–87, 8.13:1 Static CR, Australian spec
20Axxxx1A	Rover SD1	3.5-litre, 1982–87, 8.13:1 Static CR, Australian spec
21Axxxx1A	Rover SD1	3.5-litre, 1982–87, 8.13:1 Static CR, Australian spec
23Axxxx1A	Rover SD1	3.5-litre, 1982–87, 8.13:1 Static CR
24Axxxx1A	Rover SD1	3.5-litre, 1982–87, 8.13:1 Static CR
25Axxxx1A	Rover SD1	3.5-litre, 1982–87, 8.13:1 Static CR
26Axxxx1A	Rover SD1	3.5-litre, 1982–87, 8.13:1 Static CR
27Axxxx1A	Rover SD1	3.5-litre, 1982–87, 8.13:1 Static CR, hot climate spec
28Axxxx1A	Rover SD1	3.5-litre, 1982–87, 8.13:1 Static CR, hot climate spec
30Axxxx1A	Rover SD1	3.5-litre, 1982–87, 9.75:1 Static CR
31Axxxx1A	Rover SD1	3.5-litre, 1982–87, 9.75:1 Static CR
32Axxxx1A	Rover SD1	3.5-litre, 1982–87, 9.75:1 Static CR
33Axxxx1A	Rover SD1	3.5-litre, 1982–87, 9.75:1 Static CR
34Axxxx1A	Rover SD1	3.5-litre, 1982–87, 9.35:1 Static CR, Switzerland spec
36Axxxx1A	Rover SD1	3.5-litre, 1982–87, 9.35:1 Static CR, Switzerland spec

Engine code	Applications	Notes
38Axxxx1A	Rover SD1	3.5-litre, 1982–87, 9.35:1 Static CR, factory re-con
39Axxxx1A	Rover SD1	3.5-litre, 1982–87, 9.35:1 Static CR, factory re-con
10Exxxxx1A	Triumph TR8	3.5-litre, 1978–82, 8.13:1 Static CR
11Exxxxx1A	Triumph TR8	3.5-litre, 1978–82, 8.13:1 Static CR
12Exxxxx1A	Triumph TR8	3.5-litre, 1978–82, 8.13:1 Static CR, USA spec
13Exxxxx1A	Triumph TR8	3.5-litre, 1978–82, 8.13:1 Static CR, USA spec
14Exxxxx1A	Triumph TR8	3.5-litre, 1978–82, 8.13:1 Static CR
15Exxxxx1A	Triumph TR8	3.5-litre, 1978–82, 8.13:1 Static CR
486xxxxxxA	Morgan Plus 8	3.5-litre, 1968–86, 9.75:1 Static CR
30Axxxx	Morgan Plus 8	3.5-litre, 1983–90, 9.75:1 Static CR
37Axxxx	Morgan Plus 8	3.5-litre, 1983–90, 9.75:1 Static CR
37Axxxx	TVR 350i	3.5-litre, 1983–89, 9.75:1 Static CR
341xxxx1	Range Rover Classic	3.5-litre, 1970–83, 8.25:1 Static CR
355xxxx1C,D,E	Range Rover Classic	3.5-litre, 1970–83, 8.25:1 Static CR
355xxxx1F	Range Rover Classic	3.5-litre, 1970–83, 8.13:1 Static CR
359xxxx1A	Range Rover Classic	3.5-litre, 1970–83, 8.25:1 Static CR, CKD spec
398xxxx1A	Range Rover Classic	3.5-litre, 1970–83, 8.13:1 Static CR, Australian spec
11Dxxxx1A	Range Rover Classic	3.5-litre, 1970–83, 9.35:1 Static CR
13Dxxxx1A,B	Range Rover Classic	3.5-litre, 1981–85, 8.13:1 Static CR
15Dxxxx1A,B	Range Rover Classic	3.5-litre, 1981–85, 9.35:1 Static CR
16Dxxxx1A,B	Range Rover Classic	3.5-litre, 1983–85, 9.35:1 Static CR
17Dxxxx1A,B	Range Rover Classic	3.5-litre, 1983–85, 9.35:1 Static CR
18Dxxxx1A,B	Range Rover Classic	3.5-litre, 1983–85, 8.13:1 Static CR
19Dxxxx1A,B	Range Rover Classic	3.5-litre, 1983–85, 9.35:1 Static CR
20Dxxxx1B	Range Rover Classic	3.5-litre, 1983–85, 8.13:1 Static CR
21Dxxxx1B	Range Rover Classic	3.5-litre, 1983–85, 8.13:1 Static CR
22Dxxxx1	Range Rover Classic and Land Rover Discovery	3.5-litre, 1986–93, 8.13:1 Static CR
23Dxxxx1	Range Rover Classic and Land Rover Discovery	3.5-litre, 1986–93, 8.13:1 Static CR
24Dxxxx1	Range Rover Classic and Land Rover Discovery	3.5-litre, 1986–93, 9.35:1 Static CR
25Dxxxx1A	Range Rover Classic	3.5-litre, 1986–89, 9.35:1 Static CR
26Dxxxx1A	Range Rover Classic	3.5-litre, 1986–89, 9.35:1 Static CR
27Dxxxx1A	Range Rover Classic	3.5-litre, 1986–89, 8.13:1 Static CR
28Dxxxx1	Range Rover Classic	3.5-litre, 1986–89, 8.13:1 Static CR
29Dxxxx1A	Range Rover Classic	3.5-litre, 1986–89, 8.13:1 Static CR
30Dxxxx1	Range Rover Classic	3.5-litre, 1986–89, 8.13:1 Static CR
31Dxxxx1	Range Rover Classic	3.5-litre, 1986–89, 8.13:1 Static CR
10Gxxxx1	Land Rover Stage 1	3.5-litre, 1979–85, 8.13:1 Static CR
11Gxxxx1	Land Rover Stage 1	3.5-litre, 1979–85, 8.13:1 Static CR
12Gxxxx1	Land Rover Stage 1	3.5-litre, 1979–85, 8.13:1 Static CR
14Gxxxx1	Land Rover 90/110/127	3.5-litre, 1983–93, 8.13:1 Static CR
15Gxxxx1	Land Rover 90/110/127	3.5-litre, 1983–93, 8.13:1 Static CR
19Gxxxx1	Land Rover 90/110/127	3.5-litre, 1983–93, 8.13:1 Static CR, Saudi spec

Engine code	Applications	Notes
20Gxxxx1	Land Rover 90/110/127	3.5-litre, 1983–93, 8.13:1 Static CR
21Gxxxx1	Land Rover 90/110/127	3.5-litre, 1983–93, 8.13:1 Static CR
22Gxxxx1	Land Rover 90/110/127	3.5-litre, 1983–93, 8.13:1 Static CR, Australian spec
24Gxxxx1	Land Rover 90/110/127	3.5-litre, 1983–93, 8.13:1 Static CR
27Gxxxx1	Land Rover Discovery	3.5-litre, 1989, 8.13:1 Static CR
47G50Pxxxx	LDV Sherpa	3.5-litre, 1986–1989
35Dxxxx1	Range Rover and Discovery	3.9-litre, 1989–95, 9.35:1 Static CR
36Dxxxx1	Range Rover and Discovery	3.9-litre, 1989–95, 9.35:1 Static CR
37Dxxxx1	Range Rover and Discovery	3.9-litre, 1989–95, 8.13:1 Static CR
38Dxxxx1	Range Rover and Discovery	3.9-litre, 1989–95, 8.13:1 Static CR
47Axxxx1	Morgan Plus 8	3.9-litre, 1990–96, 9.35:1 Static CR
37A40Pxxxx	TVR Chimaera 400	3.9-litre, 1992–02, 9.75:1 Static CR
47A40Pxxxx	TVR Chimaera 400	3.9-litre, 1992–02, 9.75:1 Static CR
30Gxxxx1	Land Rover Defender	3.9-litre, 9.13:1 Static CR, Japanese spec
31Gxxxx1	Land Rover Defender	3.9-litre, 1997–98, 9.13:1 Static CR, 50th Anniversary LE spec
40Dxxxx1	Range Rover Classic LSE	4.2-litre, 1992–95, 8.94:1 Static CR
47A43Pxxxx	TVR Griffith 430	4.3-litre
42Dxxxxxx	Range Rover P38 and Discovery	4.0-litre, 1994–1998, 9.35:1 Static CR
44Dxxxxxx	Range Rover P38 and Discovery	4.0-litre, 1994–1998, 8.13:1 Static CR
57Dxxxxxx	Range Rover P38 and Discovery	4.0-litre, 1998–2003, 8.13:1 Static CR
58Dxxxxxx	Range Rover P38 and Discovery	4.0-litre, 1998–2003, 9.35:1 Static CR
92Dxxxxxx	Range Rover P38 and Discovery	4.0-litre, 1998–2003, 8.13:1 Static CR, Canadian spec
92Dxxxxxx	Range Rover P38 and Discovery	4.0-litre, 1998–2003, 9.35:1 Static CR, North American spec
46Dxxxxxx	Range Rover P38 and Discovery	4.6-litre, 1994–1998, 9.35:1 Static CR
48Dxxxxxx	Range Rover P38 and Discovery	4.6-litre, 1994–1998, 8.13:1 Static CR
59Dxxxxxx	Range Rover P38 and Discovery	4.6-litre, 1998–2003, 8.13:1 Static CR
60Dxxxxxx	Range Rover P38 and Discovery	4.6-litre, 1998–2003, 9.35:1 Static CR
93Dxxxxxx	Range Rover P38 and Discovery	4.6-litre, 1998–2003, 8.13:1 Static CR, Canadian spec
96Dxxxxxx	Range Rover P38 and Discovery	4.6-litre, 1998–2003, 9.35:1 Static CR, North American spec
S46DxxxxA	Morgan Plus 8	4.6-litre, 1996–2004, 9.35:1 Static CR
37A50Pxxxx	TVR Chimaera/Griffith 500	5-litre, 1993–2002, 9.75:1 Static CR
47A50Pxxxx	TVR Chimaera 500	5-litre, 1993–2002, 9.75:1 Static CR

Camshaft specifications

Camshaft	Valve Event Timing IVO/IVC/ EVO/EVC (degrees)	Intake Valve Lift @ 1.6:1 rocker ratio (mm)	Exhaust Valve lift @ 1.6:1 rocker ratio (mm)	Intake seat-seat duration (degrees)	Exhaust seat-seat duration (degrees)	Lobe Centre angle (degrees)	Overlap (degrees)	Lifters
Std. 3.5 Rover SD1	30/75/68/37	9.91	9.78	285	285	109	67	Hydraulic
Std. 3.9 Rover (ETC8686)	32/73/70/35	9.91	9.91	285	285	109	67	Hydraulic
Std. 4.0 Rover (ERR3720)	28/77/66/39	9.91	9.91	285	285	109	67	Hydraulic
Std. 4.2 Rover (ERR5925)	28/64/72/20	9.91	9.91	272	272	112	48	Hydraulic
Std. 4.6 Rover (ERR5250)	14/70/64/20	10.57	10.57	264	264	115	34	Hydraulic
Piper 255	24/68/68/24	10.67	10.67	272	272	112	48	Hydraulic
Piper 270	28/64/64/28	10.67	10.67	272	272	108	56	Hydraulic
Piper 270i	26/66/66/26	10.67	10.67	272	272	110	52	Hydraulic
Piper 285	31/65/65/31	11.18	11.18	276	276	107	62	Hydraulic
Piper 300	44/76/76/44	12.88	12.83	300	300	106	88	Hydraulic
Piper 300H	39/67/67/39	11.33	11.33	286	286	104	78	Hydraulic
Piper 320	47/79/75/51	13.64	13.59	306	306	104	98	Solid
Piper Group A	44/76/76/44	9.91	9.91	300	300	106	88	Hydraulic
Kent H180	23/59/59/23	11.20	11.20	262	262	108	46	Hydraulic
Kent H200	23/67/68/34	10.89	11.50	270	282	109.5	57	Hydraulic
Kent H214	31/73/78/40	11.9	12.44	284	298	110	71	Hydraulic
Kent H218	27/71/74/30	11.38	11.78	278	284	112	57	Hydraulic
Kent H224	41/83/86/44	12.49	13.08	304	310	111	85	Hydraulic
Kent H234	44/86/86/44	13.1	13.56	310	310	111	88	Hydraulic
Kent M228	32/68/73/37	11.78	11.94	280	290	108	69	Solid
Kent M238	34/70/73/37	12.32	12.32	284	290	108	71	Solid
Kent M248	43/77/79/41	12.85	12.85	300	300	108	84	Solid
Kent M256	48/76/87/43	13.05	13.56	304	310	108	91	Solid
Kent TVR 51	24/68/71/27	10.8	10.8	272	278	112	51	Hydraulic
Kent TVR 885	26/78/86/34	11.6	12.3	284	300	116	60	Hydraulic
Crower 50227	Unknown	10.20	10.69	246	253	112	26	Hydraulic
Crower 50229	Unknown	10.93	11.34	258	260	112	35	Hydraulic
Crower 50230	Unknown	11.34	11.46	260	266	112	39	Hydraulic
Crower 50231	Unknown	11.46	12.11	270	276	112	49	Hydraulic
Crower 50232	Unknown	12.40	12.44	276	281	112	55	Hydraulic
Crower 50233	Unknown	12.40	12.72	280	286	112	59	Hydraulic
Crower 50234	Unknown	13.00	13.37	284	290	112	63	Hydraulic
Crower 50303	Unknown	12.23	12.40	282	287	108	69	Solid
Crower 50304	Unknown	12.76	13.05	292	298	108	79	Solid
Crower 50305	Unknown	13.61	13.86	304	310	108	91	Solid
Holbay 111R	29/73/73/39	10.90	10.90	287	292	108	73	Hydraulic

INDEX